Between Evidence and Ideology

# Oudtestamentische Studiën

Old Testament Studies
published on behalf of the Societies for
Old Testament Studies in the Netherlands and
Belgium, South Africa, the United Kingdom
and Ireland

*Editor*

## B. Becking
Utrecht

*Editorial Board*

## H.G.M. Williamson
Oxford

## H.F. Van Rooy
Potchefstroom

## M. Vervenne
Leuven

VOLUME 59

# Between Evidence and Ideology

Essays on the History of Ancient Israel read at the
Joint Meeting of the Society for Old Testament Study
and the Oud Testamentisch Werkgezelschap
Lincoln, July 2009

*Edited by*

Bob Becking &
Lester L. Grabbe

BRILL

LEIDEN • BOSTON
2011

This book is printed on acid-free paper.

Library of Congress Cataloging-in-Publication Data

Joint Meeting of the Society for Old Testament Study and the Oudtestamentisch
Werkgezelschap in Nederland en België (14th : 2009 : Lincoln, England)
Between evidence and ideology : essays on the history of ancient Israel read at the joint meeting
of the Society for Old Testament Study and the Oud Testamentisch Werkgezelschap, Lincoln,
July 2009 / edited by Bob Becking, Lester L. Grabbe.
    p. cm. – (Oudtestamentische studien = Old Testament studies ; v. 59)
Includes indexes.
ISBN 978-90-04-18737-5 (hardback : alk. paper)
1. Bible. O.T.–Criticism, interpretation, etc.–Congresses. 2. Bible.
O.T.–Historiography–Congresses. 3. Jews–History–To 70 A.D.–Congresses. 4.
Judaism–History–To 70 A.D–Congresses. I. Becking, Bob. II. Grabbe, Lester L. III. Title. IV.
Series.

BS1171.3.J65 2009
221.9'5–dc22

BS
1171.3
.J65
2009

2010037332

ISSN    0169-7226
ISBN    978 90 04 18737 5

**Mixed Sources**
Product group from well-managed forests
and other controlled sources
www.fsc.org  Cert no. SGS-COC-006767
©1996 Forest Stewardship Council
FSC

PRINTED BY A-D DRUK BV - ZEIST, THE NETHERLANDS

# CONTENTS

# INTRODUCTION

Lester L. Grabbe
*University of Hall*

The present volume had its origins in the cooperation between the Society for Old Testament Study in the UK and Ireland (SOTS) and the Oudtestamentisch Werkgezelschap in Nederland en België (OTW). Lester L. Grabbe was the 2009 president of SOTS and wanted a theme relating to the history of ancient Israel for some of the papers read at the winter and summer meetings of the Society. The OTW, president Bob Becking, was scheduled to meet in the UK with SOTS (a joint meeting occurs every three years), and the specific topic of "History of Ancient Israel between Evidence and Ideology" was agreed on. As it happens, these two societies met with the European Association of Biblical Studies for a three-way joint meeting in the cathedral city of Lincoln, 26th–30th July 2009.

Not all of the papers read are published here, since some were not specifically relating to the main theme, but some of the papers by SOTS members were read in January at the winter meeting while others were read in July.[1] Even within the theme of "History of Ancient Israel between Evidence and Ideology", there was a good deal of variety. The organizing of the conference was mainly carried out by the SOTS Secretary John Jarick and the SOTS Hospitality Secretary Elizabeth Harper. The editors are grateful to both these individuals for their hard work in helping to make the conference a success. Following is a survey of the individual contributions, with observations to indicate their content and how they fit within the larger framework of debate about history and historical methodology.

---

[1] The papers by Ed Noort, Groningen, and Axel Knauf, Bern, will be published elsewhere.

## 1. Summaries of Articles

The first contribution, by Lester Grabbe, is placed as it is because it was the SOTS presidential paper and also because it treated a general theme relating to methodology of Hebrew Bible scholarship in general. "The Case of the Corrupting Consensus" perhaps makes an obvious point but one too often neglected by scholars: we should not allow research to be directed, canalized, or blocked by scholarly consensus. A consensus should be respected since it often represents the considered judgment of a large number of scholars over a long period of time. Yet how many of us senior scholars would follow the consensuses of the scholarship of our youth many decades ago? In some areas, scholarship has changed enormously. Is it because the previous generation was dull? Or is it not the case that many of these consensuses embodied important insights but are no longer tenable in the light of continued thinking and / or new data? And we have to take account of the fact that there are fashions in scholarship, and the field can even come to accept the opinion of a prominent figure without subjecting the view to the range of scrutiny normally to be expected. In other words, scholars sometimes fall victim to "authority"! The main danger, though, is that new views and the views of younger scholars can be stifled because of the weight of consensus. Yet we can all think of examples where the field advanced because of a theory that ultimately proved unsustainable. Being wrong can be a virtue at times!

OTW president Bob Becking sets the scene for the specific topic of history and ancient Israel in "David between Ideology and Evidence". He discusses principles of historiography and history writing, and then proceeds to illustrate by using the story of David. Most of the tradition about David is found in the biblical text, though in recent years several other sources of information on David have been put forward. These are examined, and there does seem to be some evidence of a figure called David, but none of the sources demonstrates the truth of the biblical stories. Archaeology also indicates some demographic growth at the time. We do have a number of short inscriptions and abecedaries from this period, which demonstrate the developing of written material for agricultural and commercial purposes, but nothing argues for a centralized, bureaucratic state. The biblical material is now recognized as being at least centuries after the alleged time of David. Based on the biblical material, however, some elements of a re-enactment of the life of David can be suggested: he was a warlord who offered his services to anyone who would pay (compared to the *apiru* of the Amarna texts); he managed to gain control over parts of Judah and Israel from his base in Hebron, but he ruled over a rather restricted area and did not really found a nation. Administration first developed out of economic growth rather than nation building.

With his "Mercator in the Wilderness: Numbers 33", John Bartlett explores an interesting corner of 16th-century biblical scholarship, that of making maps. Maps were used to tell the biblical story. Events from the exodus and the wilderness sojourn were often depicted on maps. Initially, the Ptolemaic maps provided the model for biblical cartographers. An early important contributor was Jacob Ziegler of Strassburg, whose work was drawn on by Miles Coverdale but also Girardus Mercator and Wolfgang Wissenburg. The last changes the route by drawing on Deut. 2:8, and many subsequently followed him (even Mercator in his later maps). But cartographers of the later 16th and the 17th centuries show a decline in accuracy and scholarship, and it is only in the 18th and 19th centuries that new techniques start to improve things. Yet Mercator's influence continued even into the late 19th and the 20th centuries.

Meindert Dijkstra wonders about the "Origins of Israel between History and Ideology". This is a huge topic, but he presents only some main lines, especially relating to the Egyptian connection. This includes the famous "Israel stela" of Merenptah, about which much has been learned in the last two decades. A succession of rulers copied or imitated reliefs of Ramesses II at Karnak, so that the reliefs are best seen as examples of long-term political claims about the Levant. "Israel" was on the margin of Egypt's interest until at least 1100 BCE. The stela is mainly about the Libyan war in which the Libyan leader used elements of the Sea Peoples as mercenaries. The Sea Peoples are not always easy to distinguish from the Shosu. The lower register on the wall seems to picture a standard coalition of Asiatics, Shosu, and representatives of the Sea Peoples. There is considerable doubt about a clear parallelism between the reliefs and the text, and we cannot be sure that an attempt is being made to represent "Israel". The confrontation with Israel had no lasting impact on the Egyptian politics. Egyptian rule as far north as Damascus seems to have continued perhaps even until about 1100 BCE—longer than assumed in the past. The vacuum was initially filled not by Israel but by the Philistine and Phoenician harbour cities. The Phoenician cities seem to have taken the Levant coast south to Dor perhaps with the Yarkon as the border between them and the Philistines. Between them the Philistines and Phoenicians limited Israelite settlement and the developing states to the highland region, perhaps even until the Iron IIa. Environmental factors may have been an important factor, leading not only to a decline of Egypt in the Late Bronze (because of a series of low Niles, etc.) but also an increase in population in marginal areas in Palestine because of increased rainfall. The "mixed multitude" picture of early Israel (Exod. 12:38) may contain a good deal of truth. Israel may not have taken Gezer into its borders until about 950 BCE, which would mean that even that late most of the coastal region and lowlands remained outside the incipient Israelite state.

In "Three Hasidisms and their Militant Ideologies: 1 and 2 Maccabees, Psalms 144 and 149", Harm van Grol takes a theme that belongs to the later history of Israel. He presents a thesis about the *Asidaioi* of the books of Maccabees, often referred to as *Hasidim*. He argues that the information there should be combined with information from Psalms 144, 145, and 149, which mention the *Ḥāsidîm*. In his view the information in the sources can be put together to reconstruct a sectarian group that was "a well-defined religious movement, characterized by piety and militancy ... active from about 200 BCE onwards, [who] participated in the revolt against the Jewish Hellenists and the Seleucids (167–161 BCE), and disappeared from the scene after the confrontation with Alcimus (161 BCE)." A study of the book of Psalms suggests, "These observations could lead to a larger construct in which the Hasidim are seen as the redactors/writers of the closing Hallel, Psalms 146–150, and, in an earlier stage, of the David prayer book, Psalms 137–145."

Since his target is one Lester Grabbe (who pointed out the lack of information about the *Asidaioi*–and he was not the only one), it seems fair to pose some questions. The common view that the "pious" were all against Hellenization is little supported in the sources. None of our sources mention that anyone criticized the Hellenistic reform of Jason or that a problem was found with Hellenistic culture until *after* Antiochus attempted to suppress Judaism. Thus, why should we assume that a sect of the *Asidaioi* was already active by about 200 BCE? How secure is the late dating of these Psalms? Many would see nothing in them that precludes a rather earlier date. Finally, why is the group led by Judas the Maccabee, who is conducting the war against the Seleucids, said to be the *Asidaioi*? 2 Maccabees 14:6 seems to refer to all Judas' followers as *Asidaioi*. But van Grol is correct that the arguments of Grabbe need to be scrutinized as much as his own, and questions on both sides need to be debated.

In "The Old Testament as a Diachronic Corpus", Marinus Koster surveys the various sections of the Bible to show the diachronic aspects, from the creation story thorough Judges, Samuel, and Kings to the prophetic literature, the psalms, and the wisdom literature. Not everyone will agree with his conclusion that the Bible "should not be downgraded to a secondary source" but that it is "a primary source for writing its own history, the history of ancient Israel". But many are likely to agree that there is both "story-like history" and "history-like story" in the biblical text. Of course, the tricky part is to determine which is which.

With "Pharaoh Shishak's Invasion of Palestine and the Exodus from Egypt", Andrew Mayes may seem to be doing the impossible by connecting the exodus and the invasion of Shishak. He surveys some of the recent scholarship on the inscriptions of Shoshenq (or Sheshonq) and the biblical account of Shishak's coming against Jerusalem. As has long been discussed, the form of the Pharaoh's name and dating of his reign suggest that the biblical account can only be referring to Shoshenq, yet the Egyptian inscription makes no mention of any Judean highland site, much less Jerusalem. The most recent study confirms that Jerusalem is not mentioned in Shoshenq's list of cities and towns, nor is it likely to have existed in damaged parts of the inscription. Yet it has been suggested the Shishak's investment of the Jezreel Valley may have been an important stage in the rise of the northern kingdom. The exodus tradition seems to have been a "charter myth" of the northern kingdom, a collective cultural memory that helped it to establish its own identity. Regardless of its actual origins, the exodus story would have reminded the Israelites of the "slavery" (forced labour) they endured under Solomon, from which they were delivered by Jeroboam. If there was a Pharaoh of the exodus, he was Shishak!

In "The Greek Esthers and the Search for History: Some Preliminary Observations", Jill Middlemas suggests that the historical reading of the book was first accepted in the Greek versions, the Septuagint (LXX) and the Alpha text (AT). This is indicated by some of the "additions" found in the Greek texts, especially two edicts that are quoted. The scribes dealt with historical questions by showing the action of the divine in events, the efficacy of prayer, and divine determinism. These three points become clearer in the Greek "additions". The Additions C and D give a more detailed description of the religious life of Modecai and Esther. Additions A and F serve as a prologue and epilogue to provide a cosmic dimension and reveal a prophetic understanding of history. The effect of the LXX and AT expansions is to assimilate the Esther story to the "scriptural norm" (including the exodus story, the Joseph story, Daniel, and Jeremiah 28), and to align Mordecai and Esther with characters of the biblical story.

These suggest an attempt to make the Esther story more traditional. The composers of the Greek versions understood history as coming from scriptural traditions. There is evidence that the Greek versions update the story to make it more contemporary (e.g., using Macedonian dates) and also to give a defence of Judaism. These points need to be taken into account when evaluating texts for real history.

Nadav Na'aman asks, "Does Archaeology Really Deserve the Status of a 'High Court' in Biblical Historical Research?" While recognizing the advances in archaeology, he wants to know whether some researchers are justified in giving preference to archaeology when it differs from the textual data, and looks at a number of case-studies: the Amarna letters and cities in Palestine; Jerusalem in the Iron IIa; the walls of Jerusalem in the 9th–8th centuries; Jerusalem in the Persian period; Gibeah of Benjamin, and Bethel. He notes several reasons why the archaeology may not show settlements that in fact existed: the problem of dating the beginnings of archaeological strata, the destructive of evidence by later building activity, and the high bedrock in the highlands which meant that new builds often removed previous levels down to bedrock. From Mesopotamia we know of important cultic sites (such as Nippar and Eridu) for which the city settlement declined and came to include only cult personnel. Thus, without in any way detracting from the importance of archaeology, it should be treated with caution when dealing with multi-strata highland sites in times of the supposed "United Monarchy" and the Babylonian and Persian periods. The limitations of both text and archaeology need to be recognized.

Klaas Sprong looks at "Prophecy and History in the Book of Judges". The first part of the article investigates the use of "prophet" in the book of Judges, but then it asks about the historical background for these statements about prophets. Several examples are used to demonstrate the difficulty of finding a historical context of the book. B.G. Wood thought he had found evidence of the Eglon story (Judges 3) by appeal to the Jericho excavations of John Garstang, but he does not deal with several important questions that must be answered before historicity can be established. As for the Ashkelon ostracon, a translation that finds references to Samson's head seems almost to be a spoof, until you recognize that the scholar proposing it is deadly serious—if rather blinkered in his desire to find history in the story of Samson. Yet an attempt by M. Liverani to find a Persian-period context for Judges 19–21 runs into similar difficulties. A number of scholars put Judges in the Persian period, and a plausible case is made for a Persian dating of the events of these chapters. Yet the problem is finding evidence that rules out other periods—that cannot be dated to any but a very narrow time frame. Perhaps the reference to Zorah (Judges 13:2) is a start, if the archaeological identification is correct, since it seems to have existed only in the period from Sennacherib to the fall of Jerusalem in 586 BCE.

Like J. Bartlett, maps are the concern of Keith W. Whitelam in "Resisting the Past: Ancient Israel in Western Memory". His study is part of an investigation into the subject of collective memory and forgetting. The image of Palestine's past is a powerful one, pushing away critical engagement not only for the lay person but also for many scholars. John Speed's atlas of 1611 included a map of Palestine. Surprisingly, rather than a map of the kingdom of David and Solomon, it focuses on the journeys of Abraham and on the tribes of Israel. This might seem strange, but this lack of interest in the monarchy seems to reflect the situation in England at the time. Palestine was treated as a county of England. At that time there was a particular concentration on local issues that largely ignored royal power. The local landed gentry and merchant families had an interest in their own histories, and books were produced to fill this need. The map of Palestine simply imbeds this outlook into the history of ancient Israel. This imaginary geography was very real to the users of the map, with the remembered biblical scenes forming a living present for the map readers. The power of the remembered past continues to shape our view of Israel's history and to mould scholarly debate.

## 2. Concluding Observations

The overall theme of "The History of Ancient Israel between Evidence and Ideology" was well borne out by these contributions. Most of them dealt in some way with the question of history and discussed evidence and ideology in trying to understand the history of Israel. It is interesting to see how more than one essay covered a particular topic or took a particular starting point. For example, two essays dealt with maps of Palestine primarily from the 16th and 17th centuries. J. Bartlett was mainly interested in how the map makers interpreted the biblical text to locate sites from the Bible (especially Numbers 33), whereas K.W. Whitelam noted how national English concerns of the time affected what type of data was emphasized in the maps (commenting especially on the failure to use the United Monarchy as a model). Whitelam's concern is collective memory, which he shares with Andrew Mayes who looks at the function of the exodus tradition as a form of collective memory that shaped the contemporary view of history, in this case how the newly emerged kingdom of Israel reacted to Shoshenq's invasion. Mayes brings in an Egyptological text (the Shoshenq inscription), as does M. Dijkstra (Merenptah's "Israel stela") who is interested in Israelite origins. Several of the papers take a section of Israelite history as a major theme: Dijkstra with Israel's origins; B. Becking with the question of the King David tradition and its historicity; K. Spronk with the book of Judges.

The place of the Bible in historical reconstruction exercises a number of the contributors. Unlike the specific studies of Becking and Sprong, M. Koster does a more generalized survey to plead for the use of the biblical text and not "downgrade" it to a secondary source. How many would follow his specific request remains to be seen, but several participants discussed methodological questions of using different sources. N. Na'aman specifically compares textual and archaeological sources to make a generalized point of recognizing the limitations of each. As someone who is known for his mastery of the use of archaeology in historical studies, Na'aman's warning is timely and has to be taken seriously. Although H. van Grol is not explicitly discussing methodology, he attempts to bring biblical and other texts together to discuss the problem of the Hasidim.

Finally, quite a few of the speakers took ideology as a theme in one way or another. L.L. Grabbe was concerned with the way modern scholarly ideology–in the form of the "scholarly consensus"–might serve to hinder the reception of new ideas or damage the careers of young scholars. How an earlier scholarly consensus about how to approach the history of Israel at various points was being given up or reshaped was exemplified in one way or another in the papers of Becking, Dijkstra, Grabbe, Mayes, Sprong, and Whitelam. Na'aman looked at an ideology affecting overall historical methodology. All in all, the conference managed to steer a clear path between evidence and ideology and, in its own small way, make a further contribution to the on-going debate about writing the history of ancient Israel.

# DAVID BETWEEN IDEOLOGY AND EVIDENCE

Bob Becking
*Utrecht University*

## 1. Introduction: Images of David

The Biblical King David is an intriguing figure and has inspired artisans through the ages to create impressive works of art.[1] Almost universally known are the marble sculpture by Michelangelo[2] and the German novel by Stephan Heym.[3] David plays a role in Shakespearean drama[4] and a recent novel by Joseph Heller is composed as the memories of David from his dying days.[5] Through the ages, David is modelled and remodelled into a wide variety of figures. All these images of David can be seen as appropriations of the Biblical character—or at least some features of him—into the cultural and societal context of the various artists.[6]

[1] A nice collection can be found in W. Dietrich, H. Herkommer (eds), *König David, biblische Schlüsselfigur und europäische Leitgestalt*, Freiburg, Stuttgart 2003.

[2] See now A. Gill, *Il giganti: Michelangelo, Florence and the David, 1492–1505*, St Martins 2003.

[3] Stefan Heym, *Der König David Bericht: Roman*, Berlin 1973; see, e.g., D. Roberts, "Stefan Heym: Der Konig David Bericht", *Journal of the Australasian Universities Language and Literature Association: A Journal of Literary Criticism, Philology & Linguistics* 48 (1977), 201–211; K.E. Attar, "Stefan Heym's King David Report: A Microcosmic Precursor". *Neophilologus* 85 (2001), 273–286 W. Dietrich, "Der Fall des Riesen Goliat. Biblische und nachbiblische Erzählversuche", in: W. Dietrich, H. Herkommer (eds), *König David, biblische Schlüsselfigur und europäische Leitgestalt*, Freiburg, Stuttgart 2003, 120–133; P. Rusterholz, "Stefan Heym—Der König David Bericht", in: Dietrich, Herkommer (eds), *König David*, 809–830; V. Tumanov, "Divine Silence in Stefan Heym's The King David Report", *Neophilologus* 93 (2009), 499–509.

[4] See, e.g., J.A. Porter, *The Drama of Speechacts: Shakespeare's Lancastrian Tetralogy*, Berkeley 1979; D. Evett, "Types of King David in Shakespeare's Lancastrian Tetralogy", *Shakespeare Studies* 18 (1981), 139–161.

[5] Joseph Heller, *God Knows*, New York 1984. See the review by J. Freidman, J. Ruderman, "Joseph Heller and the "Real" King David", *Judaism* 36 (1987), 296–301. The later novel by Allan Massie, *King David: A Novel*, London 1995, although more close to the biblical account, fails to reach the literary level of Heller.

[6] On this idea from cultural anthropology that is more and more applied in historical research see, e.g., E. Maeckelberghe, *Desperately Seeking Mary A Feminist Appropriation of a Traditional Religious Symbol*, Louvain 1991; B. Meyer, *Translating the Devil: An*

What strikes me is the inherent and ongoing ambiguity in the character of David as depicted in art. Next to the tenderness of David's hetero-
sexual love for Bathsheba as depicted by, e.g., Rembrandt and Chagall,
stands the beautiful book-length poem rewriting the story of David and
Jonathan in homoerotic terms by Stephen Schechter.[7] Leonard Cohen's
song 'Hallelujah' is full of references to King David. In this song the
paradoxical and ever changing relationship between God and the human
being is painted in lyrical words. David's ambiguity comes to the fore in
the line 'Your faith was strong but you needed proof'. Another ambiguity
in the depictions of David is that of the pious warrior. This is, I think, one
of the main themes in Heller's novel.

In the Hebrew Bible, King David is already portrayed as an intriguing
and paradoxical figure. The depiction of this king is colourful and multi-
dimensional. In the narratives of Samuel and 1 Kings, the reader meets
a character of flesh and blood. The author presents the image of a king
who is just, but nevertheless acts immorally on occasion; who is steered
by wisdom, but nevertheless falls a prey to his passion and temper. In
short this king has lived through all ambivalence of human life and
suffered from its ambiguity. Within the narrative world of the Hebrew
Bible, David is said to have established the so-called United Monarchy
of Israel and Judah and to have brought this empire-like state to its first
period of wealth and power.[8] All these artistic and Biblical images can be
classified as ideology.

The interesting question would be—for both historian and theologian—whether this ideology on David could be linked to history or—in
other words—to what degree are the Biblical pictures of David to be seen
as an ancient appropriation? Is the image original and can it be construed
as an adequate depiction of the 'historical David', or is it a repaint from
later days with none or only a few original traits?[9]

---

*African Appropriation of Pietist Protestantism. The Case of the Peki-Ewe in Southeastern Ghana*, Edinburgh 1999; E. Wasserman, "Paul among the Philosophers: The Case of Sin in Romans 6–8", *JSNT* 30 (2008), 387–415.

[7] S. Schechter, *David and Jonathan: A Story of Love and Power in Ancient Israel*, Westmound 1996; see also W. Dietrich, *David: Der Herrscher mit der Harfe* (Biblische Gestalten 14), Leipzig 2006, 233–259; A. Heacock, *Jonathan Loved David: Manly Love in the Bible and the Hermeneutics of Sex* (Bible in the Modern World), Sheffield 2009.

[8] See, e.g. W. Dietrich, *Die frühe Königszeit in Israel: 10. Jahrhundert v. Chr.* (BibEnz 3), Stuttgart Berlin Köln 1997,59–85; Dietrich, *David: Der Herrscher mit der Harfe*, 98–200.

[9] For a survey of scholarly research on the Books of Samuel, see W. Dietrich, Th. Naumann, *Die Samuelsbücher* (Erträge der Forschung, 287), Darmstadt 1995.

## 2. The Problem of Historiography

One should be careful in (re)constructing the past. Of course, it could be argued that the traditional and / or Biblical image of David is incorrect since it cannot be found in the sources. This argument, however, is fallible for several reasons that are connected to three important historiographic concepts: the character of the sources, the notion of truth, and the idea of narrativism.

### 2.1. *Sources or Evidence?*

The "sources" that are at our disposal for the period under consideration have a fragmented character. They do not inform us on all aspects of life in Judah and Jerusalem in the "Age of David". In fact the available sources can be compared with a jigsaw puzzle with too many pieces missing.

"Sources" should not be considered as hard facts. The metaphor "source"—though used widely—is as such misleading, since it yields the image of a well from which historical information is constantly flowing. In my view, the Old Testament text should be treated as evidence. The Old Testament supplies its readers with a diversity of traces of the past that are mirroring that past one way or another. The same holds for archaeological evidence and extra-biblical texts. All these traces can be and have been treated differently. The difference in the treatment is mostly related to the ideology of the historian, be it minimalistic or maximalistic, or something in between. What are generally taken as sources, in fact are pieces of evidence. In a jigsaw puzzle a green piece can be seen as part of the woods in the background, but also be placed in the meadow in front. Eventually it may turn out to be part of a shutter from an old farmhouse.

In line with Collingwood, I rather prefer to speak about evidence as traces of the past.[10] With Collingwood the methodological discussion concerning the possibility of recreating the past that centred on the antagonism between "realism" and "scepticism" has been brought an important step forward. The dichotomy between "realism" and "scepticism" should not be confused with the more recent debate between

---

[10] R.G. Collingwood, *The Idea of History: Revised Edition with Lectures 1926–1928*, Oxford 1994; see also G.R. Eltom, *The Practice of History*, Oxford ²2002.

"maximalists" and "minimalists."[11] The antagonism "realism" versus "scepticism" has to do with the character of historical knowledge. "Realism" assumes that the past is knowable on the basis of analogies in the present. "Scepticism" is based on distrust in the possibility of knowing the past. A sceptical scholar would argue that the past is closed. He or she would only build an argument on data that can be tested empirically. In the end, "scepticism" would lead either to a position in which history writing is impossible or to post-modern fantasizing.[12] Collingwood bridges this methodological gap by remarking that although the past is a foreign country,[13] traces of actors in the past are still visible. Humankind has left traces of its actions. Clay tablets in the British Museum, for instance, should be seen as traces of the past. And so should archaeological footprints. These traces, however, are not to be confused with the events as such.

In sum, history writing means the construction of the past.[14] This construction, however, is not free to take just any desired form, since it is bound by the existing evidence and needs to take account of as many traces as possible. History writing is a *narratio* that has the status of a hypothesis. This is my view on the past and I hope that I can convince you to share my view.

## 2.2. *Theories of Truth*

In current debates in the pilosophy of science, three models or theories of truth are on stage and in competition:

The correspondence theory of truth. This theory applies very easily to traditional research in physics. The truth of a theory can be established—or not—by referring to reality. Newton's law of gravity is true, since it corresponds to various phenomena in reality, such as apples falling to the ground or planets circulating around the sun. In other words, a theory

---

[11] See on this controversy D. Banks, *Writing the History of Israel* (LHB / OTS 438), London New York 2006, 205–217; P.R. Davies, *Memories of Ancient Israel: An Introduction to Biblical History—Ancient and Modern*, Louisville, London 2008, 145–172.

[12] I owe the latter phrase to my colleague in the history department of Utrecht University, Maarten van Rossem, see M. van Rossem, *Heeft geschiedenis nut?* Utrecht 2003, 11–12.

[13] See: D. Löwenthal, *The Past Is a Foreign Country*, Cambridge 1988, taking up the first line in the novel by L.P. Hartley, *The Go-Between*, London 1953.

[14] C. Lorenz, *Die Konstruktion der Vergangenheit: Eine Einführung in die Geschichtstheorie*, Köln, Wien 1997.

or a preposition is "true when there is a corresponding fact, and is false when there is no corresponding fact".[15]

The coherence theory of truth. The traditional correspondence theory is problematical in many regards especially since the concepts 'fact' and 'reality' are not that clear as traditionally assumed. Facts are only known when dressed up in language or mathematics. 'Charlemagne was crowned in 800 CE' is not a fact, but a sentence describing an event. A mathematical formula, such as $y = ax^2 + bx + c$, can only be seen as an interpretation or description of reality, not as reality itself. The coherence theory of truth assumes that propositions are always linked to other theories. The assumption that the *Higgs-particle* must exist is not true because this particle can be seen in reality, but because its assumed existence is coherent with the Standard or Grand Unified Theory of particles and forces.[16] A model of God and his attributes is true not because someone has seen God, but because the various propositions in this model cohere with each other.[17]

The pragmatic theory of truth. This third theory takes the epistomological crisis seriously. According to this approach any theory is true as long as it works or as long as it guides us successfully when we act upon it.[18] This way of approaching the truth can be seen in contemporary politics, but is also at the basis of the majority of empirical science.

The importance of this distinction for historical research becomes clear when looking at a remark made by Kyle McCarter some 20 years ago with regard to the search for the historical David:

> The Bible is our only source of information about David. No ancient inscription mentions him. No archaeological discovery can securely be linked to him. The quest for the historical David, therefore, is primarily exegetical.[19]

'No ancient inscription mentions him' should be seen as an attempt to correspond features of the life of David with the reality as described in

---

[15] Definition by B. Russell, *The Problems of Philosophy*, Oxford 1958, 129 [original edition 1912].

[16] See, e.g., S.E. Hawking, *The Nature of Space and Time*, Princeton, New Jersey 1996.

[17] See, e.g., N. Rescher, *The Coherence Theory of Truth*, Oxford 1973; O. Handlin, *Truth in History*, Cambridge MA, London 1979; W.J. Abraham, *Divine Revelation and the Limits of Historical Criticism*, Oxford 1982; F.R. Ankersmit, *Narrative Logic: A Semantical Analysis of the Historian's Language*, Den Haag 1983; R.J. Evans, *In Defence of History*, London 1997, esp. 75–102. 224–253.

[18] See basically W. James, *Essays in Pragmatism* (edited with a brief Introduction by A. Castell; The Hafner Library of Classics 7), New York 1948.

[19] P.K. McCarter, "The Historical David", *Int* 40 (1986), 117 (117–129).

ancient inscriptions, although it should be noted that ancient inscriptions do not equal the events they describe. McCarter's view on the lack of archaeological data for David can be seen as a remark in the mode of a coherence theory. It seems to me that he is opting for the position that a specific (re)construction of the life of David can be truer than another one, when it would cohere with archaeological findings or theories based on such findings. McCarter's conclusion that the 'quest for the historical David, therefore, is primarily exegetical' seems to be a pragmatic choice for two reasons. (1) When there is no other evidence the historian must work with the available sources even when it is clear that they are late and biased. (2) The propositions in the Book of Samuel on the acts of David especially when sifted by the process of interpretation are haphazard, contested and unconnected data: The historian is in need of some more general framework within which the 'data' can have their pragmatic function.

### 2.3. The Idea of Narrativism

Such a framework can be found in the idea of narrativism. 'Narrative' is a meta-syntactical idea by which texts can be classified. It hints at the form, the *Gattung* of the text and the tenses used in it. 'Fiction' has to do with the question how far away from reality a text stands.[20] To bring this point to a more fundamental discussion, I will refer to the narrativism of, e.g., Danto and Ankersmit.[21] For them the *narratio* is a form of history-writing (or re-enactment) that consciously selects and connects 'events' from the past into a narrative. The historian by profession is responsible for the selection of the material and the connection of data. When history-writing takes the form of a narrative, it is an organization of the past and not a mere description of it. A distinction should be made between the narrative as a whole and its elements. This distinction has to do with epistemology. The narrative as such cannot be verified, since it is the product of the mind of the historian. All that can be asked is internal consistency and evidence relatedness. A narrative relating history should

---

[20] See also the fundamental remarks by E.A. Knauf, 'From History to Interpretation', in: D.V. Edelman (ed.), *The Fabric of History: Text, Artifact and Israel's Past* (JSOT Sup 127), Sheffield 1991, 47–50, on this subject.
[21] A.C. Danto, *Analytical Philosophy of History*, Cambridge 1968; Ankersmit, *Narrative Logic*; see also the remarks by H.M. Barstad, *History and the Hebrew Bible: Studies in Ancient Israelite and Ancient near Eastern Historiography* (FAT 61), Tübingen 2008, esp. 13–23.

not be self-contradictory. The reader should be given insight in how the elements of the narrative are related to archival data and comparable evidence.[22] The narrative, however, contains propositions, phrased as sentences, or groups of sentences that are evidence-related. They can be verified over and against the evidence available.[23]

### 2.4. History Writing as Re-enactment based on Evidence

Recently, two 'lives of David' appeared written by Steven McKenzie[24] and Baruch Halpern.[25] McKenzie does not aim at a novelistic retelling of the David story or at some other literary representation of this intriguing figure. His goal is to (re)construct David's biography in such a way that other historians could share his proposal as an adequate depiction of the past. His starting point is the above remark by Kyle McCarter.[26] Basically, Halpern follows the same strategy, less thematically organised, however.

Although I appreciate much in the work of McKenzie and Halpern, in the light of the methodological remarks made above, their proposals are in need of refurbishment. Phrased otherwise, I would follow to some degree the recipe of the post-modern historian Hayden White.[27] White makes a clear distinction between 'research' and 'writing'. The research leads to the row-material of unconnected propositions on the past. It is the historian, who in an autonomous narrative offers a representation that by definition is not factual and must compete with other autonomous narratives. In the footsteps of both McKenzie[28] and Halpern[29]—who have shown that the postmodernist distinction between the factual and the

---

[22] See e.g. Ankersmit, *Narrative Logic*, 75–76. Le Roy Ladurie's books—e.g., *Montaillou: Village occitan de 1294 à 1324*, Paris 1975; *Le siècle des Platter 1499–1628:1. Le mendiant et le professeur*, Paris 1996—form a good example, since this historian gives the reader the possibility to check the elements of his historical stories against the evidence on which they are constructed.

[23] See Ankersmit, *Narrative Logic*, 29.75.104: Banks, *Writing the Histroy of Israel*, 1–15.

[24] S.L. McKenzie, *King David. A Biography*, Oxford 2000.

[25] B. Halpern, *David's Secret Demons: Messiah, Murderer, Traitor, King*, Grand Rapids, Cambridge 2001.

[26] In fact McKenzie analyses the three propositions implied in McCarter statement in the given order.

[27] See esp. H.V. White, *The Tropics of Discourse: Essays in Cultural Criticism*, Baltimore: Johns Hopkins University Press, 1978; H.V. White, *The Content of the Form: Narrative Discourse and Historical Representation*, Baltimore: Johns Hopkins University Press, 1987.

[28] S.L. McKenzie, *King David. A Biography*, Oxford 2000.

[29] B. Halpern, *David's Secret Demons: Messiah, Murderer, Traitor, King*, Grand Rapids, Cambridge 2001.

narrated is at least limited by the factual—I will, however, first and fore-most concentrate on the existing evidence. Not every *narratio* on David would be adequate. Not every appropriation of this king—be it in words or pictorial—can be assessed as successful. When it comes to the appli-cation of my ideas on historiography to the 'history of David', five dimen-sions need to be discussed and searched for pieces of evidence and pos-sible propositions on the past. These dimensions are: 1. Landscape; 2. Climate; 3. Archaeology; 4. Epigraphy; 5. Hebrew Bible.[30] After scruti-nizing these dimensions, I would make a proposal of my re-enactment of the life of David, trying to account for as much evidence as possible.

## 3. Landscape

It would be of great interest to discuss the landscape of Ancient Judah in full detail. For the purpose of this contribution it suffices to note that Ancient Israel / Palestine was a hilly area, that contained various and differing zones. The mountainous core of Judah was blessed with soil that as such was fertile. This core area as well as the surrounding semi-arid zones, however, was in constant need of rainwater including a technology to avoid its running off. In other words the area had great agricultural potential but needed an intelligent cultivator.[31]

## 4. Climate

Aharon Horowitz was one of the first historians to pay attention to the effect of changes in climate to the course of history. Based on palyno-logical studies of pollen from various sites in Ancient Israel / Palestine he concluded the interplay of drier and more humid periods in the history of the area. On the basis of the material available to him, he proposed that

---

[30] See also K.L. Noll, *Canaan and Israel in Antiquity: An Introduction* (the Biblical Seminar 83) London, New York 2001, 31–57.

[31] For further details see, e.g., D.C. Hopkins, *The Highlands of Canaan: Agricultural Life in the Early Iron Age* (SWBAS 3), Sheffield 1985, 27–75; O. Borowski, *Daily Life in Biblical Times* (SBL ABS5), Atlanta 2003; A.M. Maier, S. Dar, S. Safrai, (eds.), *The Rural Landscape of Ancient Israel* (BAR International Series 1121), Oxford 2003; M. Har'el, *Landscape, Nature and Man in the Old Testament: A Commentary on Biblical Sites and Events*, Jerusalem 2003.

around 950 BCE the area suffered from a period of dryness.[32] This would imply that the "Age of David" coincided with a change to a drier climate. A drier climate implies smaller agricultural produce and less food. That conclusion stands contrary to the demographic development to be discussed below.

It should be noted that Horowitz's research is quite one-dimensional since it is restricted to only one set of data. Next to that, his conclusions and his time frames are rather rough. Since the time of his research many new data have been found leading to a more sophisticated model of climate change in Iron I Judah. Recently, more elaborated methods have led to a more comprehensive view. The climate of the past can be reconstructed on the basis of the ice-layer research conducted by the GISP2-Programme.[33] In the ice-masses of Greenland traces can be found of the yearly snow fall and its variation over time. The results of this research are astonishing. They open a window into the past and its climate. It turns out that during the Holocene, or post-glacial period the global climate went through a series of climate changes. It turns out that the first half of the tenth century BCE was a period of global cooling at an even greater magnitude than we experience today.[34]

The lowering of the average temperature in a sub-tropical climate implies an increase in rainfall. This can also be deduced form the fact that the sea water level in the Dead Sea was rising in the period.[35] By implication, an increase of rainwater in combination with the improved technology in the construction of terraces leads to the presence of more

---

[32] A. Horowitz, "Preliminary Palynological Indications as to the Climate of Israel during the last 6000 years", *Paléorient* 2 (1974), 407–414; his views were adapted by Hopkins, *The Highlands of Canaan*, 99–108; see also W.H. Stiebing, 'Climate and Collapse: Did the Weather Make Israel's Emergence possible?', *BR* 10 (1994), 18–27.

[33] Greenland Ice Sheet Project http://www.gisp2.sr.unh.edu/; for an application to the Holocene see D.A. Meese, A.J. Gow, P. Grootes, P.A. Mayewski, M. Ram, M. Stuiver, K.C. Taylor, E.D. Waddington, "The Accumulation Record from the GISP2 Core as an Indicator of Climate Change Throughout the Holocene", *Science* 266 (1994), 1680–1682; S.O. Rasmussen, I.K. Seierstad, K.K. Andersen, M. Bigler, D. Dahl-Jensen, S.J. Johnsen, "Synchronization of the NGRIP, GRIP, and GISP2 Ice Cores Across MIS 2 and Palaeoclimatic Implications", *Quaternary Science Reviews* 27 (2008), 18–28.

[34] W. Dansgaard, S.J. Johnsen, J. Møller and C.C. Langway, Jr., "One Thousand Centuries of Climatic Record from Camp Century on the Greenland Ice Sheet", *Science* 166 (October 1969), 377–381; C.D. Schönwiese, *Klimaänderungen. Daten, Analysen*, Berlin 1995.

[35] Yehouda Enzel e.a., 'Late Holocene Climates of the Near East deduced from Dead Sea Level Variations', *Quaternary Research* 60 (2003), 263–273.

water for agriculture and to a better harvest. This all will lead to better conditions for living on the land.

## 5. ARCHAEOLOGY

This section will be opened by two remarks from two well-known scholars. Kyle McCarter stated that 'No archaeological discovery can securely be linked to him [David]'.[36] This view, shared by other scholars, is correct insofar as it regards archaeological findings that can indubitably be connected with the person of David. Recently, John van Seters amplified this view by stating: 'We now know with a high degree of confidence that the sociohistorical context in the Court History of David simply cannot be supported by the archaeological for the 10th century and must belong to a much later age'.[37] This view—too—is correct insofar as it regards archaeological findings that can indubitably be connected with all sorts of details from the life of David. Nevertheless, there exists archaeological evidence form the period in which David supposedly lived: the transit from Iron Age I to Iron Age II.[38] Problematical, however, is the fact that almost all of these remains have been interpreted within the United Monarchy paradigm. This view that accepted the existence of a united monarchy under David and Solomon, who supposedly reigned as

---

[36] McCarter, "The Historical David", 117.

[37] J. van Seters, *The Biblical Saga of King David*, Winona Lake 2009, xii.

[38] I leave aside the interesting discussion on high or low chronology; see on that discussion, e.g., I. Finkelstein, 'Philistine Chronology: High, Middle or Low?' in: S. Gitin, A. Mazar, E. Stern (eds), *Mediterranean Peoples in Transition. Thirteenth to Early Tenth Centuries BCE. In Honor of Professor Trude Dothan*, Jerusalem 1998, 140–147; I. Finkelstein, "Hazor and the North in the Iron Age: A Low Chronology Perspective", *BASOR* 314 (1999), 55–70; E.A. Knauf, "The "Low Chronology" and How Not to Deal With It", *BN* 101 (2000), 56–63; E.A. Knauf, "Low and Lower? New Data on Early Iron Age Chronology from Beth Shean, Tel Rehov and Dor", *BN* 112 (2002), 21–27; H.J. Bruins, J. van der Plicht, A. Mazar, "14-C Dates from Tel Rehov", *Science* 300 (11-4-2003), 315–318: A. Mazar, "The Debate over the Chronology of the Iron Age in the Southern Levant: Its History, the Current Situation and a Suggested Resolution", in: T.E. Levy, T. Higham (eds), *The Bible And Radiocarbon Dating: Archaeology, Text And Science*, London 2005, 15–30; L.L. Grabbe, *Ancient Israel: What do we Know and How do we Know it?*, London, New York 2007, 12–16; A. Mazar, "The Spade and the Text: The Interaction between Archaeology and Israelite History Relating to the Tenth–Ninth Centuries BCE", in H.G.M. Williamson (ed.), *Understanding the History of Ancient Israel* (Proceedings of the British Academy, 143), Oxford 2007, 143–171; R. Beeri, "Round Oil Presses of the 13th–10th Centuries BCE in Palestine and their Implications: Chronology, Function and Geographical Distribution", *PEQ* 140 (2008), 159–167.

kings over a vast territory supported by state bureaucracy, is no longer valid.[39] This implies that we no longer can talk about Solomon's stables at Megiddo, or David's building activities throughout the land. Recently, however, two new claims concerning archaeological findings that could be linked to David have been made.

### 5.1. *The Palace of David and the Battle with Goliath*

1. Eilat Mazar has interpreted the remains of massive walls constructed of large undressed stones—the 'Large Stone Structure'—as part of a big construction complex, which also would have included the 'Stepped Stone Structure' on the slope excavated earlier by Macalister and Duncan.[40] She dated this complex to about 1000 BCE and identified it as the palace of King David.[41] If she were correct, hard evidence for building activities in the Davidic era would be present. Her proposal, however, is open to severe challenge. First of all, her find can be seen as an example of theory-laden observation. Based on an analysis of Biblical evidence, which she takes as first hand eyewitness reports, combined with something like common sense, she earlier stated that the palace of David had to be built "on the top of the spur, northwest of the Stepped Stone Structure".[42] No

---

[39] See, e.g., G.N. Knoppers, "The Vanishing Solomon: The Disappearance of the United Monarchy from Recent Histories of Ancient Israel", *JBL* 116 (1997), 19–44; S. Bunimowitz, Z. Lederman, "The Iron Age Fortification of Tel Beth Shemesh: A 1990–2000 Perspective", *IEJ* 51 (2001), 121–147; D.M. Master, "State Formation Theory and the Kingdom of Ancient Israel", *JNES* 60 (2001), 117–131; Noll, *Canaan and Israel in Antiquity*, 170–198, C. Holden, "Dates Boost Conventional Wisdom About Solomon's Splendor", *Science* 300 (2003), Issue 5617, 229–230; R. Tappy, "Tel Zayit and the Tel Zayit Abecedary in Their Regional Context", in: R.E. Tappy, P.K. McCarter (eds), *Literate Culture and Tenth-Century Canaan: The Tel Zayit Abecedary in Context*, Winona Lake 2008, 1–44; Davies, *Memories of Ancient Israel*, 74–76; the thesis is still accepted by: J.M. Cahill, "Jerusalem at the Time of the United Monarchy: The Archaeological Evidence", in: A.G. Vaughn, A.E. Killebrew (eds), *Jerusalem in Bible and Archaeology: The First Temple Period* (SBL SS 18), Atlanta 2003, 13–80; J. Uziel, I. Shai, "Iron Age Jerusalem: Temple-Palace, Capital City", *JAOS* 127 (2007), 161–170; A. Mazar, "From 1200 to 850 BCE: Remarks on some Selected Archaeological issues", in: L.L. Grabbe (ed.), *Israel in Transition: From Late Bronze Age to Iron IIa (c. 1250–850 BCE). Volume 1. The Archaeology* (LHB / OTS 491), London, New York 2008, 109; Van Seters, *Biblical Saga of King David*, 60–65.

[40] R.A.S. Macalister, J.G. Duncan, *Excavations on the Hill of Ophel, Jerusalem, 1923–1925*, London 1926.

[41] E. Mazar, *The Palace of King David: Excavations at the Summit of the City of David: Preliminary Report of Seasons 2005–2007*, Jerusalem, New York 2009.

[42] E. Mazar, "The Undiscoverd Palace of King David in Jerusalem—A Study in Biblical Archaeology", in: A. Faust (ed.), *New Studies on Jerusalem, Proceedings of the Second*

wonder, that she finds her palace on this spot. Of a more technical archaeological character is the criticism by Israel Finkelstein and others. They
argue that:

- The walls unearthed by Mazar do not belong to a single building;
- The more elaborate walls may be associated with elements uncov-
  ered by Macalister and Duncan in the 1920s and should possibly be
  dated to the Hellenistic period;
- The 'Stepped Stone Structure' represents at least two phases of con-
  struction—the lower (down slope) and earlier, possibly dating to the
  Iron IIA in the 9th century BCE, and the later (which connects to the
  Hasmonaean First Wall upslope) dating to the Hellenistic period.[43]

These remarks make the interpretation by Eilat Mazar somewhat premature. They also indicate that uncovered remains cannot be taken as
hard evidence for Davidic building activities.

2. Recent excavations at Khirbet Qeiyafa (Elah Fortress), have brought
to light the remains of a short term occupation of the site in the tenth
century BCE. The site has been identified with biblical Sha'arayim.[44]
The site is overlooking the Elah Valley where, according to the Biblical
account, David fought Goliath.[45] Sha'arayim was a key location for the
kingdom of Judah along the main road from Philistia and the Coastal
Plain to the eastern Hill Country.[46] The excavations at Khirbet Qeiyafa
are important for two reasons. (1) The pottery types found at this site

---

*Conference*, Ramat-Gan 1996, 9–20 (Hebrew); her view is supported by Mazar, "From
1200 to 850 BCE", 106–107; who primarily was sceptical A. Mazar, "Jerusalem in the 10th
Century BCE: The Glass Half Full", in: Y. Amit, E ben Zvi, I. Finkelstein and O. Lipschits
(eds), *Essays on Ancient Israel in Its Near Eastern Context: A Tribute to Nadav Na'aman*,
Winona Lake 2006, 269–270.

[43] I. Finkelstein, Z. Herzog, L. Singer-Avitz, D. Ussishkin, "Has King David's Palace
in Jerusalem Been Found?", *Tel Aviv* 34 (2007), 142–164; I. Finkelstein, A. Fantalkin,
E. Piasetzky, "Three Snapshots of the Iron IIA: The Nortern Vallyes, the Southern Steppe
and Jerusalem", in: Grabbe (ed.), *Israel in Transition*, 39–40; M.L. Steiner, "Propaganda
in Jerusalem: State Formation in iron Age Judah", in: Grabbe (ed.), *Israel in Transition*,
196–197. On the Maccabean date for the 'Stepped Stone Structure' see also M.L. Steiner,
*The Persian City Walls of Jerusalem* forthcoming. For milder criticsim see O. Keel, *Die
Geschichte Jerusalems und die Entstehung des Monotheismus* (Orte und Landschafte der
Bibel 4,1–2), Göttingen 2007, 147.

[44] A. Mazar, C. Bronk Ramsey, "14C Dates and the Iron Age Chronology of Israel: A
Re-sponse", *Radiocarbon* 50 (2008), 159–180. Y. Garfinkel, S. Ganor, "Khirbet Qeiyafa:
Sha'arayim", *JHS* 8 (2008), # 22.

[45] 1 Sam. 21,9.

[46] As is reflected in 1 Sam. 17,52.

differ from the pottery excavated at the Philistine city of Gath, located seven miles west, from the same period. This might indicate distinct ethnic identities of the two sites.[47] (2) At Khirbet Qeiyafa an ostracon with five lines of an ancient Hebrew text in black ink were discovered. The dyktus of the inscription hints at a date in Iron IIA.[48] The language of the inscription is as yet not established and might be Phoenician or Ancient Hebrew. Conclusions have to wait the proper publication of this inscription. All in all, Khirbet Qeiyafa makes clear that the site was inhabited in Iron Age IIA; the excavation, however, does not deliver proof of the historicity of David's battle with Goliath.

### 5.2. Demographic Developments in Iron IIA

In fact, the excavation at Khirbet Qeiyafa reinforces an observation made by Paula McNutt on demographic developments during Iron IIA in Judah.[49] In her view, based on a variety of excavations, an increase of population in the area of Judah in Iron IIA can be detected. The climate change mentioned above could have been instrumental in this development. This view concurs with (1) a risen insight and (2) a recent finding.

### 5.3. Improvement of Terrace Building

All agriculture is dependent on three features: a fertile soil, enough water and the presence of a cultivator. In the Levant, the construction of

---

[47] As has been suggested by Ethan Bronner, "Find of Ancient City Could Alter Notions of Biblical David", in the *New York Times* of October 29, 2008.

[48] See below 6.2.3.

[49] P. McNutt, *Reconstructing the Society of Ancient Israel* (Library of Ancient Israel), London, Louisville 1999, 108–112; see also the essays in I. Finkelstein, N. Na'aman (eds), *From Nomadism to Monarchy: Archaeological and Historical Aspects of Early Israel*, Jerusalem 1994; Dietrich, *Frühe Königszeit in Israel*, 127–133; McKenzie, *King David*, 20–23; Halpern, *David's Secret Demons*, 427–478; for comparable evidence see S. Gibson, "Agricultural Terraces and Settlement Expansion in the Highlands of Early Iron Age Palestine: Is there any Correlation between the Two?", in: A. Mazar (ed.), *Studies in the Archaeology of the Iron Age in Israel and Jordan* (JSOT Sup 331), Sheffield 2001), 113–145; A. Fantalkin, I. Finkelstein, "The Sheshonq I Campaign and the 8th-Century BCE Earthquake: More on the Archaeology and History of the South in the Iron I–IIa", *Tel Aviv 33* (2006) 18–42; Finkelstein, Fantalkin, Piasetzky, "Three Snapshots of the Iron IIA", 35–41; R.E. Tappy, "East of Askelon: The Setting and Settling of the Judean Lowlands in the Iron Age II A", in: J.D. Schloen (ed.), *Exploring the Longue Duree: Essays in Honor of Lawrence E. Stager*, Winona Lake 2009, 449–463.

terraces on hill slopes has very ancient even pre-historic roots.[50] During the Early Bronze Age I the technology was implemented on a larger scale.[51] This technology helped to arrest the run-off water and to make it useful for agricultural purposes. A second advantage has been that more horizontal surfaces for agricultural use came into existence, which made the work for the cultivator much easier. Next to that a system of terraces is very helpful in avoiding erosion.[52]

Within the history of terracing there are only few technological improvements. The application of iron for agricultural tools and their introduction on the terraces of Judah most certainly would have lead to greater control over the various phases of the agricultural cycle.[53] Next to that the number of agricultural terraces increased during Iron II A.[54] It goes without saying that a better form of arresting run-off rainwater would lead to a larger outturn in harvest and hence to more food, which could have been the material basis for the demographic development mentioned above.

### 5.4. *Apiculture at* Tēl Reḥōv

Excavations at Tēl Reḥōv have brought to light the remains of an Iron Age apiary. A large number of beehives from the tenth to the early ninth century BCE were found.[55] The remains make the impression of an almost industrial production of honey. The number of beehives gives the impression that honey was produced not only for the local market, but also or even especially for reasons of export.[56] Mazar and Panitz-Cohen assume that such a large scale production of honey needed a "central

---

[50] From the Natufian site Hahal Oren four architectural terraces are known that supported a settlement of about 13 hut-dwellings, see M. Stekelis, T. Yizraeli, "Excavations at Nahal Oren: A Preliminary Report", *IEJ* 13 (1963), 1–12.

[51] See N. Glueck, "Further Explorations in Eastern Palestine", *BASOR* 86 (1942), 14–24; P. de Miroschedji, "Tel Yarmut, 1992", *IEJ* 42 (1992), 265–272.

[52] See, e.g., Hopkins, *The Highlands of Canaan*, 173–186; H.J. Bruins, M. Evenari, U. Nessler, "Rainwater-harvesting for Food Production in Arid Zones", *Applied Geography* 6 (1986), 13–32; K.W. Butzer, "Environmental History in the Mediterranean World: Cross-Disciplinary Investigation of Cause-and-Effect for Degradation and Soil Erosion", *Journal of Archaeological Science* 32 (2005), 1773–1800.

[53] See, e.g., Hopkins, *The Highlands of Canaan*, 173–186.

[54] See Gibson, "Agricultural Terraces and Settlement Expansion in the Highlands of Early Iron Age Palestine".

[55] A. Mazar, N. Panitz-Cohen, "It is the Land of Honey: Beekeeping at Tel Reḥov", *Near Eastern Archaeology* 70 (2007), 202–219.

[56] Mazar, Panitz-Cohen, "It is the Land of Honey", 211, calculated "an annual yield of about three to five hundred kilograms of honey and fifty to seventy kilograms of beeswax".

authority to carry out broad-scale economic and administrative policies such as would have been required to set up and maintain this apiary".[57] In other words, they see the apiary at Tēl Reḥōv as evidence for the early emergence of a state with administrative abilities in Judah and / or Israel. They assume that it is only by the directives of a central power that a more complex system of production and distribution could emerge. A counter-argument against that view can be found in the fact that during the Early Bronze Age, nomadic groups were able to organize factorylike copper-melting activities in the Faynan area of Jordan. The metal-forging and the distribution of commodities took place without the support of the nearby city states.[58] In my view, economies can blossom without the impulse from a central organization and it is only a complex and blossoming economy that could ask for a central organization in order to defend the grown interests. A zooarchaeological analysis of a large sample of animal bones from the domestic quarters of Iron Age Tēl Reḥōv has revealed interesting aspects of the foodways of the inhabitants of the site: The regular partaking of gourmet portions of sheep and goat meat from young animals; wild-boar hunting. The consumption of gourmet portions of livestock animals and the practice of wild-boar hunting suggest that Iron Age Reḥov was inhabited by a socioeconomic elite.[59] At Tēl Reḥōv three paleo-Hebrew inscriptions were found in connection with the apiary.[60] They will be discussed below.

### 5.5. Fish bones in Jerusalem

During excavations at the rock-cut "pool" near the spring in Jerusalem 7,392 fish bones from Iron IIA have been found. About one third belonged to a particular family of species. No less than 2,300 bones belonged to maritime fish. From the available evidence it can be deduced

---

[57] Mazar, Panitz-Cohen, "It is the Land of Honey", 211–212.

[58] See R.B. Adams, "Copper Trading Networks across the Arabah during the Later Early Bronze Age", in: P. Bienkowski, K. Galor (eds), *Crossing the Rift. Resources, Routes, Settlement Patterns and Interaction in the Wadi Arabah* (Levant Supplementary Series Volume 3), Oxford 2006, 137–144.

[59] N. Marom, N. Raban-Gerstel, A. Mazar, G. Bar-Oz, "Backbone of Society: Evidence for Social and Economic Status of the Iron Age Population of Tel Rehov, Beth She'an Valley, Israel", *BASOR* 354 (2009), 55–75.

[60] A. Mazar, "Three 10th–9th Century BCE Inscriptions from Tēl Reḥōv", in C.G. den Hertog, U. Hübner, S. Münger (eds), *Saxa Loquentur: Studien zur Archäologie Palästina / Israels. Festschrift fur Volkmar Fritz zum 65. Geburtstag* (AOAT 302), Munster 2003, 171–184.

that some sort of a fish market existed in the era near one of the city gates.[61] The presence of the remains of maritime fish implies some sort of trade network that could function without the presence of a bureaucratic state. The consumption of fish and its proteins would have helped the physical condition of the inhabitants of Iron IIA Jerusalem. I construe it to be one of the factors for the demographic development.

## 6. Epigraphic Evidence

In this section, two kinds of evidence will be discussed and analyzed. Firstly, attention is paid to inscriptions from the Iron Age that supposedly refer to David. Secondly, I will look at inscriptions that, although they do not mention David, are of importance since they roughly stem from Iron Age IIA.

### 6.1. *Inscriptions Mentioning David*

Three pieces of inscriptional evidence will be discussed.

### 6.1.1. *The Tel Dan Inscription(s)*

On 21 July 1993 a basalt-stone with an ancient North West Semitic inscription was unearthed during an archaeological campaign at Tel Dan, formerly Tell el-Qādi. About one year later two other inscribed fragments were found at the same site. The inscriptions admirably quickly published by Biran and Naveh[62] occasioned an intense and sometimes heated[63] discussion among scholars on questions like the authenticity of the text(s), the date and language—Hebrew, Aramaic or a mixed dialect—of the

---

[61] See R. Reich, E. Shukron, O. Lernau, "The Iron Age II Finds from the Rock-Cut "Pool" near the Spring in Jerusalem: A Preliminary Report", in: Grabbe (ed.), *Israel in Transition*, 140–141.

[62] A. Biran, J. Naveh, 'An Aramaic Stele Fragment from Tel Dan', *IEJ* 43 (1993), 81–98; A. Biran, J. Naveh, 'The Tel Dan Inscription: A New Fragment', *IEJ* 45 (1995), 1–18.

[63] As especially reflected in the titles of the following papers: H. Shanks, ''David' found at Dan', *BAR* 20/2 (1994), 26–39; P.R. Davies, ''House of David' Built on Sand: The Sins of the Biblical Maximizers', *BAR* 20/4 (1994), 54–55; A.F. Rainey, 'The 'House of David' and the House of the Deconstructionists', *BAR* 20/6 (1994), 47, who warns the reader in his subtle subtitle 'Davies is an amateur who can 'safely be ignored''; see also; H. Hagelia, *The Tel Dan Inscription: A Critical Investigation of Recent Research on Its Palaeography and Philology* (Studia Semitica Uppsalensia 22), Uppsala 2006.

inscription(s), the possibility of a join between the fragments known and the identity of the morpheme ביתדוד—'House of David' or 'Temple of the deity Dôd'—in line 9 of the inscription.[64] I will not repeat or summarise the discussion here but only state that a consensus has not been reached yet.

A great number of scholars accept the historicity of the inscription as well as the standard 'join' of the fragments A + B1 and B2 to one coherent text.[65] This implies that in their view about a century and a half after the alleged life of David, this king was known as the founding father of the dynasty that ruled the southern part of Israel. In other words, the Tel Dan inscription is seen as an independent witness to the historicity of David. Nevertheless, McKenzie for instance warns his readers that 'names are not stories'. The historicity of David does not imply automatically the trustworthiness of the stories in 1 and 2 Samuel.[66]

The recent analysis of the inscription by George Athas, however, underscored the view that the three fragments (A; B1+B2) should be regarded as pieces of one and the same inscription. Fragment A contains the remnants of the upper part of the inscription while fragments B1 + 2 should, however, be placed below fragment A at about 20–25 % from the bottom.[67] Athas' view also has implications for the historical context of

---

[64] An outline of the most important contributions to the debate is found on pp. 11–14 of A. Lemaire, 'The Tel Dan Stela as a Piece of Royal Historiography', *JSOT* 81 (1998), 3–14. See now G. Athas, *The Tel Dan Inscription: A Reappraisal and a New Interpretation* (JSOT Sup, 360), Sheffield 2003; L.J. Mykytiuk, *Identifying Biblical Persons in Northwest Semitic Inscriptions of 1200–539 B.C.E.* (SBL Academia Biblica, 12), Atlanta 2004, 110–132; Hagelia, *The Tel Dan Inscription.*

[65] E.g., Biran, Naveh, 'The Tel Dan Inscription: A New Fragment'; W.H. Schniedewind, 'Tel Dan Stela: New Light on Aramaic and Jehu's Revolt', *BASOR* 302 (1996), 77–78; J.W. Wesselius, 'The First Royal Inscription from Ancient Israel: The Tel Dan Inscription Reconsidered', *SJOT* 13 (1999), 163–188; J.-L. Ska, *Les énigmes du passé: Histoire d'Israël et récit biblique* (Le Livre et le Rouleau 14), Bruxelles 2001, 99–100; Noll, *Canaan and Israel in Antiquity*, 184–185; A. Lemaire, 'Hebrew and Westsemitic Inscriptions and Pre-Exilic Israel', in: J. Day (ed.), *In Search of Pre-Exilic Israel* (JSOT Sup 204), London, New York 2004, 359–370; Mykytiuk, *Identifying Biblical Persons*, 110–132; K.A.D. Smelik, *Neem een boekrol en schrijf: Tekstvondsten uit het Oude Israël*, Zoetermeer 2006, 60–68; I. Finkelstein, N.A. Silberman, *David and Solomon: In Search of the Bible's Sacred Kings and the Roots of the Western Tradition*, New York 2006, 264–266; Hagelia, *The Tel Dan Inscription*; F.I. Andersen, R.S. Hess, *Names in the Study of Biblical History: David, Yhwh Names, and the Role of Personal Names* (Buried History Monograph 2), Melbourne 2007, 6–14; Davies, *Memories of Ancient Israel*, 95–97.

[66] McKenzie, *King David*, 11–13.

[67] Athas, *Tel Dan Inscription*, 189–191; the idea had previously been suggested by Biran, Naveh, 'The Tel Dan Inscription: A New Fragment', 11; Dietrich, *Frühe Königszeit*

the inscription. In view of the archaeological findings at Tel Dan the inscription should be construed as referring to events that took place in the early parts of the eighth century BCE. Athas makes a strong case that the 'king of ביתדוד' mentioned in A:8–9 has been Joash and that his son Amaziah is referred to in B:8.[68] His analysis not only reinforces the idea that two different military conflicts were related in the Tel Dan inscription, but also that the events narrated took place several decades after the death of Jehu. Although Athas' analysis has clarified various points from the reign of king Jehu, it has no implications whatsoever for the historicity of David.

The evidence from the Tel Dan inscription makes clear that about a century and a half after he assumedly lived, David was seen as the eponymous ancestor of the royal lineage of Judah, even from an outsider perspective. In other words: a David must have lived and ruled over what is now known as the Southern Kingdom.[69] The question of the historicity of the narratives in Samuel and Kings and their manifold propositional elements cannot be decided from the evidence of the Tel Dan inscription.

### 6.1.2. Mesha:31

Based on firsthand observations of this well-known inscription, André Lemaire proposed to read line 31 as follows:

And the House of [Da]vid dwelt in Horonen.[70]

---

in Israel, 140; now accepted by Keel, Geschichte Jerusalems, 165; Grabbe, Ancient Israel, 129–130; M. Staszak, "Zu einer Lesart und dem historischen Hintergrund des Fragments B der Stele von Tel Dan", BN 142 (2009), 67–77.

[68] Athas, Tel Dan Inscription, 255–298.

[69] See also, Halpern, David's Secret Demons, 71; Noll, Canaan and Israel in Antiquity, 223–224; Finkelstein, Silberman, David and Solomon, 264–266; Mazar, "Jerusalem in the 10th Century BCE", 268; Dietrich, David: Der Herrscher mit der Harfe, 21–26; Keel, Geschichte Jerusalems, 165; Mazar, "From 1200 to 850 BCE", 109. For a critical position see Davies, Memories of Ancient Israel, 95–97.

[70] A. Lemaire, 'La dynastie davidique (byt dwd) dans deux inscriptions ouest-sémitiques du IX. s. av. J.-C.', SEL 11 (1994), 17–19; Lemaire, "Tel Dan Stela", 10. His view is adopted by A.F. Rainey, "Following up the Ekron and Mesha Inscriptions", IEJ 48 (2000), 116–117; modified by K.A. Kitchen, 'A Possible Mention of David in the Late Tenth Century BCE, and the Deity *Dod as Dead as the Dodo?', JSOT 76 (1997), 35; mentioned by Keel, Geschichte Jerusalems, 165–166; Davies, Memories of Ancient Israel, 94–97; but critized by N. Na'aman, "King Mesha and the Foundation of the Moabite Monarchy", IEJ 47 (1997), 89. E. Gass, Die Moabiter: Geschichte und Kultur eines ostjordanischen Volkes im 1. Jahrtausend v. Chr. (ADPV 38), Wiesbaden 2009, 48, accepts the reading, but contrues DWD as freferring to an otherwise unknown southern-Moabite dynasty.

In the following, though broken lines, Kemosh—the Moabite divinity—orders king Mesha to reclaim Horonen and surroundings for the kingdom of Moab. In case Lemaire's proposal could be affirmed by an independent analysis of the Mesha inscription, then some light might by shed on 2 Kings 3.[71] In that biblical report a coalition of Israel, Judah and Edom against Moab is narrated. According to McKenzie the presence of the name 'David' in the Meša-stele is less certain than in the Tel Dan inscription. Nevertheless, it makes the historicity of David plausible, although the text does not give any information on the life of David.[72]

### 6.1.3. *Sheshonq Relief # 106*

Kitchen proposed to read in the famous relief of Pharaoh Sheshonq carved on the temple of Amun in Thebes: "the highlands / heights of David (*d-w-t*)".[73] If Kitchen's proposal were true, than 'David' would refer to a clan living in the hills of central Palestine in the ninth century BCE. His proposal, however, is quite speculative as even McKenzie accepts.[74] This implies that no historical conclusion can be drawn based upon the Sheshonq Relief.

---

[71] However, the connection between the historical propositions in the Mesha inscription and in 2 Kings 3 remain enigmatic and complicated; see, e.g., J.A. Dearman, "Historical Reconstruction and the Mesha Inscription", in: J.A. Dearman (ed.), *Studies in the Mesha Inscription*, Atlanta 1989, 155–210; K.A.D. Smelik, *Converting the Past: Studies in Ancient Israelite and Moabite Historiography* (OTS 28), Leiden 1992, 59–92.; Na'aman, 'King Mesha and the Foundation of the Moabite Monarchy', 192; Finkelstein, Silberman, *David and Solomon*, 98–101; Th.L. Thompson, 'Mesha and Questions of Historicity', *SJOT* 21 (2007), 241–260; N. Na'aman, 'Royal Inscription versus Prophetic Story, Mesha's Rebellion according to Biblical and Moabite Hitoriography', in: L.L. Grabbe (ed.), *Ahab Agonistes: The Rise and Fall of the Omri Dynasty* (LHB/OTS 421), London new York 2007, 166–176; E. van der Steen, K.A.D. Smelik, "King Mesha and the Tribe of Dibon", *JSOT* 32 (2007), 139–162; Grabbe, *Ancient Israel*, 144–146; E. Gass, 'Topographical Considerations and Redaction Criticism in 2 Kings 3', *JBL* 128 (2009), 65–84; Gass, *Moabiter*, 53–61.

[72] McKenzie, *King David*, 15. Halpern, *David's Secret Demons*, 268–269, makes no comment on Lemaire's reconstruction of the Meša-stela.

[73] Kitchen, 'A Possible Mention of David', 29–44; for mild criticism, see Keel, *Geschichte Jerusalems*, 166–167.

[74] McKenzie, *King David*, 15–16; Halpern, *David's Secret Demons*, 71–72, 266–268; on the campaign see now Fantalkin, Finkelstein, 'The Sheshonq I Campaign'; Keel, *Geschichte Jerusalems*, 339–340; Grabbe, *Ancient Israel* 81–83; R.L. Chapman, 'Putting Sheshonq I in his Place', *PEQ* 141 (2009), 4–17.

### 6.1.4. *Conclusions*

On the basis of the epigraphic evidence a clear and sound conclusion can be drawn. The references open the lane for accepting David as an historical figure, but no information on his deeds and doings is given in them. This assumption can even be phrased in the language of a correspondence theory of truth: The historicity of David as a person can be seen as true, since it corresponds to evidence from reality. This is a restricted truth, since it only holds for the figure of David, but not for the various stories on him.

### 6.2. *Tenth Century* BCE *Inscriptions*

In the framework of the discussion on the origin of the states of Judah and Israel, Israel Finkelstein and Neil Silberman stated: "Not a single trace of tenth century Judahite literary activity has been found".[75] They correctly leave aside the well-known 'Gezer-calendar' from the tenth century BCE,[76] since this was most probably not a Judahite text. Recent excavations, however, have made clear that some traces of Judahite literary activity have survived.

### 6.2.1. *Minor Inscriptions*

Half a dozen Judahite texts from tenth century BCE are now known.

(1) Two short inscriptions from Tel ʿAmal (Tell el-ʾAṣi) west of Beth Shan. The first reads לנמש, 'belonging to Nimsh(i)', and was incised

---

[75] I. Finkelstein, N. Silberman, *The Bible Unearthed: Archaeology's New Vision of Ancient Israel and the Origins of the Sacred Texts*, New York 2001, 238; in similar vein D.W. Jamieson-Drake, *Scribes and Schools in Monarchic Judah* (JSOT Sup 109; SWBAS 9), Sheffield 1991, 139–140; see the criticism by N. Naʾaman, "Sources and Composition in the History of Solomon'" in: L.K. Handy (ed.), *The Age of Solomon* (SHANE 11), Leiden 1997, 160–161; Borowski, *Daily Life in Biblical Times*, 99–107; J. Shimron, "Perceptions and Evidence of Early Literacy in Hebrew", in: D.D. Ravid, H. Bat-Zeev Shyldkrot (eds), *Perspectives on Language and Language Development: Essays in Honor of Ruth A. Berman*, Dordrrecht, Boston 2005, 453–472. McNutt, *Reconstructing the Society of Ancient Israel*, 66–69; Grabbe, *Ancient Israel*, 115–118, hold a middle position.

[76] Gez(10):1; *HAE* 1:30–37; *KAI* 182; *HI* 156–165. In my view the Gezer Calendar does not represent a Hebrew text; for discussion see D. Sivan, "The Gezer Calendar and Northwest Semitic Linguistics", *IEJ* 48 (1998), 101–105; Tappy, "Tel Zayit and the tel Zayit Abecedary", 1–44.

on the shoulder of a jar.[77] Nimshi was either the owner of the jar or, more probably, the receiver of the commodities that were in the jar. The second inscription was engraved on the rim of a jar found in a tomb: ...]חאל, 'belonging to Achy[....'[78]

(2) An inscription on the rim of a dish found at Tel Batash (Timna in the Judaean Shephala) that reads: לחנן : ב[ ...], '[the so]n of Hanan'.[79] Hanan most probably was the owner of the dish.

(3) An incised game board form Beth Shemesh with two names on it: חנן, 'Hanan', and גמען, 'Gam'on'.[80]

(4) Three short inscriptions from Tēl Reḥōv (*Tell eṣ-Ṣārem*) in the Beth-Shean Valley.[81]

   a. Inscription No. 1 was incised on a sherd found on a floor surface attributed to Stratum VI in Area B. The inscription reads לבנ[ה/א], 'belonging to the prophet', or 'Libn[ah]'..[82]

   b. Inscription No. 2 was found in room 4616 of Building B in Area E, attributed to Stratum IV. The building appears to be part of a sanctuary complex, and at its north-eastern corner, facing a spacious courtyard, a platform with a few standing stones[83] was found, with a ceramic altar nearby. The inscription was incised after firing on the shoulder of a "hippo" storage jar and reads עמ[ ] [ ]מע, 'from ... [to] ....'[84] In my view the inscription contained the name of both receiver and sender. Mazar argues that only the sender is mentioned and proposes three possible names: "from ʿAmasʿam"; "from ʿOmriʿam", or "from ʿAnerʿam".[85]

---

[77] Asi(10):1; S. Levy, G. Edelstein, "Cinq Années de Fouilles à Tel ʿAmal (Nir David)", *RB* 79 (1972), 336; *HAE* 1:29–23; *HI* 3.

[78] Levy, Edelstein, "Cinq Années de Fouille", 341.

[79] Bat(10):3; G.L. Kelm, A. Mazar, "Tel Batash (Timnah) Ezcavations: Third Preliminary Report (1984–1989)", in: *Preliminary Reports of ASOR-Sponsored Excavations, 1982–1989* (BASOR Sup 27), Baltimore 1991, 55–56; *HAE* 1:30.

[80] S. Bunimovitz, Z. Lederman, "Six Seasons of Excavations at Beth Shemesh", *Qadmoniot* 30 (1997), 22–37; on board games from Israel/Palestine see U. Hübner, *Spiele und Spielzeug im antiken Palästina* (OBO 121), Freiburg, Göttingen 1992; P. Romain, "Les représentations des jeux de pions dans le Proche-Orient ancien et leur signification", *Board Game Studies* 3 (2000), 11–38.

[81] Mazar, "Three 10th–9th Century BCE Inscriptions from Tēl Reḥōv", 171–184.

[82] Mazar, "Three 10th–9th Century BCE Inscriptions from Tēl Reḥōv", 171–173. A tenth century BCE date for this level is highly probable.

[83] To be interpreted as *maṣṣēbôt*.

[84] Mazar, "Three 10th–9th Century BCE Inscriptions from Tēl Reḥōv", 173–176.

[85] Mazar, "Three 10th–9th Century BCE Inscriptions from Tēl Reḥōv", 176.

c. Inscription No. 3 was found in Room 5425—part of an exceptional building that was destroyed by heavy fire. Like inscription No. 2, this inscription also was incised on the shoulder of
a "hippo" type storage jar. It reads נמש[ ]לשק, 'from Shaq[qu
to] Nimshi'[86] and thus contains the names of both sender and
receiver.

On these inscriptions Mazar stated: "The evidence, albeit scant, of writing
on everyday objects in Israel and Judah during the 10th–9th centuries
allows for the assumption that many more inscriptions were written
on perishable materials (papyrus and parchment). The use of writing
on everyday objects like pottery vessels is probably only the tip of the
iceberg of literacy in ancient Israel and neighbouring regions during this
period".[87] His iceberg metaphor is clear and dangerous at the same time,
since it is difficult to argue from evidence that has not yet been found.
Nevertheless, these minor inscriptions reveal that some Judahite literary
activity took place in the tenth century BCE. It should be noted that
this activity was mainly connected with the distribution of agricultural
products or related to objects of luxury—the dish and the game board.
No connections with an emerging state are assumed. Before drawing
conclusions, a final piece of evidence needs to be discussed.

### 6.2.2. The Tel Zayit Abecedary

During excavations at Tel Zayit in the Shephalah—most probably to be
equated with Biblical Libnah[88]—a paleo-Hebrew inscription was found.
The stone on which the inscription was engraved was later used in the
interior face of a wall. The building, to which this wall belonged, was
destroyed by fire near the close of the tenth century BCE. This implies
that the inscription can quite securely be dated to the first half of the
tenth century BCE. The inscription contained the 22 characters of the
west Semitic alphabet.[89] Abecedaries are known in several west Semitic

---

[86] Mazar, "Three 10th–9th Century BCE Inscriptions from Tēl Reḥōv", 176–180.
[87] Mazar, "Three 10th–9th Century BCE Inscriptions from Tēl Reḥōv", 176–182.
[88] See, e.g., Joshua 10; 2 Kings 19:8; identification with Ziklag – 1 Samuel 27–30, is also possible.
[89] R.E. Tappy, M.J. Lundberg, P.K. McCarter, B. Zuckerman, "An abecedary of the mid-tenth century BCE from the Judaean Shephelah", *BASOR* 344 (2006), 5–46; and the essays in R.E. Tappy, P.K. McCarter (eds), *Literate Culture and Tenth-Century Canaan: The Tel Zayit Abecedary in Context*, Winona Lake 2008.

languages: Ugaritic,[90] Canaanite,[91] Phoenician,[92] Ancient Hebrew,[93] Aramaic,[94] Ammonite,[95] and Arabic.[96] Even a Greek abecedary form Jerusalem from the late second temple period has been found.[97] Abecedaries can be construed as part of scribal education,[98] without however indicating the existence of a school-building.[99] The presence of an abecedary at Tel Zayit—in a borderland area[100]—in the tenth century BCE indicates a certain level of literacy. It is interesting to note that the inscription despite

---

[90] *KTU* 5.4; 5.5 (fragment); 5.6; 5.8 (partial abecedary); 5.9 (letter with two partial abecedaries); 5.13 (multiple lines of partial abecedaries); 5.14 (complete alphabet with syllabic equivalents).

[91] The Beth Shemesh Tablet: *KTU* 5.24 = 8.1—G.A. Barton, "Notes on the Ain Shems Tablet," *BASOR* 52 (1933), 5–6; see P. Swiggers, "The Bet-Shemesh "abecedary" ", in: A.S. Kaye (ed.), *Semitic Studies in Honor of Wolf Leslau on the Occasion of his eighty-fifth Birthday*, Wiesbaden 1991, 1520–1527; a South Semitic Abecedary excavated at Ugarit: *KTU* 9.426—P. Bordreuil, D. Pardee, "Un Abécédaire du type sud sémitique découvert en 1988 dans les fouilles archéologiques françaises de Ras Shamra-Ougarit," *Comptes-rendus de l'Académie des Inscriptions et Belles-Letters*, 1995, 855–860; 'Izbet Sartah-ostracon edit. M. Kochavi, "An Ostracon from the Period of the Judges", *Tel Aviv* 4 (1977), 1–13; see recently M.C.A. Korpel, "Kryptogramme in Ezechiel 19 und im 'Izbet-Sarta-Ostrakon'," *ZAW* 121 (2009), 70–86.

[92] See A. Lemaire, *Les écoles et la formation de la Bible dans l'Ancien Israël* (OBO 121), Fribourg, Göttingen 1981, 10 (fragment, written in boustrophedon).

[93] E.g., Lak(8):13; *HAE* 1:74–57 (fragment) see now J.N. Whisenant, *Writing, Literacy, and Textual Transmission: The Production of Literary Documents in Iron Age Judah and the Composition of the Hebrew Bible* (DPhil University of Michigan), 2008, 321; on the Hebrew abecedaries see Lemaire, *Les écoles et la formation de la Bible*, 7–33. For a much later period see A. bij de Vaate, "Alphabet-Inscriptions from Jewish Graves," in: J.W. van Henten and P.W. van der Horst, *Studies in Jewish Epigraphy*, Leiden 1994, 148–161.

[94] See A. Lemaire, "Abécédaires et exercices d'un écolier en épigraphie Nord-Ouest Sémitique." *Journal Asiatique* 266 (1978), 221–235.

[95] Mainly on abecedary seals, see N. Avigad, *Corpus of West Semitic Stamp Seals* (Revised and Completed by Benjamin Sass), Jerusalem1997, 366.

[96] P. Bordreuil, "The South-Arabian abecedary", *NEA* 63 (2000), 197.

[97] D. Ben-Ami, Y. Tchekhanovets, "A Greek Abecedary Fragment from the City of David", *PEQ* 140 (2008), 195–202.

[98] See: C.A. Rollston, "Scribal Education in Ancient Israel: The Old Hebrew Epigraphic Evidence", *BASOR* 344 (2006), 47–74. A connection with mantic practices can not be established, see A.R. Millard, "'BGD. Magic Spell or Educational Exercise?", *Eretz Israel* 18 (1985) 39*–42*; R. Byrne, "The Refuge of Scribalism in Iron I Palestine", *BASOR* 345 (2007), 1–31.

[99] As suggested by Lemaire, *Les écoles et la formation de la Bible*, 7–33; K. van der Toorn, *Scribal Culture and the Making of the Hebrew Bible*, Cambridge, London 2007, 96–104. For criticism of Lemaire's position see, e.g., J.L. Crenshaw, *Education in Ancient Israel: Across the Deadening Silence*, New York 1998, 100–108; Smelik, *Neem een boekrol en schrijf*, 29–38; C.A. Rollston, "The Phoenician Script of the Tel Zayit Abecedary and Putative Evidence for Israelite Literacy", in: Tappy, McCarter (eds), *Literate Culture and Tenth-Century Canaan*, 70–72.

[100] See Tappy, "Tel Zayit and the tel Zayit Abecedary", 1–44.

it being inscribed on a forty-pound stone contains characters that stagger up and down over the surface. This implies that the inscription was more of a writing exercise than a formal monument.[101] It should be noted that no connection to an emerging state and its central power can be established. Ronald Tappy has made clear that Tel Zayit and surroundings was a blossoming agricultural area in Iron II A. The area produced not only for the local market.[102] This development might explain the need for writing skills in view of the administration for the upcoming trade.

### 6.2.3. *Khirbet Qeiyafa Inscription*

As noticed above a tenth century BCE ostracon containing an inscription in Ancient hebrew has been found at Khirbet Qeiyafa. Thanks to Gershon Galil the inscription is now made readable for the scholalry world.[103] On the basis of the drawing supplied by him I would read:

1′ ‏[. . .]ת‏[א עדב ועשת על‏
2′ ‏[מ‏]תי טפש‏[‏ן‏]מלעו‏[ד‏]ב‏[ע‏] טפש‏
3′ ‏ו ל‏[ד‏]בר ללע ב‏[ר‏] רג‏[ו‏]‏
4′ ‏ךלמ דבי מקמ ן‏[מ‏]ל‏[א‏]‏
5′ ‏[ד‏]ת רג ךש דבע‏[ו‏] ןי‏[ב‏]א‏

And translate:

1′ you shall not do [it], but worship th[e . . .].
2′ Judge the sla[ve] and the wid[ow] / Judge the orph[an]
3′ [and] the stranger. [Pl]ead for the infant / plead for the po[or and]
4′ the widow. From the power of the hand of the king
5′ protect the po[or and] the slave / [supp]ort the stranger.

In my view, this text should be construed as a writing exercise—as becomes apparent from the irregular shapes of the characters, the upstairs writing of the last three letters of line 2′ and the metathesis ‏יבד‏ for ‏ביד‏ in line 4′. As for the contents, the inscription reflects an early form of social consciousness, the awakening of which was probably one of the teaching strategies in Iron IIA. It would be premature to draw far-

---

[101] See also Tappy, Lundberg, McCarter, Zuckerman, "Abecedary of the mid-tenth Century BCE", 42; Whisenant, *Writing, Literacy, and Textual Transmission*, 163.

[102] Tappy, "East of Askelon", 457–459.

[103] G. Galil, 'The Khirbrt Qeiyafa Inscription', forthcoming; see also H. Misgav, Y. Garfinkel, S. Ganor, 'The Ostracon', in: Y. Garfinkel, S. Ganor, *Khirbet Qeiyafa Vol. 1 Excavation Report 2007–2008*, Jerusalem 2009, 243–257; A. Yardeni, 'Further Observation on the Ostracon', in: Garfinkel, Ganor, *Khirbet Qeiyafa Vol. 1*, 259–260.

reaching conclusions from this inscription, other than the fact that the tenth century BCE shows an emerging literacy.

### 6.3. *Literacy, Writing and the Emerging State*

In his evaluation of the epigraphic evidence from the tenth century BCE, Seth Sanders notes that the inscriptions discussed above "challenge both the somewhat idealized reconstruction of a bureaucratized Solomonic state and the somewhat preconceived dismissal of complex culture in 10th-century Israel".[104] This statement tallies with my observation that some Judahite literary activity can be found in that period. This activity, however, was related to what I see as an upcoming agriculture that more and more supplied the non local market. Most inscriptions are to be connected to agriculture and its trade, some to luxury items and not to the functions of a central state. I therefore conclude that the epigraphic evidence from the tenth century BCE can be related to a period of demographic growth. Population growth, upcoming trade and starting literacy were signs of the time. They were not orchestrated by a central state. They can be seen as elements of a *histoire conjuncturiel*: These developments were in need of a stronger administration to defend the economic interests that came out of them. Therefore, the "Kingdom of David" better could be construed as an "ethnic entity that would become a nation"[105] or be seen as a patrimonial society.[106]

---

[104] S.L. Sanders, "Writing and Early Iron Age Israel: Before National Scripts, beyond Nations and States", in: Tappy, McCarter (eds), *Literate Culture and Tenth-Century Canaan*, 104.

[105] Quotation from S. Bunimowitz, Z. Lederman, "The Iron Age Fortification of Tel Beth Shemesh: A 1990–2000 Perspective", *IEJ* 51 (2001), 147; see also W.G. Dever, "Histories and Non-Histories of Ancient Israel: The Question of the United Monarchy", in: J. Day (ed.), *In Search of Pre-Exilic Israel* (JSOT Sup 406), London new York 2004, 65–94; Tappy, Lundberg, McCarter, Zuckerman, "Abecedary of the mid-tenth Century BCE", 41–42; Tappy, "Tel Zayit and the Tel Zayit Abecedary", 8–9; Whisenant, *Writing, Literacy, and Textual Transmission*, 165–167; Mazar, "Jerusalem in the 10th Century BCE", 255–272; Grabbe, *Ancient Israel*, 105–115; Mazar, "From 1200 to 850 BCE", 106–110; Steiner, "Propaganda in Jerusalem", 200–201; Van Seters, *Biblical Saga of King David*, 66–73.

[106] Master, "State Formation Theory", 130–131.

## 7. HEBREW BIBLE

The Hebrew Bible can be used as a source for evidence when carefully treated. Many scholars—I think—will agree with such a statement. The problem in the current debate on the use of the Hebrew Bible in (re)constructing Israel's past is given with the fact that the adverb "carefully" has been interpreted in a variety of ways. It is not my aim to rehearse or even summarise the current debate on this question. Instead, I would like to focus on some proposals of the trustworthiness of the Biblical stories on David.

In Old Testament scholarship, the narratives in the Books of Samuel and Kings are generally understood as parts of the Deuteronomistic History.[107] Scholars, however, do not agree as to the date and the extent of this literary corpus. DtrH is seen as mainly an exilic text with its final composition somewhere in the Persian era.[108] As far as the narratives on David are concerned, this late composition has traditionally been seen as based on three older narratives: 'The story of David's rise to power'; 'The succession account' and 'The ark-narrative'.[109] These stories have been construed as reports by eyewitnesses of events from the Davidic period. In other words: traditional Old Testament scholarship took them as trustworthy sources for a reconstruction of the Life of David. DtrH has a adopted these narratives with some new paint: the deuteronomists construed David as the ideal king by whose standard almost all later Judaean and Israelite kings turn out to be failures.

Rost's views, however, are no longer accepted. The stories on David are no longer generally construed as eyewitness reports. The composition of the stories is now dated much later, although a consensus has

---

[107] See—basically—the thesis of M. Noth, *Überlieferungsgeschichtliche Studien: Die sammelnden und bearbeitenden Geschichtswerke im Alten Testament*, Tübingen 1943.

[108] See for the 'Smend-school': W. Dietrich, *Prophetie und Geschichte: Eine redaktionsgeschichtliche Untersuchung zum deuteronomistischen Geschichtswerk* (FRLANT 108), Göttingen 1972; for the 'Cross-school': R.D. Nelson, *The Double Redaction of the Deuteronomistic History* (JSOT Sup 18), Sheffield 1981. A helpful overview is to be found in Th. Römer, A. de Pury, 'Deuteronomistic Historiography (DH): History of Research and Debated Issues', in: A. de Pury, Th. Römer, J.-D. Macchi (eds), *Israel Constructs its History: Deuteronomistic Historiography in Recent Research* (JSOT Sup 306), Sheffield 2000, 24–141. A new proposal for a synthesis can be found in Th.C. Römer, *The So-called Deuteronomistic History: A Sociological, Historical and Literary Introduction*, London, New York 2005.

[109] See the theory elaborated by L. Rost, *Die Überlieferung von der Thronnachfolge Davids* (BWANT 3/6), Stuttgart 1926.

not been reached. Dietrich sees in them a *Fürstenspiegel* from the time of Hezekiah that might contain some trustworthy elements.[110] McKenzie, too, accepts that the stories on David are moulded in apologetic language. He then develops two reading strategies for doing his job as a detective in search of historical truth behind the biased testimony of the witnesses. Next to a sceptic approach, he applies the technique of 'reading against the grain', or—more elegantly phrased—he bases his reading on the principle of *cui bono?* His reading of 1 Samuel 25 is a good example in case: David acts as some sort of 'warlord' who eventually profits from Nabal's untimely death.[111] Halpern applies the *Genre* of extra biblical sources as a model to read the Hebrew text.[112] The 'language' of Mesopotamian royal inscriptions, especially those from the times of Tiglath-Pileser III, helps him to detect an ideological bias as well as many hyperboles in the stories on David, next to that it allows him to rearrange the order of the events.[113] This acquired competence leads to the view that the biblical account of David is to be construed as propaganda "stemming from circles close to David and Solomon".[114] Israel Finkelstein and Neil Silberman assume a complicated process for the emergence of the biblical traditions on David. They suppose that already in the tenth century BCE some memories on David as an outlaw existed. David was remembered as a bandit leader who was active in the Judaean wilderness as well as in the Shephalah. These early memories were then transmitted both in an oral process and via folktales.[115]

While Dietrich, McKenzie, Halpern, Finkelstein and Neil Silberman still accept a pre-exilic origin of the biblical picture of David, others deny the possibility that 1 and 2 Samuel would contain any authentic material from pre-exilic times. Persian period and even Hellenistic origin of the stories has been proposed.[116] Recently, John van Seters has

---

[110] W. Dietrich, *Die frühe Königszeit in Israel: 10. Jahrhundert v. Chr.* (BibEnz 3), Stuttgart, Berlin, Köln 1997; Dietrich, *David: Der Herrscher mit der Harfe.*

[111] McKenzie, *King David*, 94–101.

[112] In fact, he is taking serious the advice by John Barton that an interpreter of texts needs to develop a literary competence for reading these texts; J. Barton, *Reading the Old Testament: Method in Biblical Study*, second edition, London 1996, 8–19.

[113] Halpern, *David's Secret Demons*, 124–132; fierce criticism has been given by S.W. Holloway, "Use of Assyriology in Chronological Apologetics in *David's Secret Demons*", *SJOT* 17 (2003), 245–267; Van Seters, *Biblical Saga of King David*, 58.

[114] Halpern, *David's Secret Demons*, xiv.

[115] Finkelstein, Silberman, *David and Solomon*, 31–59.

[116] See, e.g., N.P. Lemche, 'The Old Testament—A Hellenistic Book?', *SJOT* 7 (1993),

published an impressive monograph on King David.[117] He argues that the biblical story of David is a saga composed in the late Persian period. This implies that the image of David is a beautifully crafted and highly realistic portrayal of a typical Near Eastern monarch of that era.[118] The author of the David-saga had as his basic source an earlier version of the David story. This relatively small Deuteronomistic report presents— within the parameters of the Deuteronomistic theology—a completely idealized David as the king and founder of a unified state of the people of Israel. Dtr—in van Seters' view—first put together the story on David and although he does not exclude the possibility that Dtr used older traditions, no historical claims on these traditions can be made[119] The author of the David-saga reworked this material but took over some features of it, especially the idea that David and all his offspring, including Solomon, were unfit for rule and the cause of the state's ultimate demise. According to van Seters the David-saga is to be read as a counter document against the popular notion in the Persian era time as expressed for instance in the Book of Ezra that a single, unified and ethnically pure people of Israel would be the only way out of the crisis of Exile and Return.[120]

Although the discussion on dating the biblical traditions on David— and their assumed sources—is of great interest for the view on the emergence of the Hebrew Bible, it is not decisive for the focal question of this paper. Whether the traditions are written one or seven centuries after the supposed events, is of no importance for the historiographic question. All proposals imply that we do not have eye-witness reports of or other trustworthy documents on the life of David. Using the Hebrew Bible for the writing of a 'Life of David' is therefore a delicate enterprise. The evidence in the biblical narratives should be inter-

---

163–193; N.P. Lemche, *Die Vorgeschichte Israels: Von den Anfängen bis zum Ausgang des 13. Jahrhunderts v. Chr.* (BibEnz, 1), Stuttgart Berlin Köln 1996, esp. 68–73; Davies, *In Search of 'Ancient Israel'*, esp. 57–71; Th.L. Thompson, *The Bible in History: How Writers Create a Past*, London 1999; J.W. Wesselius, *The Origin of the History of Israel: Herodotus' Histories as Blueprint for the First Books of the Bible* (JSOT Sup, 345), Sheffield 2002. For criticism of this position see B. Becking, *From David to Gedaliah: the Book of Kings as Story and History* (OBO 228), Fribourg, Göttingen 2007, 1–22; Barstad, *History and the Hebrew Bible*, 70–89.

[117] J. van Seters, *The Biblical Saga of King David*, Winona Lake 2009.

[118] Van Seters, *Biblical Saga of King David*, 53–120.

[119] Van Seters, *Biblical Saga of King David*, 207–269.

[120] See esp. Van Seters, *Biblical Saga of King David*, 351–353.

preted within the framework of a pragmatic theory of truth. They were true because the author believed that they were true and because he succeeded to convince his audience to share a religious identity. Whether that identity was the image of a morally good civil servant in the age of Hezekiah or the position of anti-particularism in the age of Ezra is not decisive for the historiographic problem on the life of David. At most, some of the narratives can be seen in the light of a coherence theory of truth, since they sometimes present a coherent view on the character of David.

## 8. David between Evidence and Ideology: A Reenactment

To what results leads this five dimensional analysis? Firstly, the existence of David as founder of the dynasty in Jerusalem is established. Secondly, his reign coincided with demographic changes. Thirdly, the image emerges that inspired by economic blossoming and trade interests the ethnic communities embarked on a road that would lead within a century and a half to state that we now know as Judah. Against this historical minimum, I would like to present my re-enactment of the life of David. I will not do that in the form of a story, but only by indicating which elements need to integrated in such a story, if it were written:

- David is a young man from an upper middle class family
- As a younger son—and hence in the absence of economic means— went his own way.
- He wandered about as a war-lord, offering his services to anyone who would pay—be it King Saul or the Philistines—.
- He could be compared to the Hapiru form the Amarna correspondence. In doing so he built a solid power base that he later expanded through marriages and kinship networks. Using Hebron as springboard he was able to gain control over parts of Judah and Israel.
- Once ruler, he reigned over a local and rather restricted area.
- He did not really found a nation.
- Economic blossoming—and not nation-building—lead to the first forms of administration.

In short, David was a very human being who took advantage of the changes in society evoked by an increase of population and was more of a macho than the gallant image of the little shepherd-boy would suggest. The inherent ambiguity and paradoxicality[121] of this David[122] was foundational for the often paradoxical image of David in biblical and later tradition ʿad hayyôm hazzeh.

---

[121] For a definition of both concepts see T.E. Patton, "Explaining Referential / Attributive", *Mind* 106 (1997), 245–261; A. Orlandini, "Logical, Semantic and Cultural Paradoxes", *Argumentation* 17 (2003), 65–86.
[122] Dietrich, *David: Der Herrscher mit der Harfe.*

# MERCATOR IN THE WILDERNESS: NUMBERS 33

JOHN R. BARTLETT
*University of Dublin—Ireland*

## 1. INTRODUCTION

The aim of this paper is to explore an interesting corner of 16th-century biblical scholarship. This is the period when reformers were translating the scriptures into their local vernacular; the first European vernacular Bible was published in German in Strassburg in 1466; there were nearly 20 other German bibles before Luther's German New Testament appeared in Sept. 1522[1] and his Old Testament in 1534. Tyndale's English translation of the NT appeared in 1526 and his Pentateuch in 1530, Coverdale's translation in 1535, the so-called 'Matthew's Bible' (largely based on Tyndale) in 1537, the 'Great Bible' (largely Coverdale's work) in 1539 and 1540; this drew also on the work of the Hebraist Sebastian Münster, who had issued a literal German translation of the Hebrew Scriptures in 1534–1535.[2] These two decades, then, between 1520 and 1540 saw much activity by Hebraists, bible translators, printers and publishers, both in England and on the Continent, and also much activity by another group of scholars, the cartographers.

## 2. PTOLEMAIC MAPS

The printing of the Ptolemaic maps at Bologna (1477) and subsequently at Rome (1478), Florence (1482), Ulm (1486), and again Rome (in 1490) (**Map 1**), and a new edition by Martin Waldseemüller in Strassburg (1513),[3] had made scholars more aware of the importance of maps.

---

[1] See J.L. Flood, 'Martin Luther's Bible Translation in its German and European Context', in Richard Griffiths (ed.), *The Bible in the Renaissance: Essays in Biblical Commentary and Translation in the Fifteenth and Sixteenth Centuries*, Aldershot 2000, 45–70.

[2] For a detailed account see D. Daniell, *The Bible in English: Its History and Influence*, New Haven and London 2003.

[3] For bibliography of editions of Ptolemy, see H.N. Stevens, *Ptolemy's Geography: A*

Luther apparently hoped to include a Ptolemaic map, presumably of
the Holy Land, in his 1524 New Testament, though none appeared.
Somewhere between 1522 and 1525 (according to Armin Kunz) Luther's
friend and supporter, the artist Lucas Cranach the Elder (1472–1553),
produced a map of the Holy Land (**Map 2**).[4] Cranach appears to have
borrowed his outline from the Ptolemaic map 'Quarta Asiae Pars'—
one notes the coastline, the Lebanese mountain range, the shape of the
Jordan, the Sinai range running out between the Gulfs of Suez and Aqaba,
and the Arabian mountains on the southern edge of the map. Cranach
thus turned a professional cartographer's map into a means of telling
the biblical story, complete with illustrative vignettes of biblical scenes
(Cranach was, after all, an artist, not a professional mapmaker). His map
is a *view* of the Promised Land as seen from high above Arabia looking
north. The foreground and focal point of the map presents the exodus-
wilderness story as told in Exodus 12–19 and Numbers 13–21 (Cranach
does not use the list of wilderness-stations in Num. 33, or the short list
in Dt. 10:6–7, as later biblical mapmakers did[5]). Cranach begins with
*Sochot* (Succoth; Exod. 12.37), shows the Egyptian chariots pursuing
the Israelites across the Sea, locates *Ethan* (Etham, Exod. 13:20), *Marath*
(Marah, Exod. 15:23), *Elim* (Exod. 15:27), *Sur* (wilderness of Shur, Exod.
15:22), *Sin* (wilderness of Sin, Exod. 16:1), with an illustration of the
heavenly manna on the ground. At *Rephidim* (Exod. 17:1) Moses is seen
striking the rock. *Sinai* (Exod. 19:1) has Moses on top, and a calf being
worshipped below. *Cades* (Kadesh) *Barnea* and the wilderness of *Pharan*
(Paran; Num. 13:26) are illustrated by the results of Korah's rebellion,
Korah's followers being swallowed up in pits (Num. 16:34). The route

---

*Brief Account of all the Printed Editions down to 1730*, 2nd ed., London 1908; reprinted
by Theatrum Orbis Terrarum, Amsterdam 1972; C. Moreland and D. Bannister, *Antique
Maps*, 3rd ed., London and New York 1979, 301–302.

[4] A. Kunz, 'Cranach as Cartographer: The Rediscovered Map of the Holy Land',
*Print Quarterly* 12.2 (1995), 123–144. See also Arthur Dürst, 'Zur Wiederauffindung der
Heiligland-Karte von 1515 von Lucas Cranach dem Alteren', *Cartographica Helvetica* 3
(1991), 22–27. The present map was reconstructed from two blocks published by H. Röt-
tinger, *Beiträge zur Geschichte des sächsischen Holzschnittes*, Strasbourg 1921, 10–15, four
blocks published by E. Laor, S. Klein, *Maps of the Holy Land: Cartobibliography of Printed
Maps 1475–1900*, New York / Amsterdam, 1986, 28, 29, and the lower edge from the Bi-
bliotheek Vrije Universiteit, Amsterdam, published by L. Ruitinga, 'Die Heiligland-Karte
von Lucas Cranach dem Alteren: Das älteste Kartenfragment aus der Kartensammlung
der Bibliothek der Freien Universität in Amsterdam', *Cartographica Helvetica* 9 (1994),
40–41.

[5] Kunz, 'Cranach as Cartographer', 132, note 48, thinks that Cranach located Ethan
from his reading of Num. 33.

moves on past *Zin* (and Hebron; Num. 13:21), *Mount Hor* (Num. 20:22), *Salmona* (Num. 33:41), *Punon* (Num. 33:42), with an illustration of the serpents from Num. 21:6–9, *Oboth* (Num. 21:10; 33:43), *Abarim* (Iye-Abarim; Num. 21:11; 33:44), the rivers *Sared* (Zered; Num. 21:12), *Arnon* (Num. 21:13) and *Iaboc* (Num. 21:24), and the *Blachfeld Moab* (plains of Moab; Num. 22:1). Cranach also locates *Mt Pisga* (Num. 21:20) and the city of *Ar* (Num. 21:28). Cranach presents the Israelites' route as a winding curve, a zig-zag, across the mountainous region of Seir-Edom. This is in itself a considerable piece of scholarly reconstruction from the known geography and the biblical text. There is no obvious extant predecessor on whom Cranach might have drawn for this aspect of his very individual map. The choice of Cranach's map, with its theme of the Exodus and Way through the Wilderness, for the German Old Testament (mostly Luther's work) of 1525 (in which Froschauer of Zurich printed the map in reverse) and for the Dutch versions of van Liesveldt of 1526 and Vorstermann of 1528 (which corrected the error),[6] is significant; it reflects the Reformers' concern with the theme of Israel's redemption as presaging the Christian redemption.

### 3. ZIEGLER'S MAP

In 1532, about ten years after Cranach produced his picture map, the scholar Jacob Ziegler (c. 1470–1549) published at Strassburg his geographical researches with a set of very different maps in his *Quae intus continentur: Syria ad Ptolomaici operis rationem … Palestina … Arabia Petraea … Aegyptus … Schondia …: Regionum superiorum singulae tabulae geographicae*. 'Syria according to the scheme of Ptolemy's work; Arabia Petraea, Egypt, Scandinavia, …: with separate maps of the above regions'.[7] A second edition appeared in 1536, which incorporated a *Terrae Sanctae altera descriptio*, by Wolfgang Wissenburg, and an index giving biblical references for the place-names on Ziegler's maps. Ziegler was a theological controversialist, an ally of Erasmus, a mathematician with

---

[6] See C. Delano-Smith, E.M. Ingram, *Maps in Bibles, 1500–1600: An Illustrated Catalogue*, Genève 1991, 25–26, 37 (Fig. 14), 167 (Froschauer) and 38 (Fig. 15) and 137 (van Liesfeldt and Vorstermann). For the reduction process see A. Dürst, 'Die digitale Umformung von Karten als Forschunghilfe', *Cartographica Helvetica* 9 (1994), 43–44.

[7] For the manuscript of a closely related map, see K. Nissen, 'Jacob Ziegler's Palestine Schondia Manuscript, University Library Oslo, MS.917–40', *Imago Mundi* 13 (1956), 45–52.

an interest in spheres, and a biblical geographer.[8] He knew Ptolemy's work well; editions were published in Strassburg in 1513, 1520, 1522, and 1525.

Ziegler's maps took their form and orientation from Ptolemy's, with degrees of latitude on the left and right margins, and longitude along the top and bottom. While his outlines do not follow Ptolemy's exactly, there are important similarities. Ptolemy shows the Arabian Gulf bifurcated at its northern end, with the *Melani Montes* running out into a southern promontory separating the *Sinus Elanitis* to the east from the *Mare Rubrum* (our Gulf of Suez) to the west. Ziegler's seventh map (Tabula Septima) (**Map 3**) shows much the same, but with *Sinai/Horeb* at the southern end of the Melani Montes, and an illustration of the Israelites in the Mare Rubrum (Red Sea) pursued by Pharaoh's army. This map shows most of the wilderness journey of the Israelites, and on it were plotted most of the *mansiones* (stations) listed in Num. 33, according to the map coordinates which Ziegler had given them in the text of his book.[9] For the names Ziegler follows the Vulgate and the Hebrew texts rather than Luther's German text. He plots the *mansiones*, with one exception, in the order of the Numbers list, though he does not number them as Mercator later does. After crossing the sea, the Israelites head east across the Desert of *Sin* to *Alus* (no. 10) and *Rephidim* (no. 11), whence they turn north along the *Melani Montes* or the *Amoreus Mons* past *Chaseroth* (14) to *Sepher Mons*(20), *Hasmona* (26), where the Israelites loop back south to *Beeroth Ben Iahachon* (28), *Moseroth* (27), *Ghidghad* (29) before turning east to *Iothbathah* (30), *Habronah* (31), *Hesion ghaber* (32), *Sin* and *Chades Barnea* (33), *Hor Mons* (34), *Salmonah* (35), *Punon* (36), *Oboth* (37), *Hiim Hahabarim* (38), *Dibon Ghad* (39), *Halmon Dablathaimah* (40), and finally on another map (Tabula Quarta) *Habarim Mons* (41). Note that Ziegler gives no coordinates in his text for nos. 15–19 and 21–26 and no place on his map for them (except apparently for *Hasmonah* [26]); which Ziegler's cartographer, Martin Richter (without coordinates to guide him) locates vaguely north of *Ben Iahachon*. The map reflects the sequence of Ziegler's text (p. lxxx) in which *Beeroth Bene Iahachon* precedes *Moseroth* (cf. Dt. 10:6); but Ziegler's text notes the alternative read-

---

[8] On Ziegler see R. Karrow Jr, *Mapmakers of the Sixteenth Century and their Maps*, Chicago 1993, 603–611; G. and E. Wajntraub, 'Jacob Ziegler (1470?–1549?): An enlightened Man from a Dark Period', *Journal of the International Map Collectors' Society* 100 (2005), 49–54.

[9] In the sections *Marmorica et Aegyptus* (pp. lxvii–lxxv) and *Arabia Petraea* (pp. lxxvi–lxxxiv).

ing (Num. 33.30) in which the sequence is *Hasmonah, Moseroth, Bene Ben Iahachon, Ghidghad*, the sequence followed by Coverdale, Mercator and everyone else.

Ziegler is thorough, and includes in his map many sites from the other biblical wilderness accounts (especially Exod. 17–18, Num. 21): the rock at *Choreh* (Choreb; Exod. 17:6) near Rephidim; *Madian* (Midian; Exod. 18:1), *Pharan* (Num. 13:3; Dt. 1:1), *Chebron* (Hebron; Num. 13:22), *Arath* (Arad; Num. 21:1), igniti serpentes (fiery serpents; Num. 21:6, illustrated), *Zered, torrens, vallis* (Num. 21:12), *Puteus* (the well; Num. 21:17), *Mathanah solitudo* (Num. 21:18), *Nachaliel* (Nahaliel; Num. 21:19), *Bamoth* (Num. 21:19), *Vallis* (the valley in the region of Moab; Num. 21:20), *Hesion ghaber* (Ezion Geber; Dt. 2:8; Ziegler distinguishes this from the place in Num. 33:36, describing the former in his text as a *portus* (p. lxxvi), cf. 1 Kings 9:26, and giving the two places different coordinates, thus solving an awkward topographical problem). Ziegler notes also *Disahab* (Dizahab; Dt. 1:1), *Cademoth solitudo* (wilderness of Kedemoth; Dt. 2:26), *Haroher* (Aroer; Dt. 2:36; Ziegler's text says [p. liiii] 'quae est iuxta ripam (*beside* the bank) torrentis Arnon'; his maps show a town in the *middle* of the Arnon, illustrating the following words of the text '& civitas quae est in medio vallis'—'and a city which is in the midst of the valley'). Ziegler includes also *Dedan* (cf. Jer. 25:23, Ezek. 27:20), *Luchit* (Luhith; Isa. 15:5), *Albus vicus* (from Strabo), *Elana villa* (which Ziegler identifies in his text [p. lxxvi] with Haila, Elat), and *Petra regia*, which Ziegler notes (p. lxxxi) as 'dicta Sela & Arachen, … a Chaldaeis Recem, ab Hebraeis Iaktheel'. He adds a place called *Colchiel*, unknown from either biblical or classical sources; his map locates it between Disahab and Punon, both associated by Eusebius (*Onom*.114[10]) with mines, and I suspect that the *colchi* part derives from *chalkos*, cf. *chalkou metalla*, copper mines (cf. Euseb. HE viii.13:5[11]). Ziegler notes (p. xv) that his sources included the sacred history from Moses to the Maccabees, Hieronymus, the Onomasticon ('eo libro de locis Hebraicis'), Strabo, Josephus, Pliny, Ptolemaeus and Antoninus.

---

[10] The standard Greek edition is E. Klostermann, *Eusebius: Das Onomastikon der biblischen Ortsnamen* (Die griechischen christlichen Schriftsteller der ersten drei Jahrhunderte), Eusebius III.1, Leipzig 1904. See also now J.E. Taylor (ed.), *Palestine in the Fourth Century AD. The Onomasticon by Eusebius of Caesarea*, translated by G.S.P. Freeman-Grenville, indexed by Rupert L. Chapman III. Jerusalem 2003.

[11] Eusebius, *Ecclesiastical History*, translated by K. Lake (vol. 1) and J E.L. Oulton (vol. 2), Loeb Classical Library, London 1926–1932; see VIII.13.5, vol. 2, page XXX.

I find myself wondering, however, just *how* Ziegler plotted, or where exactly he found, his coordinates for the wilderness wanderings. He must have used Ptolemy, but from him he could locate only *Petra* (vaguely) and *Elana villa* (Aila). He got little help from Eusebius's Onomasticon, translated by Jerome; its one precise detail about the Wilderness route is that Maththanem (= Ziegler's *Mathanah*; Num. 21:18) was on the River Arnon 12 milestones east of Medaba (Euseb. *Onom.* 127). I suspect that Ziegler plotted his route from the starting point of the Red Sea, the central, focal point of Mt Sinai, and the end points of the river Arnon and Dead Sea, Moab and the Jordan, and that the intervening coordinates and resultant route were mainly invention. If Cranach's map was before him, he does not mention it or follow it. While Cranach illustrated several wilderness stories, Ziegler illustrated just two: the Egyptian pursuit of Israel at the sea, and the fiery serpents near Mt Hor. Ziegler aimed at cartographical precision, not biblical illustration.

Ziegler was a serious scholar, and his work influenced his three immediate cartographic successors. First, Miles Coverdale (1488–1569), whose English translation of the Bible, published in 1535,[12] contained a map entitled 'Descripcio Terrae Promissionis' (**Map 4**), strongly focused on the Exodus and the Wilderness route. Though oriented towards the south (upside down to Ziegler's map), it certainly draws on Ziegler (using his outlines of the Dead Sea and the Nile delta, and the direction lines extending to Rome, Venice, Babylon, Regensburg and elsewhere). The draughtsmanship (even if Hans Holbein the Younger was involved, as Delano-Smith and Ingram think)[13] makes the Israelites' route much harder to follow than on Ziegler's map; but Coverdale's map similarly has the Israelites proceed east from the Red Sea to *Raphidim*, where they turn north via *Hazeroth* and *Mos Sepher* to *Hasmona*; here they turn southwest and make a circle via *Mosseroth, Bne Iaekon, Gadgad, Iatbatha, Abrona, Ezeongeber* and *Elath* until they reach *Cades Barnea* (very close to *Hasmona*), where they turn east towards *Phunon, Oboth,*

---

[12] M. Coverdale, *Biblia. The Bible: that is, The Holy Scriptures of the Old and New Testaments, faithfully translated into English*, Zürich 1535; facsimile, *The Coverdale Bible, 1535, with an introduction by S.L. Greenslade*, Folkestone 1975.

[13] C. Delano-Smith, 'Maps in Bibles in the Sixteenth Century', *The Map Collector* 39 (1987), 3–14, p. 6; E.M. Ingram, 'The Map of the Holy Land in the Coverdale Bible: A Map by Holbein?', *The Map Collector* 64 (1990), 26–31. Ingram argues that Holbein contributed the pictorial elements (cartouches, vignettes, four cardinal windheads, mountains, seas) and Nicolaus Kratzer (1487–1550) or John Rudd (c. 1498–1579) the cartography.

and the region east of the Dead Sea. The southwesterly loop clearly follows Ziegler (though this map, following Ziegler's *alternative text* and not his *map*, reversed the locations of Bne Iaekon and Mosseroth so that Moseroth directly follows Hasmona on the line of march). Again, Ezeon gaber and Elath are located in the centre of the mountains, far away from the Red Sea.

### 4. MERCATOR

In 1537, a year after the 2nd edition of Ziegler's book, Girardus Mercator (1512–1594), a young man of 25, published at Louvain his first map, 'Amplissima Terrae Sanctae Descriptio ad Utriusque Testamenti Intelligentiam.'[14] This wall map (**Map 5**) of six sheets, 98.4 × 43.4 cms overall, presented the Holy Land from a viewpoint high in the air southeast of Mt Sinai; the Mediterranean coast runs in a convex curve across the top from the Nile delta to Phoenicia. His mountain chains were the same as Ziegler's, with the *Desertum Sur* connecting *Mons Casius* and the Gulf of Suez, and the *Amorrhaeus Mons* (the name Melani Montes has been dropped) running in parallel further east, culminating in *Horeb montes & Sinai mons* at the southern end. Mercator copies Ziegler's banana-shaped Dead Sea. In the centre foreground is the wilderness of Israel's wanderings. Mercator incorporates the *mansiones* of Num. 33, and numbers them on his map (the first cartographer to do so). He used Ziegler's coordinates, listing those stations for which Ziegler gave no coordinates as 'mansiones incognitae positionis' (nos. 15–19) or 'incertae notae' (21–25) (apart from no. 26, Asmona). As in Coverdale's map, Mercator makes the Israelite route turn north at *Raphidim*, and sets *Asemona vel Asmona* as the turning point for the southwesterly loop. He similarly locates *Asiongaber* in the middle of the wilderness, but avoids the need to invent another Eziongeber for Dt.2.8 by leaving the Gulf of Aqaba off his map.

---

[14]  See R. Almagià, 'La carta della Palestina di Gerard Mercatore 1537', in *Fondo Italiano per lo Studio della Palestina I*, Firenze 1927; C. Delano-Smith, E.M. Ingram, 'La carte de la Palestine', in M. Watelet (ed.), *Gerard Mercator, cosmographe*, Pt. IV, 268–283, Antwerp 1994; M. Destombes, 'Un nouvel examplaire de la carte de Palestine de Mercator de 1537', from M. Destombes, *Contributions selectionées à l'Histoire de la Cartographie et des Instruments Scientifiques*, ed. par Günter Schilder, Peter van der Koogt, Steven de Clerq, Utrecht 1987, 427–432.

Mercator makes his sources, and his scholarly purpose, clear in a Latin text in a cartouche in the bottom right corner.

> Fair reader, greeting! We have drawn this map of Palestine, and the Hebrews' route into it from Egypt through the stony regions of Arabia, from Ziegler, the most faithful cartographer of these things, his place names being adjusted, as far as possible, to the old translation of the Bible.[15]

Mercator expressly states that his major concern is the Israelites' route from Egypt, and his source is Ziegler. He sets the wilderness at the very centre of his map, giving it exaggerated space, and making the land of Israel and Judah comparatively cramped, in this perhaps following Cranach. He emphasises his theme by including a number of vignettes—the Israelite camp round the Tabernacle in the desert (Num. 2), the battle of Israel and Amalek at Rephidim (Exod. 17), the serpent in the wilderness near Salmona (Num. 21:8)—and by setting thematic quotations from Micah 6:3–4—'I brought you up from the land of Egypt ...'—and Dt. 8:7–10—'the Lord your God is bringing you into a good land ....'—at the top of the map, beneath the crucified Christ.

### 5. WISSENBURG

Lastly, in 1538, Wolfgang Wissenburg, a biblical scholar who had contributed a biblical gazetteer to Ziegler's 1536 edition, published his own larger wall map (**Map 6**), 'Descriptio Palaestinae Nova', 105 × 74.5 cms, in 8 sheets, dedicating it to a fellow reformer, Thomas Cranmer, Archbishop of Canterbury.[16] Wissenburg's map depends partly on Ziegler for its outline and other features, but in contrast it magnifies enormously the Israelites' route through the wilderness, and it gives a more accurate shape for the Dead Sea. Wissenburg follows the route of Num. 33, numbering the *mansiones* in sequence along a wide, clear path. Each halting

---

[15] This was a literal translation from the original Hebrew and Greek, made by Santes Pagninus, O.P., published in Lyons in 1528, and used by Coverdale.

[16] On Wissenburg and his work see R.W. Karrow, *Mapmakers of the Sixteenth Century and their Maps*, Chicago 1993, 587–590. For a reproduction of Wissenburg's original map, in the Bibliothèque Nationale, Paris, GEDD 2987 (10.402), see K. Nebenzahl, *Maps of the Holy Land*, New York, 1986, 74. In 1557 Giovanni della Gatta published a copy of this map in Rome (see Karrow, *Mapmakers*, 589, and E. Laor and S. Klein, *Maps of the Holy Land: Cartobibliography of Printed Maps 1475–1900*, New York, Amsterdam 1986, 249), and in 1563 Ferandus Bertellus published a simplified version, 'Palestinae sive terrae sanctae descriptio', in Venice (Karrow, *Mapmakers*, 589). See also V. and P. Bella, *Cartografia rara*, Milan 1986, 104, no. 96.

place is marked by a tent encampment; between the encampments Wissenburg shows marching columns of Israelites. He inserts vignettes of scenes en route—in the *Mare Rubrum* the wreckage of Pharaoh's chariots; in *Solitudo Sinai* a plan of the Tabernacle; on top of *Horeb* Moses, with horns (Exod. 34:35; Vulg., 'faciem ... cornutam'), and on top of *Sinai*, facing Moses, the Lord; at *Sepulchra Concupiscentiae* (Num. 11:34) a flight of quails; near *Zin quae Cades* the grave of Miriam (Num. 20:1); on *Mt Hor* the grave of Aaron (Num. 20:25–29); near *Salmonah* the fiery serpents and the bronze serpent set on a pole (Num. 21:6–9). The whole map is focused on the wilderness, with Sinai at the centre. But Wissenburg's great contribution is that he changes the route. Unlike Ziegler and Mercator, Wissenburg locates the *Aezion-gabaer* of Num. 33:35 alongside *Elath* at the head of the Elanitic Gulf of the Red Sea, and so has the Israelites, after crossing the Gulf of Suez, proceed north to march round Horeb/Sinai, then turn south to Ezion-geber, and thence northeast round Moab towards the promised land across the Jordan near Jericho. Wissenburg thus accommodates the information from Dt. 2:8, that the Israelites's route included Ezion-geber at the Red Sea. This was the route accepted in future by most cartographers. Mercator himself, in his 'Europae descriptio' of 1554 and 'Europae descriptio emendata' of 1572,[17] is influenced by this (though he does not take the Israelites quite so far south as the coast of the Red Sea).

Today's story ends here with Wissenburg, though it could go on through the 16th century with Sebastian Münster, Tilemann Stella, Abraham Ortelius and others. In fact later 16th and 17th century publishers, copying from each other, show a decline in accuracy and scholarship, until the 18th and 19th century scholars, exploring and mapping with new cartographic techniques, transform the picture. But these late Renaissance and Reformation period scholars, with their cartographical skills and biblical erudition, made a serious contribution to biblical scholarship, and we should respect them for it. Mercator's influence is still visible in the Israelite route through the wilderness given on George Armstrong's map of 1890,[18] and in Grollenberg's *Atlas of the Bible* (1956),[19] and will probably remain strong for a long time yet.

---

[17] See A. Dürst, 'The Map of Europe', in M. Watelet (ed.), *The Mercator Atlas of Europe. Facsimile of the Maps by Gerardus Mercator contained in the Atlas of Europe circa 1570–1572*, Pleasant Hill, OR, 1998, 31–41.

[18] Illustrating H.A. Harper's *The Bible and Modern Discoveries*, London: Palestine Exploration Fund (1890).

[19] L.H. Grollenberg, *Atlas of the Bible*, London 1956.

# ORIGINS OF ISRAEL BETWEEN
# HISTORY AND IDEOLOGY[*]

Meindert Dijkstra
*Utrecht University*

"Yesterday is another country, Mr.
Barnaby, borders are now closed."

Teddy in 'Vixen's Run' (Midsummer
murders)[1]

## 1. Introduction: Bible and History

This topic is a *mer à boire*. Full treatment of it would need a thousand-page volume. I can only present some main lines in summarizing my views on Israelite origins and settlement. My contribution is not meant to be another philipic in the dispute of minimalist and maximalist historians, biblical revisionists and 'Die Bibel hat doch recht' cronies.[2] I am neither suffering from Bibliophobia, biblistic or confessional ailments.[3]

---

[*] I would like to thank Dr. Karel Vriezen for discussing my views *in statu nascendi* and reading my manuscript carefully, in particular giving me early warnings for archaeological pittfalls, and also the Rev. Christopher Rigg and Dr. Cees Bons, TU Delft, providing me with literature and some insights about water supply, water management and climatic change. Christopher also corrected my 'Dunglish' for which many thanks. Of course, I am alone responsible for the views expressed here.

[1] Teddy here is referring to the historian D. Löwenthal, *The Past Is a Foreign Country*, Cambridge 1988, who took up the first line in the novel by L.P. Hartley, *The Go-Between*, London 1953.

[2] See for example A. Rainey, 'Stones for Bread. Archaeology versus History,' *Near Eastern Archaeology* 64 (2001), 140–149 (*NEA*); J. Barr, *History and Ideology in the Old Testament. Biblical Studies at the end of the Millennium*, Oxford 2000; W.G. Dever collected and reworked some articles in *What Did the Biblical Writers Know and When Did They Know it*, Grand Rapids, Michigan / Cambridge, UK 2001; reactions from N.P. Lemche, 'Ideology and the History of ancient Israel,' *SJOT* 14 (2002), 165–193; K.W. Whitelam, 'The Search for Early Israel: Historical Perspective', in: S. Ahituv, E.D. Oren (eds), *The Origin of Early Israel—Current Debate*, (Beer-Sheva 7), Beer-Sheva 1998, 41–64; esp. providing on page 44 a nice review of names and assessments used in these polemic disputes.

[3] M. Dijkstra, 'History of Israel: Progress, Problems and Prospects,' in: W.R. Farmer (ed.), *The International Bible Commentary. An Ecumenical Commentary for the Twenty-*

As always, I hope to keep my approach practical, touching upon some of
the major if not crucial questions and theories about Israelite origins and
settlement in Canaan. The greater part of the Old Testament consists of
a very diverse assortment of traditions about the origins of early Israel,
some remembered in ancient stories and narrative cycles, others memo-
rized in ancient songs such as the song of Deborah. It is, however, not an
assortment from which anyone can take a pick at random or according to
taste. A (Biblical) story is not simply history because it is told in the Bible,
as Sports preached in his burlesque sermon in 'Porgy and Bess': "It ain't
necessarily so, the t'ings that yo' li'ble to read in the Bible ..." I agree with
the Copenhagen scholars and many of my less outspoken fellow scholars
that the Bible first and foremost is a library of literature that is written
with literary means and aims. But all the same it is for the greater part
a collection of 'historiographic literature', that is historiographic in the
sense as expressed by the Dutch historian Johan Huizinga: a type of literature in which people render account of their own past.[4]

The fact that the Early Iron Age in Canaan and Jordan is very poor in
epigraphic finds, reflecting an apparently very limited production of writing,[5] supports the view that Israelite and Judean scribes did not start to
collect 'historiographic' tradition in 'books' before the Iron IIB Period. It
implies that many of the topographical remarks and territorial traditions
do not really refer to a distant past but actually reflect invented tradition about situations and changes either confirmed or established in the
recent past. An interesting example relating to the origins of Israel is the
list of unconquered cities and villages recorded in Judg. 1:18–19, 27–36.
This review has been incorporated in a late document that connected the
Book of Joshua with a pre-canonical version of Judges starting at Ch. 2,
verse 6. The idea that these chapters were once an ancient, independent
historiographic source, is now generally abandoned. The piece looks like
a *nishu*, an historical extract selected from other sources, in particular

*First Century*, Bangalore 2004, 236–243, M. Dijkstra, '"As for the Other Events ..."
Annals and Chronicles in Israel and the Ancient Near East', in: R.P. Gordon, J.C. de Moor
(eds), *The Old Testament in Its World: Papers Read at the Winter Meeting January 2003* ...,
(OTS, 52), Leiden 2005, 14–39, esp. 15–19. As far as I see, I am only once said to have a
'minimalist' view, but in the context of a positive appreciation of our book see B. Becking
*et al.*, *Only one God? Monotheism in Ancient Israel and the Veneration of the Goddess
Asherah*, (BiSe, 77), London/New York 2001 by W.G. Dever, *Did God Have a Wife?
Archaeology and Folk Religion in Ancient Israel*, Grand Rapids, Michigan/Cambridge,
UK 2005, 206.
[4] Dijkstra, 'As for the Other Events ...', 18–19.
[5] See also the paper by Bob Becking in this volume.

from Joshua, with a particular historical or theological purpose. This does not exclude that the 'negative Besitzverzeichnis' (Judg. 1:19, 21, 27–35) in it adopted and adapted, stems from a source earlier than the end of the Israelite Kingdom in 721 BCE. It is plausible that the texts are about developments in the Kingdom period, especially the expansion of Israel under the Omrid Dynasty, or perhaps the later *floruit* of Israel under Joash and Jeroboam II.

It would be unwise to ignore the Bible in our investigations simply because its history writing is biased and of a late date. Every earnest historian will admit that even late sources may contain reliable information in a disguised form. Knowledge about Canaan as a colony of Egypt lies disguised in a remarkable genealogical tradition counting Canaan as one of the sons of Ham with Egypt, Nubia and Punt in the table of nations (Gen. 10:6; 1 Chron. 1:8).[6] It was probably tradition kept alive because it puts the origins of Canaan in unfavourable light. Nevertheless, at present we know it to be reliable historical tradition, even more remarkable and reliable because in the current Old Testament stories about Israel's settlement in the promised land, the Egyptian occupation of Canaan remains out of view. The Old Testament knows next to nothing about the presence of New Kingdom Egypt in the Levant and its dealings with the Philistines and related tribes of the 'Sea People'. This lack of knowledge reveals immediately the historical distance between the history of the Late Bronze and Early Iron Age and Biblical tradition or stories about Israel's origins. The same applies to the tradition about the origins of the Philistines. Apart from a kind of standardized view about their origins from Caphtor / Crete,[7] vague memories diverted to the mist of primordial times. The confusing diversity in description and iconography of the 'Sea Peoples' as found in Egypt and in documents from Anatolia and the Levant, is absent in the Old Testament.

---

[6] See similarly the Biblical Philistines connected with Caphtor and Egypt (Gen. 10:14 // 1 Chron. 1:12; Deut. 2:23; Amos 9:7; Jer. 47:4). The secondary remark that Ham is the father of Canaan (Gen. 9:18, 22 also 1 Chron. 4, 39–40) is apparently dependent on this tradition (see Cl. Westermann, *Genesis 1–11*, (BK 1/1), Neukirchen-Vluyn 1974, 647–648; H.-J. Zobel, 'כנען', *ThWAT IV*, 229, who deem it to be ancient tradition). It could be a reminiscence of the old vassal relation of Canaan with Egypt, as also Gen. 10:14 implies for the Philistines; see E. Noort, *Die Seevölker in Palästina*, (Palaestina antiqua, 8), Kampen 1994, 37, 188.

[7] This is possibly also the background of the gloss about the Philistines in Gen. 10:14 (actually, but apparently wrongly incorporated after Kasluhim), see also Deut. 2:23 Westermann, *Genesis 1–11*, 692–694; Noort, *Seevölker*, 37, 188 etc.

In the distant mirror of time the many tribal groups who terrorized the Mediterranean shores, have been condensed into one 'people', the Peleshet, the Philistines from one origin: Crete. The distance between the events told and written tradition thus grew so large that not only historical details, but also main lines of the history of the Early Iron Age got irretrievably lost in the Biblical stories about Israel's past.[8] What survived as credible and verifiable data are often erratic blocks in the changed landscape of later tradition, nevertheless, also a tradition that is partly restorable on the basis of extra-Biblical sources from Egypt and the Levant. If we would like to know where the Israelite settlers came from, we had better start by asking first where Israel was not living at the end of the Late Bronze Age and during the Early Iron Period. The almost complete silence of Old Testament tradition about Egypt in Canaan, even if Israelite settlement was already in progress,[9] is remarkably balanced by an almost complete silence of the Egyptian sources about Israel. Such a consistent non-Israelite, or perhaps 'non-Biblical' approach, or more positively phrased: mainly Egyptian perspective on the settlement history of the Levant, is, I hope, my own contribution to the debate.

## 2. CONTRIBUTION OF ARCHAEOLOGY, THE DOCUMENTS AND THE MONUMENTS

Archaeology does not necessarily fill in the historical gap. Though many archaeologists of Palestine / Israel and Biblical scholars (often one and the same person) are honestly convinced by its 'facts' and 'data', archaeology rarely helps in reconstructing a *histoire événementielle*. But archaeology can write a *histoire conjoncturelle*, a history of settlement occasionally

---

[8] Part of such a development is also the anachronistic appearance of Philistines in Patriarchal tradition (Gen. 21:32, 34; 26:1, 8, 14, 15, 18).

[9] This remarkable silence has already been noted by a number of scholars, see for instance, D.B. Redford, *Egypt, Canaan and Israel in ancient Times*, Princeton, New Yersey 1993, 294 "In the collective memory of the Israelites of these formative years in the land, no recollection of Egypt was retained"; further I. Singer, 'Egyptians, Canaanite and Philistines in the Period of the Emergence of Israel', in: I. Finkelstein, N. Na'aman (eds), *From Nomadism to Monarchy. Archaeological & Historical Aspects of Early Israel*, Jerusalem, Washington 1994, 294; C.R. Higginbotham, *Egyptianization and Elite Emulation in Ramesside Palestine. Governance and Accomodation on the Imperial Periphery*, (Culture and History of the Ancient Near East, 2) Leiden 2000, xi; A.E. Killebrew, *Biblical Peoples and Ethnicity. An Archaeological Study of Egyptian, Canaanites, Philistines, and Early Israel 1300–1100 BCE*, (ABSt, 9), Atlanta 2005, 152.

supported by information from Late Bronze and Early Iron Age documents and monuments. In the last ten years when doing some of the
archaeological handwork,[10] I also discovered that there is no archaeological record as such. Only fragmentary material traces of the past. The
honest belief in the archaeological records applies equally to the faithful
of the 'Die Bibel hat doch recht' school as to 'the Bible is a Hellenististic
book' adepts. The first group, the theologians who worked too much as
amateur or Biblical archaeologist have been scolded enough.[11] Likewise
the lack of archaeological experience, the 'bibliophobia' and 'minimalist'
views of Van Seters, the Copenhagen group and others have been criticized enough.[12]

   Archaeology does not and cannot do what it is often required to do,
for its results always tell us too much or to too little about the Bible.
Archaeology is, in any case, digging a large 'black hole' by the sweat of
your brow.[13] What is left is a set of drawings, photographs and a video
showing mercilessly what you have done wrong in order to achieve your
goal and to fill a store full of cartboard boxes and plastic bags with
'evidence'. Yet, there is no other way to get closer to this world of yesterday
than by digging in the past. We should do our best to glance accross the
border and exploit fully the vast resources that have become available
since Napoleon went to Egypt.[14]

   Furthermore we should not give up integrating archaeological results
into Biblical interpretation even if such integration is prone to mistakes

---

[10] J. Dijkstra, M. Dijkstra, K.J.H. Vriezen, *Tall Zar'a in Jordan. Report on the sondage at
Tall Zar'a 2001–2002 (Gadara Region Project: Tall Zira'a)*, (British Archaeological Reports
International Series, 1980), Oxford 2009.

[11] E. Noort, 'Text und Archäologie: die Küstenregion Palästinas in der Frühen Eisen-
zeit,' *UF* 27 (1995), 405.

[12] B. Halpern, 'Erasing History: The minimalist assault on Ancient Israel,' *BR* 11/6
(1995), 26–35, 47; Dever, *What Did the Biblical Writers Know, passim*; W.G. Dever,
'Merenptah's "Israel," the Bible's, and Ours,' in: J.D. Schloen (ed.), *Exploring the Longue
Durée. Essays in Honor of Lawrence E. Stager*, Winona Lake 2009, 89–90; Rainey, 'Stones
for Bread,' 144–145; J.M. Monson, 'The Role of Context and the Promise of Archaeology
in Biblical Interpretation from Early Judaism to Post Modernity,' in: J.K. Hoffmeier,
A.R. Millard (eds), *The Future of Biblical Archaeology*, Grand Rapids 2004, 315–316 to
mention just a few.

[13] Compare Rainey, 'Stones for Bread,' 140–141 "… archaeology is the science of
digging a square hole and the art of spinning a yarn from it."

[14] In my Egyptian years (1980–1989) I had enough time to think about the Levant
from Egyptian perspective and to study for myself the Karnak reliefs of Seti I, Ramesses II,
Merenptah, Shishak and those of Ramesses III at Medinet Habu. M. Dijkstra, 'Reading the
Old Testament in Cairo,' in: H. Lems (ed.), *Holland Mission. 150 Years Dutch Participation
in Mission in Egypt*, Utrecht 2005, 149–155.

and new discoveries confirm the old saying *dies diem docet*. I am not going to stir up the 'pots and people' discussion, but indicate in passing just a few, much debated examples of pottery as 'ethnic marker': the 'Philistine' bichrome ceramics and terracotta coffins as expressions of Philistine culture, ethnicity and territory and, similarly, the 'Israelite' association of the collared-rim jar.[15] Integrative study of archaeology, history and Biblical Interpretation remains one of the basic requirements of Biblical Studies.[16] There is always a gap to bridge between a text that writes a *histoire événementielle*, that is: tells a 'story of events' and an archaeological study of context which offers basically an *histoire conjoncturelle*.[17] History emerging from the data of modern settlement archaeology normally reflects the *longue durée* and only exceptionally might archaeology contribute to understanding of events. A well-known example is the interpretation of so-called destruction-layers in the discussion about the dilemma of 'Conquest or Settlement'. Recent studies have shown that archaeology cannot prove a 'Blitzkrieg' of Joshua. It may help, however, to reconstruct the settlement history of a new emerging society. Someone who does not accept such basic historical distinctions and insights of Braudel *et al.* is deemed to repeat a history of failure to understand what archaeology can do for reading the Bible. In such a

---

[15] See H. Weippert, *Palästina in vorhellenistischer Zeit*, (Handbuch der Archäologie. Vorderasien II/1), München 1988, 373–382; Noort, *Seevölker*, 113–137; idem, *UF* 27 (1995),418–419, 421–428; A.E. Killebrew, *Biblical Peoples and Ethnicity. An Archaeological Study of Egyptians, Canaanites, Philistine, and Early Israel 1300–1100 BCE*, Atlanta 2005, 197–231 about the coffins esp. 218; Killebrew is more inclined to maintain a typology of Philistine Pottery, actually only Mycenaean IIIC:1b signifies the appearance of the Philistines. The bichrome pottery belongs then to the later creolization of Philistine material culture. Another example is the ongoing debate about the 'ethnicity' of the collared-rim jar, see such divergent views as expressed in Killebrew, *Biblical Peoples*, 177–181; Dijkstra *et al.*, *Tall Zar'a in Jordan*, 49–50 and the efforts to rescue the 'Israelite association' in A. Faust, *Israel's Ethnogenesis. Settlement, Interaction, Expansion and Resistance* (Approaches to anthroplogical Archaeology), London 2006, 191–205.

[16] Karel Vriezen, Ellen van Wolde and I organized a seminar in 2007 and 2009 in Utrecht/Tilburg about exactly this topic for research master and postgraduate students of NOSTER (The Netherlands School for Research into Theology and Religion).

[17] As far as I know R.B. Coote, K.W. Whitelam, *The Emergence of Early Israel in Historical Perspective*, (SWBAS, 5), Sheffield 1987, introduced Braudel into the Biblical Archaeology debate; further I. Finkelstein, 'The Rise of Early Israel. Archaeology and Long-Term History', in: *The Origin of Early Israel—Current Debate*, 11; I. Finkelstein, N.A. Silberman, *The Bible unearthed—Archaeology's New Vision of Ancient Israel and the Origin of Its Sacred Texts*, New York 2001; Becking, 'Chronology: A Skeleton without Flesh?' 2002, 71; Dijkstra, 'As for the Other Events …', 2005, 16–17. Unfortunately, the title of Lawrence Stager's Festschrift *Exploring the Longue Durée* (see note 17) promises more than it contains on this subject.

reconstruction of settlement, many factors of development and change are involved, such as physical geography, climatic variation, economic relations and exchange, and agricultural and artistic skills. In such a contextual approach, Israelite settlement cannot simply be viewed only as a development *sui generis* from within but, as Coote and Whitelam remarked, should place confidence in a panoramic view of history to support a multicausal interpretation of the emergence of early Israel in the long term.[18]

### 3. ISRAEL FROM AN 'EGYPTIAN' PERSPECTIVE

This contribution is about 'Israel' between history and ideology. Therefore I start where this name appears first in a clearly dated context and undisputedly refering to a group of people on the alleged 'Israel' stele from Merenptah's 5th year (1208 BCE).[19] It is not the first occurrence of the name of Israel. As a West Semitic personal name it existed long before it became a tribal or a geographical name. This is not without significance, though is it rarely mentioned. We learn of a *maryanu* named *yšr'il* (*Yišrā'ilu) from Ugarit living in the same period, but the name was already used a thousand years before in Ebla.[20] The word Israel originated as a West Semitic personal name. One of the many names that developed into the name of the ancestor of a clan, of a tribe and finally of a people and a nation. There is nothing unhistorical here. Thanks to

---

[18] Coote, Whitelam, *Emergence of Early Israel*, 9.

[19] Fine surveys are found with M.G. Hasel, *Domination and Resistance. Egyptian Military Activity in the Southern Levant ca. 1300–1185*, (PÄ, 11) Leiden 1998, 194–200; K.W. Whitelam, 'The Identity of Early Israel: The Re-alignment and Transformation of Late Bronze–Iron Age Palestine,' *JSOT* 63 (1994), 57–87 esp. 68–76; Singer, 'Egyptians, Canaanites and Philistines,' 286–287.

[20] Hasel, *Domination and Resistance*, 195; M. Dijkstra, 'Jacob,' *²DDD*, 460. Hebrew *yiśrā'ēl* and Ebla *Iš-ra-ilu (AN)* are a perfect vocalisation for Ugaritic *yšr'il* (*Yišrā'ilu) RS 19.049B = *²KTU* 4, 623 PC room 81, as already noted, for instance, by Virolleaud, *PRU* 5, 97; and F. Gröndahl, *Die Personennamen der Texte aus Ugarit*, (StP, 1), Rom 1967, 146. It is also corroborated by Egyptian group-writing *yi=s-ra-'i-ra det =*Yisra'ila (J.E. Hoch, *Semitic Words in Egyptian Texts of the New Kingdom and Third Intermediate Period*, Princeton, New Yersey 1994, 27). Note that the Ugaritic name is contemporary with the 'Israel' stele. We find in Salmanasar III Monolith inscription also the gentilic *Šir-'i-la-ay(a)* with the name of King Achab. All these spellings seem to reflect an original West Semitic PN *yiśrā'il(u)**, which derives from a verb ŚRY 'to contend, strive (with)'. There is no reason to mistrust the traditional etymology in Old Testament tradition, see H.-J. Zobel, יִשְׂרָאֵן, *ThWAT III*, 988–989.

the accuracy of the Egyptian scribal art, the name was written in group-writing and provided with a determinative, which make perfectly clear that we have here a group of people, men and women of foreign origin from an Egyptian perspective.[21] Usually they were also enemies, as the added 'boomerang' sign implies (T 14). By way of comparison, wandering groups such as the Peleshet and Shakalush, or the Libyan Meshwesh are classified in exactly the same way as this 'Israel', but it did not lead to a clash of speculations about their ethnicity, provenance and whereabouts.

What's in a name? The name 'Israel' stele is a misnomer, but an interesting one. It still reveals something of the historical 'tunnel vision' often found in the interpretation of this document. I found an example on the website of the Israel Ministry of Foreign Affairs: "The victory stele of Merenptah ... for the first time specifically mentions 'Israel' as a nation, which was defeated and *goes on* (Italics mine!) Canaan was plundered and Gezer captured." Ideology sneaks in easily. Not ancient Israel, but ancient Libya or actually Pharaoh Merenptah, the great 'Prince of Peace' is the topic of this document. The stele was made to commemorate the greater glory of this Pharaoh and was erected at several places to immortalize his victory over the Libyans and their allies.[22] As such it was also part of the assemblage of texts with which this Pharaoh and his successors adorned the *Cour de la Cachette* in the Karnak Temple of the god Amun-Re.[23]

## 4. 'Israel' stele in the Context of Egyptian Royal Ideology

The real war which Merneptah had to fight in his 5th year, was the Libyan war. In Old Testament studies or the search for the prehistory of Israel, we hardly deal with 'Barbarians' such as the Libyans and their allies. This is, however, detrimental for our understanding of Levantine

---

[21] Dever, 'Merenptah's "Israel"', 89, repeatedly speaks about a determinative sign 'foreign country' preceding [sic!] the name. That the double determinative added (!) to the name of Israel is a sole exception (ibidem, 89), is not correct either.

[22] The most complete stele found by Petrie (1896) in the remains of Merenptah's mortuary temple (Qurna), is now in Cairo (JE 34025 verso). A fragmentary version is in steliform included among the inscriptions of the inner eastern wall in the *Cour de la Cachette* Karnak. See below.

[23] Colleen Malassa, *The Great Karnak Inscription of Merneptah: Grand Strategy in the 13th Century* bc, (Yale Egyptological Seminar, 5), New Haven 2003.

history in the long term. Merenptah's victory hymn is since its discovery known as the 'Israel' stele, as if the primary focus of this text. That might be true for Biblical scholars and even the Foreign Ministry of Israel,[24] but Egyptologists know better and historians should know better.

In the last twenty years much effort was invested in extracting more information about Merenptah's 'Israel' from a concentric literary structure detected in the 25th and last strophe of the Victory hymn.[25] As so often in structural exegesis, there is no consensus about this structure. I am not going to discuss the findings in detail, but there are at least two basic outcomes which lead to a minimalistist and maximalistist historical interpretation about what Israel is in this text. In other words: to make a distinction between the major and minor enemies of Egypt in Palestine. The maximalist analysis reckons Israel with the larger enemies of Egypt as a major threat to the *pax aegyptica*, Israel representing a people and even a territory. By contrast, Ahlström believes that in the stele Canaan or Kharu / Khuru represents the well-populated lowlands and Israel the Central Highlands. In the minimalist view, Israel goes with the lesser

---

[24] As far as I know, the Palestinian Authority has not yet used this early occurrence of the Peleshet people to prove that here for the first time in the Egyptian texts the 'Palestinian nation' is mentioned.

[25] For convenience, this note includes not only literature about this literary analysis, but also about the Karnak battle scenes of Merenptah's Palestinian Campaign (see below § 6). G.W. Ahlström, D. Edelman, 'Merenptach's Israel,' *JNES* 44 (1985), 59–61; G.W. Ahlström, *The History of Ancient Palestine from the Palaeolithic Period to Alexander's Conquest* (edited by Diana Edelman; JSOT Sup, 146), Sheffield 1993, 284; F.J. Yurco, 'Merenptah's Canaanite campaign,' *JARCE* 23 (1986), 189–215; L. Stager, 'Merenptah, Israel and Sea Peoples,' *ErIs* 18 (Nahman Avigad Volume) (1985), 56*–64*; I. Singer, 'Merenptah's Campaign to Canaan and the Egyptian Occupation of the Southern Coastal Plain of Palestine in the Ramesside Period,' *BASOR* 269 (1988), 1–10; F.J. Yurco, '3,200-Year-Old Picture of Israelites Found in Egypt,' *BArR* 16/5 (1990), 20–28; J.J. Bimson, 'Merenptah's Israel and Recent Theories of Israelite Origins,' *JSOT* 49 (1991), 3–29; G.W. Ahlström, 'The Origin of Israel in Palestine,' *SJOT* 2 (1991), 19–35; M.G. Hasel, 'Israel in the Merenptah Stela,' *BASOR* 296 (1994), 45–61; J.K. Hoffmeier, *Israel in Egypt: The Authenticity of the Exodus Tradition*, Oxford 1997, 28–31; K.A. Kitchen, 'The Physical Text of Merenptah's Victory Hymn (The "Israel"),' *JSSEA* 24 (1997), 71–76; F.J. Yurco, 'Merenptah's Canaanite Campaign and Israel's Origins,' in: E.S. Frerichs and L.H. Lesko (eds), *Exodus: The Egyptian Evidence*, Winona Lake 1997, 27–55; A.F. Rainey, 'Israel in Merenptah's Inscription and Reliefs,' *IEJ* 51 (2001), 57–75; M.G. Hasel, 'The Structure of the Final Hymnic-Poetic Unit on the Merenptah Stela,' *ZAW* 116 (2004), 75–81; K.A. Kitchen, 'The Victories of Merenptah, and the Nature of Their Record,' *JSOT* 28 (2004), 259–272; U. Zerbst, P. van der Veen (eds), *Keine Posaunen vor Jericho. Beiträge zur Archäologie der Landnahme*, Holzgerlingen 2005, 39–41.

enemies, the cities of Askelon, Gezer and Yanoam, with Israel together sandwiched between Canaan and Khuru, as Kitchen nicely put it.[26]

We better try another avenue first, looking at the architectural structure and historical context of this monument. The full building history of the Karnak Temple in the New Kingdom and the Third Intermediate Period is better left aside here. The construction of the Great Ramesside Hypostyle and adjacent courts, the 'Bubastic Gate', *Cour de la Cachette* and its reliefs in their original and reworked versions, should be considered in their constructive and conceptual coherence and not in splendid isolation, as has happened with the battle scenes of 'Merenptah' on the walls of the *Cour de la Cachette*, originally attributed to Ramesses II.[27] In particular, the battle scenes on the western outside wall of the *Cour de la Cachette* were reinterpreted as evidence for Merenptah's war in Palestine. According to Yurco's analysis, the two other cities depicted on this wall behind Askelon (Scene 1), are Gezer and Yano'am (Scenes 2 and 3) and subsequently the enemy in the upper register about to be massacred in the open field must be the Israelites (Scene 4), Israelites here depicted as Asiatics in Egyptian fashion. The theory that these scenes and 'writing on the wall' are a vivid illustration of the last strophe of Merenptah's Victory stele, now lives its own life in the debate about Israel's origins.

The battle scenes and texts are very damaged and open to multiple interpretation. Some of these texts and reliefs are even palimpsests which aggravates their interpretation considerably. Some Egyptologists raised grave objections against Yurco's interpretations, which can hardly be ignored.[28] First, the battle scenes are very similar to those of Seti I on the north wall of the Hypostyle. Second, there are clear indications that redecoration of these walls in the north-eastern corner of the great court of the Chons Temple was started under Ramesses II's son and royal heir Khaemwese. The facial features of the Pharaoh in the slaying-the-

---

[26] Kitchen, 'Victories of Merenptah, and the Nature of Their Record', 74.

[27] P. Barquet, *Le Temple d'Amon-Rê à Karnak*, Le Caire 1962, 272–279; F. Le Saout, 'Reconstitution des murs de la Cour de la Cachette,' *Cahiers de Karnak VII 1978–1981*, Paris 1982, 213–248 pls. I-IX; for a summary of Merenptah's inscriptional work in Karnak, see H. Sourouzian, *Les Monuments du roi Merenptah*, (SAÄK, 22), Mainz am Rhein 1989, 142–150.

[28] Sourouzian, *Merenptah*, 150; D.B. Redford, *Egypt, Canaan and Israel in ancient Times*, Princeton, New Yersey 1993, 275 n. 1; see esp. D.B. Redford, 'The Ashkelon Relief at Karnak and the Israel Stela,' *IEJ* 36 (1986) 188–200; cautiously, also Singer, 'Egyptians, Canaanites and Philistines,' 287, in particular because several observations of Mrs. Le Saout, *Reconstitution*, 228–233 about scenes 4a–c (Pls IV, IX) = Yurco's scenes 9–10 were neglected.

enemies scene on the western exterior wall are typically Ramesses II, different from the one of Merenptah depicted on the eastern interior wall of the *Cour the la Cachette*.

The stele of the Hittite-Egyptian or 'eternal treaty' (1258/1259) and the partly preserved corniche with Ramesses II cartouche included on the same wall are ample proof of the immediate provenance of its adjacent reliefs.[29] The 21st year most probably suggests for them *a terminus post quem*, a detail suprisingly often overlooked or not taken into account. A date in the second part of Ramesses' II reign tallies also with the inscriptions and scenes on the outside of the south wall of the Great Hypostyle.[30] On the inside western wall of the *Cour de la Cachette*, we find also reliefs and records that were started under Ramesses II, but later taken over by Seti II. Here also a decree for the temple issued by Ramesses II is included in the wall,[31] perhaps by his son, heir and builder Khaemwese between about 1258/1259 and 1225.[32] In the same period, the further decoration of this inner court was marked by a 'portrait' of the royal heir between the paws of a sphinx in relief.[33] The inside eastern wall was decorated after Ramesses' II death with inscriptions of the Libyan war and

---

[29] Like the southern outside wall of the Hypostyle, the reliefs on this wall were worked twice, a process apparently marked by the inclusion of the stele with the 'eternal treaty'. On the southern wall, the new relief was worked over the Battle of Qadesh, see Le Saout, *Reconstitution*, 228–229, Kitchen *et al.* as also noted by Yurco, *JARCE* 23 (1986), 206. Note that the reconstruction of the western outside wall of the *Cour the la Cachette* by Mrs. Le Saout is completed with a scene Ramesses II slaying the enemies before Amun-Re (Pl. IV 4a–b).

[30] The relief on the left (west) and right (east) of the entrance clearly have the famous triumphal scene of slaying the enemies before Amun-Re, but is a palimpsest over earlier scenes, depicting the Battle of Qadesh.

[31] Le Saout, *Reconstitution*, 224–225.

[32] To assume here a pictorial representation of an unknown son of Merenptah, Khaemwese II, instead of the well known royal heir Khaemwese, son of Ramesses II, does not really strengthen Yurco's theory (Sourouzian, *Merenptah*, 150). Of course, it is not impossible, for Ramesses III had also a son Khaemwese (Tomb 44 Valley of the Queens). However, the argument that Khaemwese had a carreer as (High)-priest (Yurco, *JARCE* 23 (1986), 206) is rather weak. There are quite a number of scenes showing that Khaemwese like his brothers had military training and was involved in battles in the early part of his father's reign (Nubia [Beit el-Wali], Qadesh, Dapur, Qode, Moab?). Is his depiction here perhaps a survival of the Battle of Qadesh?

[33] Souzourain, *Merenptah*, 142, 149 observes repeatedly that the cartouches in front of the sphinx were reworked to receive the cartouches of Merenptah and not one of his successors (*pace* Yurco, *JARCE* 23 (1986) 197). It either infers that the prince depicted between the paws is Merenptah himself (so Souzourain) or Khaemwese. Reworking with Merenptah's cartouches could also be the work of Seti II to present himself as the royal heir like on the outside wall (Le Saout, *Reconstitution*, 232, 4c Pl. IX).

adjacent to the south the standard triumphal scene depicting Merenptah slaying the enemies before Amun, also including the Karnak version of the Victory stele.[34] Sourouzian remarks that Merenptah apparently did not develop plans for his own architectural additions to the Temple of Karnak, but accepted the completion of the decoration of the existing 18th Dynasty *Cour de la Cachette* with those of his father and his own Libyan War Memorial. His successors, in particular Seti II followed suit. Perhaps, the Great War inscription was already started during his reign, whereas the Victory stele summarizing this war and other campaigns, was included after his death.[35] The Great Karnak War inscription is only about the Libyan war, but the triumphal scene mentions also the defeat of the Nubians. It is difficult to explain why Merenptach illustrated in detail his punitive action in Palestine, but devoted hardly a picture to the wretched Libyans.

Only when viewed in isolation from the broader architectural and conceptual context of the Karnak Temple, a short cut is possible between the Askelon depicted in relief and the Askelon mentioned in the Victory stele. Because they copy so much in lay out and details, the battle scenes of Seti I, the battle scenes of Ramesses and successors are hard to pin down to a particular known event in the Ramesside Period after the Battle of Qadesh. For some reason in the Karnak Temple, Ramesses II had the reliefs reworked, apparently focusing on his peace enforcement in the Levant. It was rather easy for Merenptah to adopt and claim the battle scenes of his father for his own glory and the glory of the Dynasty. The same is true for Amenmese and Seti II. Because there is more ideology than history written and depicted on the walls, the reliefs are better to be construed as specimens of a long-term history of political claims about the Levant.

Historical interpretation is also hampered by the ambiguity and vagueness of topographical terminology, for instance the different shades of meaning of Canaan and Kharu / Khuru in Merenptah's stela and other historical texts. Scholars differ about the question whether or not Pi-Canaan denotes in Merenptah's victory hymn the city of ancient Gaza only, the region of South Palestine or even the whole country on both

---

[34] Ch. Kuentz, 'Le Double de la Stèle d'Israël à Karnak,' *BIFAO* 21 (1923), 114–116; K.A. Kitchen, G.A. Gaballa, 'Ramesside Varia II,' *ZÄS* 96 (1969), 23–28, Kitchen, *RI IV*, 12–19 (synopsis); Sourouzian, *Merenptah*, 144–145.

[35] Like the Victory stela erected in his mortuary temple. If the stele were included later, the dating refers to the Libyan War only as in the Great War inscription and the 'Athribis' inscription of Kom el-Ahmar (Kitchen, *RI IV*, 19–20).

sides of the Jordan south of Syria and Libanon. Since the inscriptions of Seti I, it can mean both the city and the region, of which Pi-Canaan = Gaza is the provincial capital. Whatever the extension of the territory called Canaan, it basically refers in 2nd Millennium texts to the coastal area of the Levant and commercial activity of its inhabitants.[36] By contrast, Khuru/Kharu is more often associated with the Levantine Highlands and hinterland.[37] Some even think it includes the Province of Upe (Egyptian dominated region around Damascus) and the region of Bashan (Gaulan/Geshur/Hauran).[38] In the first stele of Seti I, Khuru/Kharu seems to include the region around the Lake of Gennesareth,[39] whereas the battle scenes associate Khuru/Kharu with the Shosu People, the Hill Country and the Transjordanian Uplands. In view of this variety of Egyptian topographical names for the Levant and Levantine names used in Egypt, which have roots in demographic changes in the Middle Bronze period,[40] it is rather improbable that a new name: Israel, would suddenly appear with similar demographic ramifications.[41] In addition, it is probable that the stele parallels Pi-Canaan, Askelon and Gezer opposite Yano'am, Israel and Kharu/Khuru from south to north and from the coastal plain to the hinterland. This alignment seems also true of the battle reliefs on the wall of the *Court de la Cachette*, following a traditional scheme which is also present in the battle scenes of Seti I.

In view of the ideological set up of these battle scenes and also in the immediate historical context of the Libyan War, the operation in Palestine, the last strophe of the twenty-five in this poem,[42] is only a kind of footnote. Because 'Israel' is mentioned, it implies that its presence was

---

[36] See the survey of H.-J. Zobel, כנען, *ThWAT IV*, 226–229.

[37] The evidence A.H. Gardiner, *Ancient Egyptian Onomastica I*, London 1947, 180–187.

[38] V. Fritz, 'Conquest or Settlement. The Early Iron Age in Palestine,' *BA* 50 (1987), 99; Rainey, *IEJ* 51 (2001), 65 with reference to pAnastasi III, 1:9–10 and Wen-Amun, both rather late testimonies (12th–11th Century BCE).

[39] About the Horites in Northern Palestine, see De Vaux, *Histoire*, 133–134.

[40] Ahituv, 'The Origins of Ancient Israel', 136–137.

[41] It has been suggested to read the name Israel on a topographical fragment from Amenophis II or III (Ägyptisches Museum Berlin No. 21687), M. Görg, 'Israel in Hieroglyphen,' *BN* 106 (2001), 21–27; Zerbst, Van der Veen, *Keine Posaunen vor Jericho?*, 40. In my opinion the damaged name could better be rendered as the lowland city of 'a-=š-[ta]-'i-=r, אשתאל, Eshtaol.

[42] See the strophic translation of E. Hornung, 'Die Israelstele des Merneptah,' in: M. Görg (ed.), *Fontes atque Pontes. Fs H. Brunner*, (Ägypten und Altes Testament, 5), Wiesbaden 1983, 224–233.

noted and of some importance to the Egyptians.[43] As such they were there on the outskirts of Canaan, either in Galilee, or in the Yarmuk estuary. However, not in the centre but in the margin of Egypt's interests and, as far as we know, it would remain so till the end of Egyptian rule about 1100 BCE.

## 5. 'ISRAEL', A FOOTNOTE IN MERENPTAH'S LIBYAN WAR

The 'Israel' stele is about the war with King Meri of the Libyan Meshwesh and his allies from the North, bands of Sea People who supported Tehenu to push Egypt into a corner. Besides this major threat from the Western Desert, there were also skirmishes with the Nubians. Whether at this stage these satellites meant an unexpected, additional threat to the Egyptians, is difficult to assess. The Libyan leader Meri, whose crimes are floridly exaggerated and whose defeat is graphically sung in the Victory Hymn used the services of *Šardinu* (Sherdanu) and *Šakaluš* (*Šikila/Šikaliya*),[44] who have been attested before the Libyan war as mercenaries on either side of the border. Also the *Aqa(y)waš, Turša* and *Lukku*, until then unknown, are mentioned as Egypt's adversaries.[45] For the *'I-qa/gá-(=y)-wa-ša Aq/ga(y)waš*, an association with the people of the *Aḫḫiya(wa)* 'Aegaeans / Achaeans' cannot be excluded.[46]

It is not always easy to distinguish tribes of Sea People and the bands of Shosu. They are sometimes confused, even by scholars such as Staubli,

---

[43] Faust, *Israel's Ethnogenesis*, 163.

[44] This group is probably equal to Egyptian *Tkr/l* (*ti₂/ta*-*-(k)ka-la/li/lu*) E. Edel, 'Die Sikeloi in den Ägyptischen Seevölkerteksten und in Keilschrifturkunden,' *BN* 23 (1984), 7–8; M. Dietrich, O. Loretz, 'Das 'seefahrende Volk' von Šikila,' *UF* 10 (1978), 53–56; G.A. Lehmann, 'Die Šikilāju—ein neues Zeugnis zu den "Seevölkern"-Heerfahrten im späten 13. Jh.v.Chr. (RS 34.129)', *UF* 11 (1979), 481–494; Noort, *Seevölker*, 85–86; I. Singer, 'A political history of Ugarit,' in: W.G.E. Watson, N. Wyatt (eds), *Handbook of Ugaritic Studies (HUS)*, (HO I, 39), Leiden 1999, 722. The question remains why both designations are used in the inscriptions of Medinet Habu, not, however, in the pHarris where *šklš* is often emended instead of *šrdn*, (Noort, *Seevölker*, 83). The idea that the name of the tribe Issachar is historically related to the *Šklš/tkr* and the *Dnyn/Danuna* with the tribe of Dan (Y. Yadin *et al.*), did not find scholarly acceptance.

[45] W. Helck, *Die Beziehungen Ägyptens und Vorderasiens zur Ägäis bis ins 7. Jahrhundert v.Chr.*, (Erträge der Forschung, 120), Darmstadt 1979, 132–144; Helck spells Turuš, but *Tu₃=r-ša* following the transcript system of Hoch is more plausible.

[46] See Helck, *Beziehungen Ägyptens und Vorderasiens zur Ägäis*, 134. Later the name 'Akiš /'Akayuš / Ikausu is still found for kings of Ekron in the 7th Century BCE, E. Lipinski, *On the Skirts of Canaan in the Iron Age, Historical and Topographical researches*, (OLA, 153), Leuven 2004, 36–42, 51–52.

Yurco and Rainey. Noort made it plausible that the group *Mützenträger I*, with a kerchief folded into a bonnet bound by a headband at the front whereas it is open at the back of the head showing there a protruding shock of hair, are Shosu. Warriors wearing any type of feather crown are Peleshet, Denyen or Tjeker/l.[47] By contrast, the group *Mützenträger II*, with a beret or turban dented in the middle, most probably belong to the Tursha or, in any case, to a different group of the Sea People (Aegaeans?).

When we return to the outside wall of the *Cour de la Cachette* armed with this knowledge, we discover that in the reliefs reworked by Seti II/ Seti-Merenptah, not only Canaanite soldiers and Shosu warriors are depicted,[48] but also Sea People, perhaps the Tursha. In the lower register with the city of Askelon and to the north an unidentified town, perhaps Gezer[49] we surprisingly discover alongside the ubiquitous Canaanite people and the Shosu also a clan of Sea People. Indeed, the reliefs are less well preserved than those of Seti I and also of lesser workmanship, but some of the Sea People warriors are quite easy to identfy by means of their dented beret/turban and round shields.[50] Just as remarkable is that they are lacking in the upper register as far as preserved. Here, further inland in my opinion, only Asiatic/Canaanite warriors are seen as Yurco, Stager and Rainey have already observed.

As noted by several scholars, the lay-out of the reliefs in lower, middle or upper register, basically imitates the battle reliefs of Seti I. In the lower register of scenes, warriors are depicted, who might be identified as Tursha because of their beret, bandaged upper body and large

---

[47] Noort, *Seevölker*, 94–112, also Helck, *Beziehungen Ägyptens und Vorderasiens zur Ägäis*, 133–134; Killebrew, *Biblical Peoples*, 202–203, though she is much less specific on the different groups of Philistines.

[48] See especially Yurco, *JARCE* 23 (1986), 207; idem, *BArR* 16 (1990), 35 and *passim*, with some modifications accepted by Stager, Staubli, Hasel *et al*. Also Rainey, *IEJ* 51 (2001), 68–75, but he rightly remarks that the warring Canaanites should not be identified with the Israelites (ibidem, 69).

[49] Thus Yurco, but Rainey: Yano'am. Comparison with the battle scenes of Seti I would favour Yurco's option, but a *non liquet* at such a controversial identification seems more advisable.

[50] W. Wreszinski, *Atlas zur Ägyptischen Kulturgeschichte*, Leipzig 1923–1938, Volume II, Pls 57–58; Staubli, *Image der Nomaden*, Abb. 39; see photograph Rainey, *IEJ* 51 (2001), 74, Fig. 7 identifying them all as Shosu, though clearly also a Canaanite and some Sea People prisoners appear, most probably representatives of Noort's *Mützenträger II* = Tursha. Apart from there, Shosu and Tursha are also shown together in Medinet Habu (Noort, *Seevölker*, 78 Abb. 21; 81 Abb. 24) and perhaps the new fragment from Tel el-Borg (Note 53). On the Askelon relief a warrior with such a beret is falling head down, carrying a round shield and wearing a kilt. This is definitely not a Canaanite and hardly a Shosu warrior, as was also noted by Stager, *ErIs* 18 (1985), 56–64*.

medaillon / amulet, alongside Shosu.[51] Actually, on second thought, these Shosu and Tursha together pose an iconographic, if not historical, problem for archaeologists and Biblical scholars who directly read these texts and depictions as historical documents. Most Egyptologists are more cautious in their assessment. The appearance of Shosu and Tursha together seems almost a kind of standard picture. They are also depicted together in Abydos (Seti I), Beit el-Wali,[52] Wadi es-Sebua, Luxor-Temple (in the Battle of Qadesh); Abu Simbel, Ramesseum (all Ramesses II), and perhaps now also Tell el-Borg.[53] Hardly surprisingly therefore, that this group of *Mutzenträger II* was first thought to be Shosu too.[54] Nevertheless, the rather strict canon of the Egyptian artist took the trouble to depict them differently, because they were, after all, a group independent of the Sea People bands,[55] even when they became part of a kind of standard image. The reliefs of Ramesses III hardly allow any other conclusion than that they belong to the 'Tursha of the Sea'. In other words, in the lower register on the wall of the *Cour de la Cachette* we once more encounter a standard Levantine coalition of Asiatics, Shosu and representatives of the Sea People.

---

[51] However, the medaillion is also found on Shosu (Noort, *Seevölker*, 76 Abb. 19; 82 Abb. 25; 89 Abb. 26; 100 Abb. 35).

[52] H. Ricke *et al.*, *The Beit el-Wali Temple of Ramses II*, ... Pl. 10–13; Staubli, *Image der Nomaden*, Abb. 36; the warriors of both groups are armed with spears and a spear thrower or boomerang.

[53] J.K. Hoffmeier and L. Pinch-Brock, 'A New Royal Chariot Scene from Tell el-Borg,' *JSSEA* 32 (2005) Fig. 4 TBO 0129, behind a Shosu with a duck-bill axe, is a fragment of a face (nose, eye and cap), which may be wearing a kind of beret / tulband like the Tursha.

[54] So R. Giveon, *Les bédouins Shosou des documents égyptiens* (DMOA, 12) Leiden 1971, *passim*; Staubli, *Image der Nomaden*, Abb. 32–37; Rainey, *IEJ* 51 (2001), 74–75, Fig. 7. Noort's (*Seevölker*, 103) remark that the *Mutzenträger II* (*trš*?) are an exception to the rule that Sea People appear both as enemies and auxiliary forces in the Egyptian records, is not correct (Noort, *Seevölker*, Abb. 21; Staubli, *Image der Nomaden*, Abb. 45 Medinet Habu) and is now also contested by the Tell el-Borg fragment in which they appear as mercenaries alongside Shosu (Note 53).

[55] I will not discuss whether all groups subsumed under Sea Peoples came from 'overseas', or were also of Anatolian and Aegaean provenance. See the apposite contributions in S. Gitin *et al.*(eds), *Mediterranean Peoples in Transition: Thirteenth to Early Tenth Centuries* BCE. *In Honor of Professor Trude Dothan*, Jerusalem 1998. If the Tursha be a group related to the Lukku from the southern coast of Western Asia, their designation as 'Tursha from the Sea' is still adequate.

## 6. 'Israel' Depicted on the Wall?

Staubli, Redford, Rainey and Kitchen—though some of them have been convinced about the Merenptah connection—expressed grave doubts on this point. Not only is it tricky to assume a clear parallellism between the text and the reliefs, because the names of the other two cities beside Askelon are no longer legible or otherwise identifiable. Even if it be accepted that they are the cities of Gezer and Yanoʻam, the problem remains that all the people resisting the Egyptians in the upper register are traditionally depicted as Semites / Asiatics / Canaanites or whatever one would like to call them. If we find here 'Israel', the Egyptian artist would not know about or see a difference from other peoples in Canaan. Perhaps, some scholars would see this as a confirmation that 'Israel' originated from Canaan, even in Egyptian perspective, but for the time being it seems better to decide for a *non liquet*. What ever the aftermath of Merenptah's war with the Libyans, the encounter with 'Israel' remained an unexpected and transient incident that as yet cannot present the evidence of major demographic changes in the region. The successors of Ramesses II, who revised and completed the reliefs and inscriptions in the *Cour de la Cachette*, meant first of all to reinforce a long-term view on the domination of the Levant.

This does not imply that a punitive action into Canaan by Merenptah, or, more probably, by his generalissimo and royal heir Seti II did not take place.[56] It probably happened after a Nubian rebellion in the 6th year.[57] The stele from Nubian Amada from the 6th year, or somewhat later,[58] adds to the royal titles of Merenptah *wʻf Qa/Gá-ḍa-=r* 'who curbed

---

[56] We know from other sources that Merenptah and Seti II became politically more active in the Levant responding to the rapid decline of the Hittite Empire, (Singer, 'Egyptians, Canaanites, and Philistines,' 286–289; idem, *HUS*, 708–715). See also Merenptah's letter to Ammurapi of Ugarit (S. Lackenbacher, 'Une correspondance entre l'administration du pharaon Merenptah et le roi d'Oegarit,' in: M. Yon *et al.* (eds), *Le pays d'Ougarit autour de 1200 av. J.-C., Actes du Colloque international (Paris, 1993)* (Ras Shamra-Ougarit, 11) Paris 1995, 77–83; Singer, *HUS*, 709–710; S. Lackenbacher, 'RS 88.2158 Un Égyptien annonce l'envoi d'artisans et de fournitures diverses à Oegarit,' in: M. Yon, D. Arnaud (eds), *Études Ougaritiques I. Travaux 1985–1995* (Ras Shamra-Ougarit, 14) Paris 2001, 239–247.

[57] Compare the remark in lines 23–24 of the Merneptah Victory stele that everything is quiet on the southern front and that the Madjoi, a kind of (Nubian?) police active as a border patrol, could sleep quietly again (also Singer, *BASOR* 269 [1988], 3).

[58] Kitchen, *RI IV*, 1:9, the rendering of the date line is not completely secure, see A.A. Youssef, 'Merenptah's Fourth Year Text at Amada,' *ASAE* 58 (1964), 273–280. The 4th Year found on the most complete stela of Amada, is probably a mistake. The Amara

Gezer'. Singer may be correct that the main purpose of this operation was a show of force to secure once more in southern Canaan the military and commercial roads to the north of the Levant. The medium was the message to keep Egypt's main door and highways open now that Hatti was on the verge of collapse. It had always been a long term concern of the Egyptian foreign policy. Centuries later, Pharaoh Neko II would do the same on the verge of the collapse of the Assyrian Empire. Merenptah outflanked the coastal settlements around Gaza and recaptured the crucial cities of Askelon and Gezer to secure the southern approach of the *Via Maris* and the junction of the road at Gezer to the Jordan Valley and beyond,[59] turning them once more into Egyptian Highways. And then, somewhere in the margin 'Israel' appears, but it is clear that the confrontation with this 'Israel' had no lasting impact on Egyptian politics and administration in the years to come of the 12th Century BCE, as the actions of the Sea Peoples and the Shosu did. In the regions of Canaan dominated by the Egyptian government and their allies, that is outside the Highlands of Canaan, there was as yet no place for Israelite settlement or expansion.

## 7. The End of Egypt's Domination over Canaan

This review of Israelite origins set off from the observation that the silence of Israelite tradition about the Egyptian presence in Canaan in the Late Bronze and Early Iron Age is balanced by an almost equal silence of Egypt about Israel. Israelite settlement and territorial expansion apparently got momentum only after the collapse of Egyptian rule. This turning point was not reached before the latter years of the 12th Century BCE. The Egyptian occupation of Canaan was not really endangered during the reign of Ramesses III, even during the troubles of the transition from the 19th to the 20th Dynasty. Evidence of the continued Egyptian prestige in the Levant since the conclusion of the 'eternal treaty' is confirmed by new archaeological discoveries and research. I mention the discoveries

---

version has the correct text: 6th Year 1st month of Akhet, Day 1, that is a year and three months after the battle against the Libyans of Meri, see Sourouzian, *Merenptah*, 201. It suggests that the operation in Palestine had taken place in the mean time.

[59] In Merenptah's 3rd year, there was already a stronghold on the mountain range near Jerusalem 'The Wells of Merenptah' perhaps identical to *Ma'yan Me=Naftoah* (Liftha Josh. 15:9; 18:15), see about this 'Border Journal': *ANET³*, 258; Yurco, *JARCE* 23 (1986), 211; Singer, 'Egyptians, Canaanites and Philistines', 288.

of new stelae of Ramesses II, one in Kiswe near Damascus from the 56th year, the other a basalt fragment from et-Turra in Jordan (near Tell esh-Shihab).[60] We mention also new documents from Ugarit, especially correspondence of Merenptah and Seti II (his vizier Biya!) from the Urtena archive addressed to the last king of Ugarit, Ammurapi (ca. 1215–1190 BCE). This increasing prestige was undoubtedly also the result of the rapid decline of Hittite domination in the northern Levant. The revision of the reliefs in the Karnak Temple by Seti II, heir-apparent and generalissimo, is not without significance in this development.[61] It suggests the confident continuation of the geopolitical claims of the New Kingdom, claims which cannot just be put aside as an empty love of display.

Another indication for Egyptian presence is the continuity of officials, who managed bureaucracy and military control of Canaan and conducted royal commerce and traffic between Egypt and Canaan. Eileen Hirsch reconstructed a series of officials with the title 'overseer of the northern foreign countries' during the 19th and 20th Dynasty which perhaps goes on to the reign of Ramesses IV (1153–1146 BCE) and even

---

[60] The Turrah fragment is to be published by S. Wimmer, who kindly gave me a copy of his article, see now also Dijkstra, Dijkstra, Vriezen, *Tall Zar'a in Jordan*, 68 n. 2. The Kiswe fragment is significant not so much because of its contents, but because of the date. The 56th Year of Ramesses II was perhaps the first year of Merenptah as Ramesses' royal heir after Khaemwese's death in the 55th year. Perhaps the person depicted after the Pharaoh is Merenptah, the crown prince. The city of Merenptah in Pi-Aram mentioned in the 'Border Journal' may be identified as a stronghold in Upe where this stele once was erected, or perhaps even Damascus itself (Helck, *Beziehungen*, 231 n. 40; Singer, 'Egyptians, Canaanites and Philistines,' 289).

[61] The punitive campaign into Canaan could have been his work, so that he rightly claimed the reliefs in the *Cour de la Cachette* for his own glory after the death of his father, Merenptah. Two joining loose blocks (Le Saout, *Reconstitution*, 232, pl IX 4c; Yurco, *JARCE* 23 (1986) Fig. 21) showing prince Seti-Merenptah on his chariot, almost certainly belongs to the battle Scene 9 (above Scenes 7–8). Usually the period of the transition from the 19th into the 20th Dynasty is depicted as a period of rapid decline, influenced by the picture painted in pHarris about 'a Syrian interregnum' (e.g. *ANET*[3], 260). By contrast, it is interesting that recent discoveries seem to rehabilitate Seti II and his spouse, regent and later Pharaoh Ta-usret and witness a strong presence in Pi-Ramesse (e.g. at Qantir: tiles, door frames, moulds, foundation bricks, reconstruction of stables). In contrast to Merenptah, Seti II and Ta-usret set up their residence in Raämses / Pi-Ramesse. Further, activitity may be noted in Sinai (Fortress A 289 = Huravit, mines at Timna and in Serabit-el-Khadim, the redecorated Pylon of Tutmoses III), in southern Canaan (Khirbet el-Msas = Tel Masos, Tell el-Far'a (S) etc) and in diplomatic exchange (Deir 'Allã, Ugarit) may be noted. After initial troubles with Amenmesse, which ended in year 4, Seti II and Ta-usret had their hands free for building projects and renewed diplomacy in Canaan and Syria.

after him.[62] Parallel to them is also evidence about the 'envoy to the foreign countries', the 'deputies of the Treasury' and numerous military commanders on mission in the Levant. Once more, the evidence from Merenptah's reign to which one may count also the stele from the 56th year of Ramesses II, gives us reasonably firm evidence that Canaan up to the region of Damascus (Upe) was still under Egyptian control, a *conditio sine qua non* for the relief transports of grain to Ugarit and its famine-striken hinterland of Hatti.[63] This continuing presence is further corroborated by Egyptian residences, temples, administrative hieratic ostraca, Egyptian sculpture, ceramics,[64] and, lest we forget, at least two largely Egyptian cemeteries at Deir el-Balah and Beth Shean, and quite a number of terracotta coffin burials on different sites in Palestine and Jordan.

In summary, it becomes increasingly evident that Egyptian rule held on longer in the coastal and lower regions of Canaan than assumed in the past, perhaps even until about 1100 BCE,[65] though the Empire was on the retreat in certain areas during the 12th Century BCE, for instance in the north retreating to Beth Shean and in the south retreating inland leaving cities like Gaza, Asdod, Askelon and Ekron to the Philistine

---

[62] E. Hirsch, 'Die Beziehungen der ägyptischen Residenz im Neuen Reich zu den vorderasiatischen Vasallen. Die Vorsteher der nördlichen Fremdländer und ihre Stellung bei Hofe', in: R. Gundlach, A. Klug, *Der ägyptische Hof des Neuen Reiches. Seine Gesellschaft und Kultur im Spannungsfeld zwischen Innen- und Aussenpolitik. Akten des internationalen Kolloquiums vom 27.–29 Mai 2002 an der Johannes Gutenberg-Universität Mainz*, Wiesbaden 2006, 119–189. To these officials also an unknown 'overseer' may be added from the beginning of Ramesses' II reign. For his restored stela from Serabit el-Khadim, Sinai 300 + 297, see M. Dijkstra, 'A Chief of the Bowmen, Overseer of the Foreign Lands at Serabit el-Khadim (Sinai 300 + 297) and the "Dwelling of Sesu" (Tell el-Borg)*', *Ägypten und Levante* 19 (2009), 121–125.

[63] Singer, *BASOR* 269 (1988) 1–10; Singer, *HUS*, 708–725.

[64] Higginbotham, *Egyptianization and Elite Emulation*, 6–7 and Killebrew, *Biblical Peoples*, 53–55 reconstructed a socio-political history of Egyptian domination as a kind of 'indirect rule' characterized as elite emulation, though Killebrew makes an exception for "formal" imperialism under Ramesses III (ibidem, 81). I am still inclined to adhere to the views of Redford, Na'aman, Weinstein, Singer and Bunimovitz *et al.* that Egyptian dominination during the 19th and 20th Dynasty involved direct military and administrative rule over a large part of Canaan up to Damascus.

[65] For the material evidence during the 20th Dynasty see M. Bietak, 'Zur Landnahme Palästinas durch die Seevölker und zum Ende der ägyptischen Provinz Kana'an,' *MDAI.K* 47 (1991), 40–41; Higgenbotham, *Egyptianization and Elite Emulation*, 57–73 and E. Lipinski, *On the Skirts of Canaan in the Iron Age, Historical and Topographical researches*, (OLA, 153), 2004, 45–48.

settlers.[66] But about 1100 BCE, Egyptian rule collapsed rather suddenly because of great internal turmoil in Egypt itself. Neither Israel, nor the Philistines, Ammonites, Moabites or even the Shosu became too much for Egypt, but Egypt's power fell finally victim to an internal administrative and economic crisis. The real nails in the coffin of the Egyptian administration of the Levant may have been years of crop failure, shortage of food, civil war and the ongoing Libyan migration into the Delta. It were, however, not the ancestors of Israel who first took advantage of this new political vacuum but the newly established Philistine and Phoenician harbour cities.

## 8. EXPANSION OF THE PHOENICIAN CITIES IN THE EARLY IRON AGE

History emerging from modern settlement archaeology normally reflects long-term developments, the *longue durée* of Ferdnand Braudel. In particular, the spatial analysis of settlement archaeology as presented by surveys of Galilee, the Palestinian Westbank, the Negev and Transjordan may help to fill in the large spatial and temporal gaps left by defective historical records. Part of such a panoramic view supported by data from settlement history would be the more prominent role of the Phoenician city-states in the coastal region and western Galilee, in particular their nascent commonwealth during the Early Iron Age and Iron Age II. From the reconstruction of the settlement history of the Acco Plain and its hinterlands in the Valley and the Hill Country of western Galilee, we may learn that Acco and Tyre dominated the area north of Carmel in the close

---

[66] See Bietak, *MDAI.K* 47 (1991), 35–50; L. Stager, 'The Impact of the Sea Peoples in Canaan (1185–1050),' in: T.E. Levy (ed.), *The Archaeology of Society in the Holy Land*, London 1995, 332–348; Bunimovitz, 'Sea Peoples in Cyprus and Israel,' 107. Nevertheless, such a retreat can hardly have resulted in a *cordon sanitaire* (*pace* Bunimovitz). It happened apparently with Egyptian consent, because Ramesses III negotiated the establishment of an Egyptian Temple in Pi-Canaan / Gaza, which at least seems to imply a kind of nominal rule as observed by Albrecht Alt, Uehlinger, Wimmer *et al.* It is odd however, that this 'Egyptian presence' no longer is translated in material evidence in the Philistine settlements, as Bietak and Stager clearly demonstrated. Unless, of course Philistine settlement started much later, as for instance, Finkelstein suggested—see I. Finkelstein, 'The Date of the Settlement of the Philistines in Canaan,' *Tel Aviv* 22 (1995), 213–239; I. Finkelstein, 'Philistine Chronology: High, Middle or Low?' in: S. Gitin, A. Mazar, E. Stern (eds), *Mediterranean Peoples in Transition. Thirteenth to Early Tenth Centuries BCE. In Honor of Professor Trude Dothan*, Jerusalem 1998, 140–147.

of the Late Bronze Age and that this situation continued at least until Iron Age II. However, as elsewhere in the Central Hill Country of Canaan and Transjordan, new villages appear during the Early Iron Age in the mountains of western Galilee. They were traditionally the territory of the tribe of Asher, which may be one of the few tribes and tribal areas mentioned in Egyptian sources even before the emergence of Israel in this region of the Levant.[67] M. Dothan and others thought of a symbiosis of Canaanites, Sherdani and Israelites in the ethnic composition of the Acco Plain,[68] but I agree with G.E. Markou, E. Lipinski and others in their survey of cities in the Phoenician homeland that Acco and its surroundings remained essentially Canaanite / Phoenician territory through the Early Iron Age.[69]

In the Early Iron Age from the mid-12th Century onwards the coastal area saw the quick re-emergence of Phoenician trade and expansion and evidence of a 'Phoenician' material culture spreading southward through the Acco plain to the region of Dor.[70] Material evidence, supported

---

[67] Gardiner, *Ancient Egyptian Onomastica*, I, 193*; II, 265*, who advances arguments to think here of Asher instead of Assur; Edelman, 'Asher', *AncBD* 1, 482–483, E. Stern, *Dor. Ruler of the Seas*, Jerusalem 1994, 89. It is interesting that many scholars have difficulty in accepting this identification, perhaps because it seems not very compatible with Biblical evidence. Indeed, the identification is not settled yet. From a number of hints in Biblical tradition, it may be inferred that Asher was seen as a 'bastard' if not almost foreign tribe more inclined to the coastal area and its Phoenician cities than central Israel (Judg. 1:31–32; 5:17).

[68] M. Dothan, 'Notes and News: Akko', *IEJ* 31 (1981), 111; idem, 'Archaeological Evidence for Movements of the Early "Sea Peoples" in Canaan', *AASOR* 49 (1989), 64–65; Singer, *BASOR* 269 (1988), 2; idem, 'Egyptians, Canaanites and Philistines', 297–298; A. Raban, 'The Philistines in the Western Jezreel Valley', *BASOR* 284 (1991), 17–27, esp. 25, but see now G. Lehmann, 'Phoenicians in Western Galilee: First Results of an Archaeological Survey in the Hinterland of Akko', in: A. Mazar (ed.), *Studies in the Archaeology of the Iron Age in Israel and Jordan*, (JSOT.S, 331), Sheffield 2001, 65–112.

[69] G.E. Markou, *Phoenicians*, (Peoples of the Past), Los Angeles 2000, 194–195; Lipinski, *On the Skirts of Canaan*, 163–164, 175–176; also Lehmann, 'Phoenicians in Western Galilee', 90–93, stating that Tyre was the actual power in northern Israel in the Iron II period, at least in the western part. I leave aside the question of Solomon's cessation of the land of Cabul to King Hiram of Tyre (1 Kings 9:11–13).

[70] Stern, *Dor*, 98–99, 103–104; idem, 'The Relations between the Sea Peoples and the Phoenicians in the Twelfth and Eleventh Centuries BCE', in: *Mediterranean Peoples*, 345–352, esp. 348–349; Gilboa, 'Iron I–IIA Pottery Evolution at Dor—Regional Contexts and the Cypriot Connection', in: *Mediterranean Peoples*, 413–423, esp. 418; Markou, *Phoenicians*, 26–32; A. Gilboa, I. Sharon, 'Between the Carmel and the Sea. Tel Dor's Iron Age Reconsidered', *NEA* 71 (2008), 146–170, esp. 161. Note that Gilboa and Sharon are almost dismissive about a particular *škl* presence and material evidence in Dor! Like Markou, Noort noted that the decline and eventual destruction of inland Late Bronze and Early Iron Age cities and the Sea People incursions did not affect the harbour cities, Noort, *Seevölker*, 157–159, also Lipinski, *On the Skirts of Canaan*, 163.

between the lines by Wen-Amun's story, reveals thriving commercial activities between Cyprus, the southern Levantine coast, Egypt and in the homeland itself Tyre, and in particular Sidon and Byblos. All three were apparently dominated from central Phoenicia. Dor was also part of their maritime commercial entrepeneurship and even business with Egypt continued apparently unhindered during the 21st Dynasty, as shown by large amounts of Egyptian ceramics and other *Aegyptica*.[71] As said, archaeology seems to confirm these unbroken international cultural ties and commericial activities between Cyprus, the Levant and Egypt. The most dramatic evidence for 'Phoenician' expansion is perhaps found in the mid-11th Century BCE destruction of the fortified Tjeker/Šikil town, not by the Israelites, but by a superseding Phoenician occupation, that is if 'Phoenician' is construed as a society that differs from Israelite and Philistine settlement, in that it originated from the Levantine coastal population mixed with new ethnic elements from overseas.[72] So the much later statement of Judg. 1:31–32 about Asher not driving out those living in Acco or Sidon and so on, might after all reveal a political reality that remained actual during the Iron II Period.

## 9. PHOENICIANS AND PHILISTINES

When and where did the Phoenician expansion to the South meet borders of Philistine and Israelite settlement? Maps of the Iron Age tend to show an empty space between Carmel and the territory of the nascent Philistine Pentapolis with a Tjeker enclave at Dor. There is now a rather broad consensus that the initial settlement of different tribes of the 'Sea People', later subsumed under the general name Philistines (Peleshet), about 1050 BCE included the harbour of Yapu/Jaffa with inland Tell Qasileh, whereas Apheq on the river Yarkon in the hinterland was at least a bone of contention (1 Samuel 4–6).[73] At that time, the harbour town of Dor was ruled by a tribal chief from the Tjeker/l. Further, hardly any tradition about the incursions of Sea People is known. It becomes increasingly evident that their arrival on the Phoenician coast, in the Acco Plain and in the Sharon Plain remained transient in historical and

---

[71] Gilboa, Sharon, *NEA* 71 (2008), 159.
[72] Gilboa, Sharon, *NEA* 71 (2008), 161.
[73] For instance, the map in Faust, *Israel's Ethnogenesis*, 140 Fig. 14.1.

archaeological evidence.[74] The few Philistine pot-sherds found in Dor did not make it part of Philistine culture. What is evident is a gradual change from Late Bronze Age 'Canaanite' to Iron Age 'Phoenician' culture in the Sharon Plain, as happened elsewhere to the North. So some time after 1050 BCE, 'Philistines' and 'Phoenicians' inhabited the coastal strip south of the Carmel with perhaps the Yarkon as the border between them. Biblical tradition says also that Dor belonged to 'the land that yet remained' (Judg. 1:27).

Renewed excavations at Dor reveal no evidence of an abrupt change in the material culture of Dor until Iron Age IIA, which might imply that the city did not become Israelite before late in the Kingdom Period. As part of a Phoenician commonwealth, it started a new *floruit* of economical activity and growth throughout the Early Iron Period until Iron II expanding its contacts as far as Tel Masos, Egypt and Cyprus. Egyptian involvement apparently never completely stagnated, even after the Wen-Amun experience. Before the return of Sheshonq I and successors, presumably around 950 BCE commercial activity of the Tanite Dynasty is not only attested by abundant Egyptian ceramics, but also by 'mass-produced' stamp-seal amulets, some of them bearing the name of Si-Amun (986–967).[75] This *floruit*, establishing the backbone of economical maritime expansion of the central Phoenician cities in the eastern Mediterranean later in the Iron II Period, also incorporated Dor and penetrated the Emek-Valley (Tell Abu Hawam, Tell Keisan, Acco, etc.) and the hinterland of Galilee and the Beqa Valley. We have reason to believe with Gilboa and Sharon "... that the new 'Phoenician' expansion meant a new society in the coastal region down to the Philistine land in the proper sense of an indigenous early Iron Age population with ethnic elements from overseas leading up to the maritime power of the Iron II period."[76]

In summary, recent research suggests that the majority of the harbour cities of the Levant survived the cultural, economical decline of the Late Bronze Age rather unscathed. Like Egypt itself, the Phoenician

---

[74] Markou, *Phoenicians*, 23–25; Lipinski, *On the Skirts of Canaan*, 163; Gilboa, Sharon, *NEA* 71 (2008), 159–160. Even more so, if Myc IIIC-1b pottery, the precursor of bichrome pottery, is the only clear ethnic marker of Sea People/Philistine presence, see Killebrew, *Biblical Peoples*, 219–230.

[75] S. Munger, 'Egyptian Stamp-seal Amulets and their implications for the Chronology of the Early Iron Age', *Tel Aviv* 30 (2003), 66–82. A. Gilboa, I. Sharon, J. Zorn, 'Dor and Iron Age Chronology: Scarabs, Ceramic Sequence and 14C,' *Tel Aviv* 31 (2004), 32–60; the dating of Si-Amun is now established on firmer ground by E. Hornung *et al.*, *Handbook of Ancient Egyptian Chronology* (HdO I, 83), Leiden 2006, 474, 493.

[76] Gilboa, Sharon, *NEA* 71 (2008), 161.

cities from Acco to Byblos and further north, quickly recovered from the incursions of 'Sea People' and other 'Barbarians'. The tragic fate of Enkomi on Cyprus, and the city of Ugarit was apparently not decisive for the southern Levant, or even for Cyprus and the northern Levant in as much as places like Tell Sukas, Ras Ibn Hani and commercial centres on Cyprus survived or quickly recovered from the blow. Perhaps we should surmise that in the coastal regions up to Byblos, Egypt's presence had a moderating effect on the 'Sea People's fury' in 12th Century BCE. Contrary to all earlier stories about a devastating 'Seevölkersturm' the 'Philistine settlement' in southern coastal strip of Palestina advanced fairly peacefully. Philistine and Phoenician cities and their hinterland took over the domination of the coastal area and the lowlands of Canaan from the Egyptians and limited Israelite settlement and the nascent Israelite states for the time being to the Highlands until the beginning of Iron Age IIA. Such a view of things implies a *caveat* for any new theory about the waves of settlements in the Negev, Beer-Sheva Plain, the central Highlands, Galilee and northern Transjordan. Settlements that would result into the emergence of 'early states' in the region, including late-comers Israel and Judah. Another enemy than the Sea Peoples or the Shosu was apparently needed to cause the demographic and political changes in the Early Iron Age.

## 10. IMPACT OF CLIMATIC CHANGE AND VARIATION

Recent studies of climatic change, hydrology and palaeometeorology in Egypt and North Africa have indicated correlations between solar activity, rainfall, Nile flooding and climatic change. Climatic change or variation affects environment and civilization.[77] Not only the sudden collapse of the Old Kingdom followed from a series of catastrophically low Nile floods due to abrupt climatic change, but also the decline of the New Empire in the 12th Century was accompanied by low floods and serious crop failure in the period 1170–1100 BCE and even famine about 1090 under Ramesses XI (1107–1078/77).[78] The transition from the 20th

---

[77] F.A. Hassan, 'Historical Nile Floods and their Implications for Climatic Change,' *Science* 212 (1981), 1142–1145; F.A. Hassan, 'A River Runs Through Egypt: Nile Floods and Civilization,' *Geotimes* April 2005; also Redford, *Egypt, Canaan and Israel*, 61–62, 64.

[78] J. Vandier, *La famine dans l'Égypte ancienne* (Recherches d'archéologie, de philologie et d'histoire, 7) Le Caire 1936, 23–27; F. Barguet, *La Stèle de la famine à Sehel*, Le Caire 1953; *ANET³*, 31–32; the collapse of the Old Kingdom (about 2150 BCE) was also marked

to the 21st Dynasty in Egypt was marked by severe political confusion, social turmoil and recession, which brought Egypt in the Levant and home to founder.

What does it tell us about the situation in the Levant? Documentary sources show that famine in Anatolia or Syria did not immediately imply problems in Egypt. In the 13th Century BCE, Egypt was still the major food basket in the region. This situation would only change in the course of the 12th Century because of lower Nile inundation and crop failure. At that time, however, the Levant had entered again—as we will see below—a period of increased rainfall. What conclusions about demographic change may be drawn from these variations in rainfall and humidity? For instance, Stiebing assembled impressive evidence for the decline in rainfall during the Late Bronze Age all across the ancient Near East and the Eastern Mediterranean basin.[79] In his view this decrease led to a decline in food production causing the Canaanites of the coastal plain to go up into the mountains to settle there. There are, in addition to Rainey's objections,[80] several problems with his theory. First, inundation of the Nile is not dependent on annual rainfall in the Mediterranean Basin. Only the Egyptian Delta may benefit from a Cyprus Low and subsequent

---

by severe social unrest and famine according to contemporary records. This collapse coincided with the fall of the Empire of Akkad (H. Weiss *et al.*, 'The Genesis and Collapse of Third Millennium North Mesopotamia Civilization,' *Science* 261 (1993), 995–1004). A large decrease in precipitation rates in North Africa, the horn of Africa and the Middle East suggests a climatic factor in this disastrous period (also a tremendous lowering of the Dead Sea level 2200–1400 BCE). From this period stem many of the reliefs showing starving people (Oenas pyramid, e.g the collection *apud* Staubli). For texts, see F. Breyer, 'Die Inschrift des Anchtifi aus Mo'alla,' *Texte aus der Umwelt des Alten Testaments. Neue Folge Band* 2, Gütersloh 2005, 187–196, including a new translation of the 'tomb biography' of Anchtifi, a local prince from Mo'alla during the First Intermediate Period (about 2150 BCE); L. Morenz, 'Hungersnote zwischen Topos und Realität,' *Discussions in Egyptology* 42 (1998), 84–97. Similar testimonies are known from the later years of the 20th Dynasty (about 1100 BCE), for instance from reports about tomb robberies and the letters of a certain scribe Tuthmosis about the strikes in the Royal Necropolis under Ramesses X. For the 'strike papyri' of the scribe of the Tomb, Amennakht, a half century earlier, see R.J. Demarée, '"Wij hebben honger". De stakingen in het jaar 29 van Ramses III,' in: R.J. Demarée, K.R. Veenhof (eds), *Zij schreven geschiedenis. Historische documenten uit het oude Nabije Oosten* (2500–100 v.Chr.), (Mededelingen en Verhandelingen van het Vooraziatisch-Egyptisch Genootschap "Ex Oriente Lux", 23), Leiden / Leuven 2003, 238–250.

[79] Stiebing, *Out of the Desert*, 167–187. W.H. Stiebing, 'Climate and Collapse: Did the Weather Make Israel's Emergence possible?,' *BR* 10 (1994), 18–27.

[80] A.F. Rainey, 'Remarks on Donald Redford's Egypt, Canaan and Israel in Ancient Times,' *BASOR* 295 (1994), 81–85, esp. 84.

winter rainstorms entering the southern Levant.[81] Second, even if rainfall decreases in the Levant, or its coastal plains, less rain still flows to the lower parts. A way to cope with such a shortage of rain and food is not to move in mass from the lowlands to the hill country, but to enlarge the cultivated areas into more marginal land. This might have happened at the lowest ebb of annual rainfall: farmers and pastoralists exchanging labour and skill to produce food also in areas less attractive for agriculture (see below).

This long-term impact of the environmental factors in decline during the Late Bronze and Early Iron Period as well as during earlier spells of climatic change in the ancient Near East has come to light only recently in studies on the origins of Israel.[82] We have already mentioned Stiebing, but climatic change was also discussed by D.C. Hopkins, apparently with conflicting conclusions about palaeometeorological and hydrological evidence produced from dendroarchaeological, pollen analysis. To begin with, there is no justification for the view that the climate of Canaan or the wider Levant has changed profoundly in the Post-Glacial or Pleistocene period. However, even if one accepts that the term 'climatic change' is a misnomer, there is climatic variation.[83] Small second-order changes or variation in the eco-system of Egypt and Northern Africa also affected agriculture in the Levant, even if agriculture there was dependent on different environmental and climatic factors from those in Egypt, in particular the annual rainfall.

Finkelstein and Silbermann see periods of drought in the long term as one of the major causes of renewed sedentarization of seasonal agro-pastoralists in the hill country of either side of the Jordan.[84] The crucial

---

[81] Y. Enzel *et al.*, 'Late Holocene Climates of the Near East Deduced from Dead Sea Level Variations and Modern Regional Winter Rainfall', *Quaternary Research* 60 (2003), 263–273; esp. 270–271 Figs. 8, 9 and 10.

[82] A.S. Issar, 'Climate Change and the History of the Middle East', *American Scientist* 83 (1995), 350–355; A.S. Issar, H. Tsoar, D. Levin, 'Climatic Changes in Israel During Historical Times and Their Impact on Hydrological, Pedological and Socio-Economic Systems', in: M. Leinen, M. Sarnthein (eds), *Paleoclimatology and Paleometeorology: Modern and Past Patterns of Global Atmospheric Transport*, Dordrecht 1989, 525–541; A.S. Issar, M. Zohar, *Climate Change-Environment and Civilization in the Middle East*, Berlin / Heidelberg 2004. One of our students at Utrecht University broke here some ground, too, in researching the relation between settlement and water supply and management, J.C. Rigg, *Settlement in Palestine and Transjordan in Relation to Water Supply and Management in the Transition from Bronze Age to Iron Age* (unpublished master thesis), Utrecht 1998.

[83] D.C. Hopkins, *The Highlands of Canaan*, (SWBAS, 3) Sheffield 1985, 100.

[84] Finkelstein, Silbermann, *The Bible Unearthed*, 143–145. In his studies of the Iron I

question here is whether there were changes in the precipitation pattern lasting long enough to trigger or enhance the assumed sedentarization of agro-pastoralists from about 1200 BCE onwards. With Stiebing, Rainey noted a decline in annual rainfall in the Eastern Mediterranean and assumed a decline in food production, resulting in a reduction in urban Canaanite population. Pastoralists could no longer barter their products for grain and withdrew into the relatively unoccupied highlands, where they started to produce grain for their own subsistence and gradually settled.[85] The problem with such theories of connecting historical events with environmental conditions is that they are subject to circular reasoning.[86] Unfortunately, apart from palaeoclimatic and archaeological environmental evidence,[87] no direct historical sources are available here to confirm a relationship between climatic variation and socio-economic disturbances like those we have for Egypt, let alone a relationship between climatic variation and the emergence of Israel at the end of the 2nd Millennium. The question is even more complicated if one realizes that settlement can be viewed either as a result of the decrease of annual rainfall, or as the result of an increase, as well as of moister conditions in the highlands.

---

resettlement of the Negev, however, Finkelstein does not think that climatic changes were relevant, see I. Finkelstein, A. Perevolotsky, 'Processes of Sedentarization and Nomadization in the History of Sinai and the Negev,' *BASOR* 279 (1990), 67–88, esp. 73–74; idem, *Living on the Fringe* 1995; but see Z. Herzog, 'The Beer-Sheva Valley: From Nomadism to Monarchy,' in: *From Nomadism to Monarchy*, 122–149, esp. 124–126; Issar, Zohar, *Climate Change*, 177–182 for a different view.

[85] Rainey, *BASOR* 295 (1994), 84; E. Bloch-Smith, B.A. Nakhai, 'A Landscape Comes to Life: The Iron I Period,' *NEA* 62 (1999) 68; Dijkstra, 'History of Israel,' 238–239; Zerbst, van der Veen, *Keine Posaunen vor Jericho?*, 28.

[86] De Vaux, *Histoire ancienne d'Israel*, 30; Issar, Zohar, *Climate Change*, 37.

[87] About the relation between annual rainfall and fluctuations in the Dead Sea level, see Enzel *et al.*, 'Late Holocene Climates of the Near East,' 263–273, and the speleothem record of the Soreq Cave, M. Bar-Mathews *et al.*, 'The Soreq Cave Speleothems as Indicators of Palaeoclimate Variations. Geological Survey of Israel,' *Current Research* 8 (1993), 1–3; M. Bar-Mathews, 'The Eastern Mediterranean Palaeoclimate as a Reflection of Regional Events: Soreq Cave, Israel,' *Earth and Planetary Science Letters* 166 (1998), 85–95; Issar, Zohar, *Climate Change*, 35–37; the general trend unto a more dry climate in Mediterrean region confirm H. Wanner *et al.*, 'Mid- to Late Holocene Climate Change: An Overview,' *Quaternary Science Reviews* 27 (2008), 1791–1828, esp. 1795, Fig. 2A. There are two long periods of extreme fall in the level 2200–1400 BCE and 500–800 AD, but also a series of shorter falls between 1175–1100, 1000–950, and 875–800 BCE. The record of fauna and flora, and tree rings shows the same evidence of drying up.

Arie Issar summarizes the climatic changes of the second half of the 2nd Millennium BCE as follows. There was a warm dry period from about 1500 BCE onwards, which affected the fringes of the desert—semi-arid areas with the average of 200 to 400 mm / year—in receiving less rain, whereas it influenced the hydrological regime of the Nile positively. Later there was a colder and more humid phase commencing about 1300 BCE, which became more extreme towards the end of the 2nd Millennium, i.e. during the Early Iron Age. This spell of more humid weather had a positive effect on the Levant, whereas Nile floodings failed due to the weakening of the monsoon system feeding the Nile. Issar viewed this as a moister period in view of precipitation rates based on data from the Soreq Cave.[88] This curve indeed shows a sharp increase in average rainfall from about 475 to 550 mm / year between 1400 and 1000 BCE in the Central Highlands of Palestine. But there was an obvious period of stagnation in the increase during the 12th Century BCE and even a dip at the end of this period.[89] This fluctuation in annual rainfall is confirmed by long-term variation in the Dead Sea level.[90] This curve shows more or less the same steep decline after about 2000 BCE, reaching it deepest point about 1400 BCE (Fig. 1).

Issar and Zohar see the permanent settlement of the Israelite (former Habiru-Shasu) tribes as the outcome of improved climate conditions in the Early Iron Age. It leads them to a remarkable amalgam of Biblical and environmental history.[91] The problem with the scheme of Finkelstein, Rainey and others is how to construe a decline in annual rainfall, droughts and stagnation in food production in the Levant with a niche of sufficient water supply in the highlands to allow at least some new settlements and dry farming to be established. However if there was a major increase in settlements in the highlands of Ephraim, Judah and Gilead, and in the semi-arid plain of Beer Sheva, the transition of the early pastoralist settlers into a new agricultural society becomes more credible as a result of improved climate conditions from about 1200 BCE onwards as Issar, Herzog *et al.* suggest.

---

[88]  Issar, Zohar, *Climate Change*, 35–39, 180–188.

[89]  Bar-Mathews *et al.*, 'The Eastern Mediterranean Palaeoclimate as a Reflection of Regional Events', 85–95; Issar, Zohar, *Climate Change*, 186–187.

[90]  Enzel *et al.* 'Late Holocene Climates of the Near East', 263–273, esp. Fig. 2A.

[91]  For example, the interpretation of Josh. 16:10 that the Canaanites of Gezer were allowed to stay once they consented "to serve under tribute" as a hint that they helped the settlers to do the heavy fieldwork and terracing (Issar, Zohar, *Climate Change*, 178).

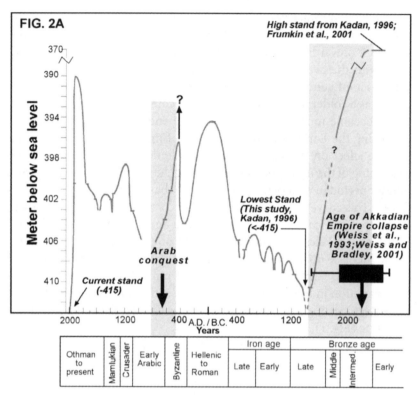

*Fig.* 1: Dead Sea level and Climate variation[92]

Setting Finkelstein's (and also Lehmann's) diagrams of settlement os-
cillations in the Central Hill Country, Transjordan and western Galilee
alongside precipitation rates based on the Soreq Cave and the slow, inter-
mittent rise in the level of the Dead Sea is striking and convincing evidence (Fig. 2). We see indeed everywhere a steep rise in the number of
new villages, which correlates with an increase of precipitation rates.[93]
People living on the fringe saw their living conditions gradually improv-
ing and could apparently change their lifestyle from bare pastoral and
agricultural substistence into that of a farming community answering
the demands for the high investments to exploit their patrimonial pos-
sessions as agricultural land. Naturally, such a transformation in lifestyle
did not take place overnight. There must have been a kind of symbio-

---

[92] Enzel *et al.*, *Quaternary Research* 60 (2003), 265, Fig. 2A.
[93] Issar, Zohar, *Climate Change*, 186–187 Figs. 10–11.

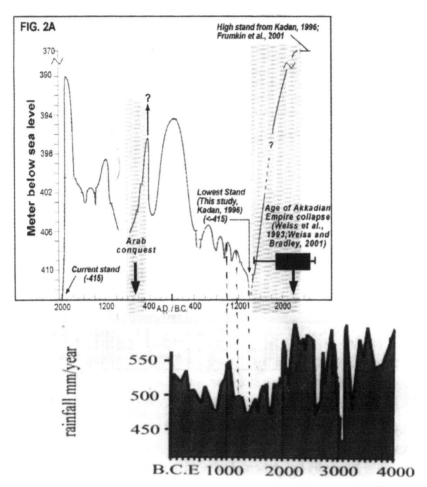

*Fig.* 2: Comparison curve Dead Sea level and rainfall Soreq Cave[94]

sis and cultural continuity in the transition from the Late Bronze to the
Early Iron Age. Some (or all?) of the famine-traditions in the patriarchal
stories and the story of Ruth may reflect a single or different spells of disastrous droughts causing periods of decline in agricultural production, if
not crop failure, in Canaan that made the Levant heavily dependent on
Egyptian grain supplies (Gen. 12:10; 26:1; 41:53–57; 42:1; 47:13–15) and
even caused migration.

---

[94] Enzel et al., *Quaternary Research* 60 (2003) 265 Fig. 2A combined with adapted
figure from Bar-Matthews *et al.*, 1998; Issar, Zohar, *Climate Change*, 186 Fig. 10.

## 11. WAVES OF SETTLEMENT IN THE HIGH LANDS OF CANAAN

Egyptian domination, and Philistine and Phoenician expansion, did not leave much room for the expansion of Israelite settlement to the Canaanite lowlands and coastal areas in the Early Iron Age. There is no written record about this settlement outside the Bible. However what is not yet historically recorded might be detectable in archaeological evidence of long-term socio-cultural and demographic changes. For demographic changes took place from about 1200 BCE onwards outside the direct control of the Egyptian authority but still—so to speak—under their noses: economic decline and impoverishment of urban communities, insecurity in rural areas and a horde of poor people, starving local shepherds and farmers and foreign migrants on the move.

Finkelstein and others convincingly showed that settlement of the Central Hill Country of Canaan took place intermittently. There were three periods of settlement with two intervals of decline in the 3rd and 2nd Millenia BCE. He assumed that the settlers of the Early Iron Age might have been the offspring of the Middle Bronze farmers. Remarkably he criticises Dever for the view that the rise of early Israel was as a singular event of population shift from the sedentary lowlands to the empty highlands.[95] We will not discuss here the long-term oscillation of settlement and nomadism. However, such cyclic patterns do not mean that Iron I settlement was a single event. On the contrary, history does not repeat itself, even not in the same environment and under similar conditions. In the Iron I Period, it was a process during decline of Egyptian domination, expansion of the newly created Phoenician commonwealth to the south and settlement of Philistine and related groups in the southern coastal area.

Just as the Egyptian withdrawal from the Levant happened in different phases and at different rates, the settlement of Israelite and other tribes may have been a far from unique and uniform process. Historical developments are always more pluriform, multicausal and complicated than

---

[95] I. Finkelstein, 'Ethnicity and Origin of the Iron I Settlers in the Highlands of Canaan: Can the Real Israel Stand Up?' *BA* 59 (1996), 209; idem, 'The Rise of Early Israel: Archaeology and Long-Term History,' in: *The Origin of Early Israel*, 11, 14–16. However at the end of his review of Tel Masos and of Finkelstein's views, Dever clearly stated that the case of Tel Masos should warn us against pressing all the possible evidence for the Israelite Settlement into a single mould …, W.G. Dever, 'Archaeology and Israelite Origins: Review Article,' *BASOR* 279 (1990), 95.

any theoretic model. Once more it is between the lines that Biblical tradition itself repeatedly affirms the complex ethnogenesis of early Israel. Even the collective memory of Biblical tradition knows that Israel's origins were of suspicious nature (Ezek. 16:3). Hebrews augmented by a large company of every kind (Exod. 12:38), in other words a "Mixed Multitude".[96] These heterogeneous origins are also expressed in the concept of 'bastard tribes' of Dan, Naftali, Asher and Gad. Moreover, the strong tradition that pre-Israelite Canaan was inhabited by a cultural and ethnic amalgam of seven peoples: Canaanites, Horites, Hivites, Jebusites, Perizzites, Hittites and Girgashites. Some of these names are familiar also from extra-Biblical sources. Others are as yet not identifiable, but they seem sound tradition, amplified by a large score of different Egyptian names for territories and people of the Levant.

Such standard traditions are not immediately translatable into demographic history, but they certainly reveal a deep-rooted awareness of a fragmented, multicultural population in Canaan through the ages. Many documents from the Late Bronze Age such as the Amarna letters, reports and narratives create the confusing picture of a small strip of land populated by city states, wandering tribes and gangs of bandits, different cultures, languages and societies, difficult to grasp for Egyptian scribes and usually viewed with disdain. This regional and cultural diversity and complex social and political stratification has remarkably consonant parallels in the Books of Judges and Samuel. Names such as Upper and Lower Rethenu, Djahi, Upe, Qedem, Amurru, Geshur, Maaka, Apiru / Habiru, Shosu, Sutu, Asher, Canaan, Aram, Tahas, Kharu / Khuru / Hor, Moab, Edom perhaps represent only the peak of the iceberg of geographical and demographic diversity in the Levant during the Late Bronze and Early Iron Age. Even more significant from an Egyptian perspective is the appearance of new names alongside the old names, e.g. Kharu / Khuru, Aram, Moab, Edom, Asher and in the brink of time also Israel as an 'afterthought' at the end of the Late Bronze and the beginning of the Early Iron Period. From such a viewpoint of diversity, Israelite settlement is best viewed as a complex and pluriform process which took place in different waves of migration and settlement, especially if also the other side of the Jordan is given its prominent role in the *longue durée*.

---

[96] See the fine synthesis of Killebrew, *Biblical Peoples*, 149–185.

Though in later tradition, northern Jordan, Biblical Gilead, is viewed as a backwater, hardly part of Israel any more or even treated as a foreign country,[97] there is also the awareness that 'Biblical Israel' once settled on both sides of the Jordan, or even that the ancestors of Israel migrated into Canaan from the East. If a chronological and geographical pattern may be detected in the waves of settlement, the movement and spread of new (proto-) Israelite settlements is basically first detected in Galilee, the Hill Country of Ephraim and Northern Jordan going south along both sides of the Jordan and ending up in the Valley of Beer Sheba and the Negev. It is hardly probable that these waves of migration and settlement comprise a single ethnic related group of tribes or peoples. In due course, these settlers would group themselves into different tribal confederations, chiefdoms and even a number of separate early states. Globally the pattern of settlement moves from north to south and from east to west.[98] Besides socio-economic changes, this move of settlement may have followed micro-environmental changes: an increasing annual rainfall and moister winters. Higher regions around the Lake of Gennesareth perhaps became available somewhat earlier for settlement and agricultural development because annual precipitation there has always been somewhat higher than in the south of Palestine. While the Late Bronze period continued for about half a century at certain places in the lowlands and the Jordan Valley, the Early Iron Age started elsewhere in the highlands with many new settlements and occasionally in the ruins of abandoned Late Bronze cities.[99]

Who were these settlers? Several theories are considered. Firstly, some suggest that impoverished and marginalized elements from the centres of urban Canaanite culture in the coastal area and lowlands, *nolens volens* looked for a better life in the highlands. Some would think that these new settlers were offspring of the farmers of the Middle Bronze Age who returned to an agriculture way of life after centuries of a wandering lifestyle as shepherds keeping sheep and goats. Finally, other scholars view pastoral tribes, especially the Shasu / Shosu, as invading from the

---

[97] E. Noort, 'Transjordan in Joshua 13: Some Aspects,' in: A. Hadidi (ed.), *Studies in the History and Archeaology of Jordan III*, Amman 1988, 125–130.

[98] Not including the settlement of Philistine tribes who migrated from overseas, Egypt and the northern coast of the Levant.

[99] Also in our sondage at Tall Zar'a, we noted the cultural decline of the Late Bronze Age ending in an interval of abandonment before a very low key settlement and pit digging in the collapsed Late Bronze remains, see Dijkstra, Dijkstra, Vriezen, *Tall Zar'a in Jordan*, 7–8, 75.

semi-arid regions of the Hejaz, Negev and Sinai, and giving birth to Israel. The problem is that often one of these options is accepted and propagated exclusive of other options. History is much more complex, certainly not as simple as ideology, and so the 'mixed throng' approach to describe the origins of Early Israel is more promising.[100] It does not seem wise to press all the evidence into a single mould. New communities of settlers were established and former arable land was reclaimed, because there was apparently an economic need to increase the agricultural area to produce at least the same amount of food to support the population.

Recent studies have shown beyond doubt that the lowland population never approached 'carrying capacity', which might have caused economic migration. Nevertheless the decline in culture of Canaanite cities, their surroundings and the population suggests heavy economic malaise, crop failure and food shortage. If the annual rainfall did not suffice to produce the required crops, new marginal areas would often be reclaimed to meet shortages. Also other more labour-intensive methods of dry farming would be tried and less water-demanding crops such as barley cultivated. This reclamation did not start with terracing, not even as an Israelite technical innovation as some scholars have suggested.[101] On the contrary, Iron I settlement began in areas of the Hill Country that did not require the construction of terraces. Dry farming of cereals does not ask for fields and soil deeper than about 20 cm. Reclamation of new farming ground might have started only as a temporary measure to meet immediate food shortages.

However that may have happened, and whichever settlers started this process, it demanded initially skill in cattle farming and ploughing and, in due course when the climate became more humid and settlement proved to be successful, a means of investment in terrace building. No evidence supports the theory that there was a direct correlation between settlement of the Central Hill Country and terrace building. Large-scale terrace building in ancient Israel did not begin before the 9th Century

---

[100] Killebrew, *Biblical Peoples*, 184–185; idem, 'The Emergence of Ancient Israel: The Social Boundaries of a "Mixed Multitude",' in: P. de Miroschedji, A.M. Maeir (eds), *I Will Speak the Riddles of Ancient Times (Abiah chidoth minei-kedem—Ps 78:2b): Archaeological and Historical Studies in Honor of Amihai Mazar in the Occasion of his Sixtieth Birthday*, Winona Lake, Ind. 2006, Volume 2 ....

[101] See now, however, Finkelstein, 'The Rise of Early Israel,' 11–12 and especially: S. Gibson, 'Agricultural Terraces and Settlement Expansion in the Higlands of Early Iron Age Palestine: Is There Any Correlation between the Two?' in: *Studies in Archaeology*, 113–146.

BCE.[102] It is incredible that the 'subdued population' of Canaan, either the inhabitants of Gezer or the local farmers of the Gibeon area, who were allowed to stay after they had consented 'to serve under tribute' (Josh. 16:10), were forced to become just 'woodcutters and water carriers for the entire community' of Israel (Josh 9:21).[103] Could it be a somewhat veiled, ideologically phrased admission that the early Israelite settlers were dependent of the agricultural skills of the former inhabitants?

## 12. Israelite Settlement at the Coast in the Early Iron Age

Egyptian rule in Canaan ended about 1100 BCE because of internal economic problems and turmoil in Egypt. At the time of this collapse, the coastal strip was already occupied up to Dor by Philistine tribes and the Acco Plain was part of the emerging Phoenician commonwealth. Most probably, Mount Carmel was the initial border between, but about 1050 BCE the 'Phoenician–Canaanite' expansion probably extended to the area of Dor. Like the 'Phoenician–Canaanite' coastal cities, surviving Canaanite lowland cities such as Lachish, Gezer, Yoqne'am, Megiddo and Beth Shean were ready for take-over of the surrounding lowlands.[104]

---

[102] C.J.H. de Geus, 'The Importance of Archaeological Research into the Palestinian Agricultural Terraces', *PEQ* 107 (1975), 65–75; Gibson, 'Agricultural Terraces and Settlement Expansion', 140, though terrace building was not a new invention and newer studies suggest that some terraces go back to the Middle Bronze Age.

[103] It is difficult to assess the implications of these menial tasks. Usually a connection is made with provisions for the temple and cult. Perhaps, it is too farfetched to find here a reference to deforesting in order to reclaim agricultural land and watering of the crops. Zertal suggested once that the large collared-rim pithoi were especially developed for agriculture to meet the water supply problems. It may be of interest that he developed this view because another classic assumption that the Israelites were able to settle in the Highlands because of the invention of plastered cisterns turned out to have no strong archaeological support, A. Zertal, 'The factor of Water and its Influence on the Israelite Settling of the Hill Country of Manasseh', in: S. Bunimovitz *et al.* (eds), *Settlements, Population and Economy in Eretz Israel in Ancient Times*, Tel Aviv 1988, 126–145; Issar, Zohar, *Climate Change*, 186; see however on the improbability of this and other suggestions for the use of the collared-rim jar as a mean of transport, Faust, *Israel's Ethnogenesis*, 193–202.

[104] Perhaps it is too farfetched to speak of a 'New Canaan' for the cities in Northern Canaan (mainly in the western Jezreel Valley), as Finkelstein suggested (I. Finkelstein, E. Piasetzky, 'Radiocarbon Dating and the Late-Iron I in Northern Canaan,' *UF* 39 (2007), 247–260 and references) as long as it remains unclear whether this revival was also supported by continued Canaanite rural settlement. See the earlier critical remarks of A. Ben Tor, *ErIs* 27 (2003), 50–54 (Hebrew).

In other words, the available historical and archaeological data do not favour the idea that Israelite settlement extended to the lowlands or arrived at the Mediterranean coast before the 10th Century BCE.

What exactly David's wars with the Philistines achieved in territorial expansion remains unclear. The only story that contains some credible information, suggests that David threw them back beyond Gezer (2 Sam. 5:7–25),[105] which may imply that he moved the border of Israelite settlement just beyond the city. It does not necessarily infer that the city itself was taken. It may still have continued to exist as a Canaanite enclave until it was destroyed in one of Sheshonq's campaigns. Though Solomon appointed a son-in-law as governor in the area of Dor (1 Kgs 4:11), this was perhaps more a territorial claim than reality. It is improbable that the city came under Israelite dominion in the Early Iron Age. What little we know about Dor in the Early Iron Age is that it was ruled by a Tjeker/l (Šikil/Šikilaya?) chief about 1075 BCE,[106] but that the harbour city went over to the nascent 'Phoenician–Canaanite' commonwealth about 1050 BCE and experienced peace and prosperity well into Iron Age II. It is more probable that a peaceful Israelite take-over took place under the Omrid Dynasty or perhaps the Dynasty of Jehu, so that the Israelite province of Dor was transformed into an Assyrian province after the conquest and abolition of the Israelite Kingdom. A similar fate may be assumed for the harbour city of Yapu/Joppa.[107] It would imply that Israel expanded to the Mediterranean Sea only in the later period of the Kingdoms if ever.

The city of Gezer has a crucial position in the history of Israelite settlement. The precarious fate of this city in the political and economic forces at the end of the Late Bronze Age and in the Early Iron Age ought to be reflected in the results of archaeological research. However, though

---

[105] Noort, *Seevölker*, 44; Schipper, *Israel und Ägypten*, 31–34. If David conquered and destroyed the city itself as Schipper suggested, the tradition about Gezer as a wedding gift from the Egyptian Pharaoh to Solomon becomes incredible, but see A. Lemaire in *Festschrift* Amihai Mazar 2006.

[106] As recorded in the Story of Wen-Amun, see B. Sass, 'Wen-Amun and his Levant', *Ägypten und Levante* 12 (2002), 247–255, esp. 252; B.U. Schipper, *Die Erzählung des Wenamun* (OBO, 209), Freiburg, Göttingen 2005; Lipínski, *On the Skirts of Canaan*, 163–164 thinks his name is Semitic. This would indeed comply with the mixed population of the city (Gilboa, Sharon, *NEA* 71 (2008), 160).

[107] In 2 Chron. 2:14, Joppa/Jaffa is mentioned as the harbour for the cedar lumber sent by King Hiram of Tyre and destined for the Temple of Jerusalem. It has been suggested that Tell Qasileh was the riverine harbor of Yapu/Joppa, see however A. Raban, 'Near Eastern Harbors: Thirteenth-Seventh Centuries BCE,' in: *Mediterranean Peoples*, 430–432.

Gezer is one of the best investigated cities of the 20th and 21st Centuries so far, it has not led yet to a neat consensus about its occupational history. In particular, the interference of the Davidic Dynasty with the city and Solomonic building activity at the site is still debated.[108]

Like so many inland cities, Gezer of the Late Bronze Age IIB (13th Century BCE) was in decline. The ceramic repertoire became limited and imported wares virtually ceased. In many respects, this decline previews the quiet beginnings of the Early Iron Age, as found elsewhere. Some disturbance in this transitional period at the end of the 13th and beginning of 12th Century was observed, perhaps connected to Merenptah's campaign in Palestine, but it was evidently not a major incursion from whichever side. If Merenptah took Gezer, the event was apparently a rather quiet and peacefull surrender more in line with his Amada epithet $w'f\ qa/gá$-$da$-$=r$, 'he who curbs Gezer'.

In fact, not until the mid 10th Century BCE a major break in occupation is attested. Dever describes two successive destructions of Gezer with an interval of about 25 year. He and other scholars ascribe these destructions to Egyptian campaigns during the 21st (ca. 950 BCE) and 22nd Dynasties (ca. 926 BCE) allegedly both recorded in the Bible (1 Kgs 9:15–17, 14:25–28).[109] If so, it reveals an increasing effort and involvement of Egypt to keep the 'coastal corridor' open. Dever connects the destruction of the 'Solomonic' four-room gate in Field III (Level VIII) to Sheshonq's campaign. The low chronology, however, would suggest setting the destruction before the building of this gate to Sheshonq and date its destruction somewhere in the 9th Century.[110]

There is hardly reason to deny the involvement of Sheshonq, but whether the first campaign was due to a 21st Dynasty Pharaoh, who presented Gezer as a dowry to King Solomon, is a matter of debate. Schipper, for instance, attributed the first destruction to David, whereas

---

[108] The renewed excavations were announced as 'The New excavations of King Solomon's City of Gezer', though the project goals and strategy are less outspoken on this point!

[109] Repeated recently by Dever, *What Did the Biblical Writers Know*, 131–138; also K.A. Kitchen, *On the Reliability of the Old Testament*, Grand Rapids, Cambrigde, 2003, 108–110. See, however, about the questionable interpretation of the scene with Si-amun slaying his enemies from Tanis, P.S. Ash, *David, Solomon and Egypt: A Reassessment* (JSOT Sup, 297), Sheffield 1999, 38–48, Schipper, *Israel und Ägypten*, 19–28; Gilboa *et al.*, *Tel Aviv* 31 (2004), 50–51; Lipinski, *On the Skirts of Canaan*, 96–97.

[110] I think that the general destruction layer of Field II and VI and the one below the 'Solomonic' gate in Field III could be the same, both attributable to Sheshonq.

the second is put down to the account of Sheshonq. However it is also possible that both destructions should be dated later, that is the first to Sheshonq and the second on a later occasion when the first 'Solomonic' gate was destroyed.

Commercial relations between Egypt and the Phoenician commonwealth were restored during the 21st Dynasty. Apparently the Phoenician cities undertook to ally themselves once more with Egypt because of a number of aggressive Assyrian campaigns in Syria.[111] For the Egyptian rulers, it implied restoration of ancient prestige in the area and breaking any sign of resistance in the coastal corridor. A major target in the Sheshonq campaign(s) was obviously the Philistine cities including the Canaanite enclave of Gezer. In the course of his operations, King Rehoboam of Judah may have submitted himself to Sheshonq and bought his and Jerusalem's freedom with a large tribute (1 Kgs 14:25, 26). In the coastal area, only Askelon was left unharmed, whereas Ashdod and Jaffa / Tell Qasileh were quickly restored, now apparently as allied harbour cities under Egyptian–Phoenician supervision.[112]

## 13. RETURN OF EGYPT IN THE LEVANT

Suddenly around 950 BCE, Egypt was back in the Levant. All of a sudden? By now we should know that things suddenly happen only in an events-history, but hardly so a in long-term history. Because of internal turmoil, economic malaise and political setbacks about 1100 BCE, Egypt had to surrender its Levantine provinces but that does not mean that they gave up their long-term ideological rights and commercial ties. As far as we know, they never did, even not in the 1st Millennium.

During the 10th Century and part of the 9th Century BCE, a Philistine–Canaanite–Phoenician corridor along the Mediterranean coast linked up

---

[111] Markou, *Phoenicians*, 37. In the light of the prevalence of Egyptians ceramics, he suggested that Dor was a primary stop-over for Egyptian commerce during the 21st Dynasty and later. So mutual trade may never have ceased (Gilboa, Sharon, *NEA* 71 (2008), 159).

[112] See also Schipper's review of the archaeology of the Philistine area including Gezer, ascribing most destructions to Sheshonq (Gaza, Ashdod+Tel Mor, Eqron, Tell el-Batash, Tell Qasileh), Schipper, *Israel und Ägypten*, 28–35. This change in Egyptian policy is quite interesting, because Egyptian commercial ties with Philistia and sites near to it were stronger than with any other region during the Early Iron Age, see J.M. Weinstein, 'Egyptian Relations with the Eastern Mediterranean World at the End of the Second Millennium', in: *Mediterranean Peoples*, 188–196; esp. 191–192.

to the Phoenician homeland. Presumably, Sheshonq I, his predecessors Si-Amun and Psusennes II of the 21st Dynasty and his successors helped to maintain this status quo when reviving commercial ties with the Levant[113] and finally, when renewing ancient Egyptian prestige along the Via Maris by a series of military campaigns. Recent scholarship has started to dismiss the idea that Sheshonq started his new foreign policy in the Levant only at the end of his reign. The large stele erected in Megiddo and the throne-base of a half-life-size statue erected in the temple of Baalat Byblos by Abibaal (ca. 935 BCE) suggest that he and his successors had more than an ephemeral presence in mind. It is probable that as Commander-in-Chief under Psusennes II, he took an active role in the efforts to renew Egyptian control in the Levantine scene for commercial and political reasons.[114]

It is no coincidence that the only extant manuscript of the Wen-Amun story is dated to the 22nd Dynasty and came from the city and temple that Sheshonq I and his successors built at al-Hiba. Wen-Amun told posterity the story of what went wrong with the prestige of Egypt and the cult of Amun in the Levant. Once a report of what had happened during his efforts to acquire timber (possibly cedar-wood) for the processional barque of Amun-Re, it became also a political document, containing the *casus belli* for Sheshonq's reconquest of Palestine.[115] It was an insult to Amun himself. So Sheshonq was called on to restore Amun's prestige. He made his presence felt, in particular as some of his

---

[113] Gilboa, Sharon, *NEA* 71 (2008) 159.

[114] Indeed the fragment of the battle scene of Si-Amun slaying his enemies does not prove a campaign against Gezer at all (so Kitchen, *On the Reliability of the Old Testament*, 280–283; K.R. Veenhof, *Geschichte des Alten Orients bis zur Zeit Alexander des Großen*, (ATD Ergänzungsreihe Band 11), Göttingen 2001, 222 etc., but see Schipper, *Israel und Ägypten*, 19–35) or Dor (so Lipinski, *On the Skirts of Canaan*, 95–98), but it still proves the aspirations and ideology of Egyptian domination. That this domination also covered the 'Asiatics' seems to be implied by the depiction of the weaponry of enemies (perhaps a Hittite shield, as even Schipper, *ibidem*, 26 has to admit, which is also attested in the Levant and even Egypt itself, Qantir).

[115] While Wen-Amun has long been thought of as an actual historical account, Egyptologists and others see it now more as a work of historical fiction. See the study of Benjamin Sass on the political dimension of the Wen-Amun story, B. Sass, 'Wenamun and his Levant—1075 BC or 925 BC', *Ägypten und Levante* 12 (2002), 247–255, Schipper, *Die Erzählung von Wenamun*, .... Also palaeography indicates the 22nd Dynasty. Both the stele and the triumphal inscription seem to imply Asiatic provocations, but it ought to be observed that they are more or less standard ancient phrases in this type of inscription.

predecessors had done, by erecting a stele in a place that was supposed to be turned into a new Egyptian stronghold, Megiddo.[116] In an earlier campaign, he probably had captured the Canaanite enclave of Gezer, but left it to be integrated into the nascent Israelite state. If the reference to a Pharaoh who conquered Gezer be credible (1 Kgs 9:16), Sheshonq either as generalissimo or as a Pharaoh early in his reign is as good a candidate as any of his predecessors.[117] Studies on the war inscriptions of Sheshonq I in the Karnak temple almost automatically take the 5th year of Rehoboam for granted (about 926 BCE) and assume Sheshonq's battles to be the result of one campaign, even if it consisted of several distinctive operations.[118] The inscriptions are not actually dated. They contain three different groups of towns, which suggest separate operations, of which the one described in 1 Kgs 14:25-28 might be the last that apparently was not included in the inscriptions.[119] From an Egyptian perspective, the war inscriptions of Sheshonq and his successors on the Bubastic Gate may represent the result of a new lifelong foreign policy which attempted to revive Ramesside aspirations. For an unknown number of years, the Libyan dynasty made Egypt's presence once more felt in Palestine, Phoenicia and Israel, but that is a different story.

---

[116] On this stela and its reconstruction, see Schipper, *Israel und Ägypten*, 129–132 and 297 Abb. 7–8; R.L. Chapman III, 'Putting Sheshonq I in his Place', *PEQ* 141 (2009), 4–17, esp. 14 Fig. 5.

[117] Redford, *Egypt, Canaan and Israel*, 313–315; Schipper, *Israel und Ägypten*, 35; Lipinski, *On the Skirts of Canaan*, 99–101.

[118] The common assumption repeated by Schipper, *Israel und Ägypten*, 125–132; Kitchen, *On the Reliability of the Old Testament*, 32–34; see, however, Wente, *JNES* 35 (1976), 275–279 and especially H.M. Niemann, 'The Socio-political Shadow of the Biblical Solomon', in: L.K. Handy et al., *The Age of Solomon. Scholarship at the turn of the Millennium*, Leiden 1997, 252–299, esp. 297; E.A. Knauf, 'The "Low Chronology" and How Not to Deal With It', *BN* 101 (2000), 62, and Lipinski, *On the Skirts of Canaan*, 99–104, esp. 100, who all assume that his inscription reflects the result of different campaigns.

[119] See, however, on the nature of this historical note, M. Noth, 'IV. Die Schoschenkenliste', in: M. Noth, *Aufsätze zur biblischen Landes- und Altertumskunde Band 2* (H.W. Wolff ed.), Neukirchen-Vluyn 1971, 74–75; Schipper, *Israel und Ägypten*, 122–125. There are reasons to believe that the inscriptions at the back of the Bubastic Gate at the Karnak Temple between the 2nd Pylon and the temple of Ramesses III, next to the battle scenes of Ramesses II on the south wall of the Hypostyle Hall, was finished before the work on the 'broad court' (Gebel el-Silseleh text of year 21 (922 BCE)) started, see Redford, *Egypt, Canaan and Israel*, 312, note 1. There is another similar smiting the enemy and topography scene of Sheshonq in the Temple of al-Hibah, but unfortunately very damaged, E. Feucht, 'Relief Scheschonqs I. Beim erschlagen der Feinde aus El-Hibe', *SAÄK* 9 (1981), 105–117, Tafel II; Redford, *ibidem*, 314 n. 12.

If the nascent Israelite state received the city of Gezer inside its borders about 950 BCE at the end of the early Iron Age, the inference seems to be that most of the Philistine–Canaanite–Phoenician coastal region and lowlands still remained outside the borders of Israelite settlement or of the recently created Israelite kingdom.

# THE CASE OF THE CORRUPTING CONSENSUS[*]

Lester L. Grabbe
*University of Hull*

With apologies to the authors of *The Corrupting Sea*, which was an answer to Braudel's work on the Mediterranean,[1] I would like to address a topic that I think is important to us as a society and as a dedicated group of scholars. It is a topic difficult to come to grips with because it is somewhat nebulous; indeed, it is not so much a topic as an attitude. It is an attitude that we all suffer from. I do not mean that *you* or *some of you* suffer from it but that *we all*–that includes me—have a problem. How often have we said, 'So-and-so has this thesis. I've read it (or heard a paper on it or had comments whispered to me in a dark alley) and it is (or isn't) very well presented; it does (or does not) have good arguments for it, but in the final analysis I don't think it stands up. One point not taken into account is such and such.' And so on. Or maybe the comment is, 'I can't put my finger on it yet, but I think there is a major flaw in there somewhere.' If we were forced at gunpoint to give a show of hands of who had said words to that effect, I would be the first to have to put up my hand. We are scholars; this is our first and normal reaction.

By this I do not mean that we are always negative to new ideas or theses. But a healthy sense of scepticism—a 'show me' attitude—listening with our arms folded—this is our metier. It is our job to evaluate arguments, to probe them, dissect them, and pull them apart for weaknesses: whether student essays, dissertations or theses; or articles or manuscripts that come to us as editors of journals and monograph series; or just in scholarly debates in defending our own ideas and attacking the opposition. It would be wrong to give this up. I am not issuing a plea to be nicer to one another—most of us in this country are so polite you sometimes

---

[*] This paper was originally presented as the presidential address to the Society for Old Testament Study, 5 January 2009. I offer my grateful thanks to the Society for electing me as President for 2009. Although this version has had footnotes added and some other revisions applied, it still retains the original style for oral delivery.

[1] Peregrine Horden and Nicholas Purcell, *The Corrupting Sea: A Study of Mediterranean History*, London 2000.

have a hard time knowing whether someone is actually disagreeing with you or not—it can be like being mugged by Shaun the Sheep.

But what I have in mind is a general institutional mind-set of the academy. This is to overvalue consensus. It can be subtle, slow, and ponderous, but before you know it this relentless academic bulldozer has a way of grinding down new ideas, especially radical ones, and especially of crushing new scholars who may espouse radical ideas. Unfortunately, this process of bringing people to heel begins when we are students. You quickly learn which ideas are accepted, which are radical but harmless, and which are eccentric and can be laughed out of court. We learn that there are certain ideas you can ignore but others you dare not challenge.

As students you were always conscious of where the consensus lay, or at least the point of view favoured by your *Doktorvater*. Some academics had the courage—or was it just bloody-mindedness?–to differ from the consensus. It was an interesting exercise to see how these mavericks were evaluated. For their students, they were almost always seen as the wave of the future, or at least as a martyr to the truth. In some cases other scholars did not follow them but nevertheless openly respected them. Others quickly gained the *sobriquet* of 'individualist', 'eccentric', or even 'crank'.

It is also frequently the case in some parts of the world that students of a particular individual form a 'school'. I do not know that the students are told they all have to believe the same thing, but it certainly seems to work out that way in practice. I shall not name any names, but one in particularly makes me cross. After coming to the UK I was not able to attend the annual meeting of the Society of Biblical Literature for about 10 years. When I finally managed to get to a meeting, I saw a session on textual criticism of the Hebrew Bible, for which I had a particular interest, and attended. It was awful. It was dominated by recent Harvard PhDs, and they were all spouting Frank Cross's line on the Hebrew Bible text, one which I thought was wrong and still think so. I mentioned this to my friend Eugene Ulrich, who is himself a student of Cross, and he acknowledged that 'Frank does tend to be a dominant individual' or words to that effect. But he did point out that as time went on, most Cross students did learn to take a more independent line, and I must say that he himself is evidence of it.

A few years ago I got an invitation to apply for a post at my alma mater. I was not sure I wanted to return to that part of the world, but I duly filled in an application and sent it off. After a few weeks we began to near the time that the SBL annual meeting took place. It was often the case that candidates would be interviewed at the meeting, before a short list was drawn up. But I had heard nothing. So I got in touch with someone at the institute who made some inquires. The word came back that they had decided not to consider my application because they felt that they already had too many of their own people on the staff.

This was particularly annoying since my experience was probably more varied and catholic than that of some of the people they would be interviewing. But as a general rule of operation, I could not quarrel with it. A number of institutions limit the number of their own graduates on their staff. Interesting, some of those regarded as leading institutions in North America—and in this country, I may say—do not have such a rule. Indeed, I understand that some Ivy League institutes will not hire any but Ivy League graduates. One particular institution is said to have a penchant for hiring its own graduates, though I cannot confirm this. Yet as a general rule, there is nothing that can stifle the field so rapidly as the dead hand of academic nepotism.

Of course, we often appeal to a consensus to save time. We cannot begin every issue from first principles. In some cases we ourselves have thoroughly examined certain issues, come to a conclusion, and we want to build on it—not go over the same ground again. But no individual can examine every aspect of OT scholarship for themselves: we all depend on what have become accepted views because of what previous generations have done, or what certain specialists in a particular area have concluded. Fair enough. Except that this often becomes a part of the argument: it's not usually worded so simply as, 'Everybody knows', but it is often no more sophisticated than that in reality.

I want to illustrate my point by taking some examples from the area of the history of ancient Israel. A number of people here were postgraduate students in the early 1970s and a few gray-beards in this audience were already lecturers! It is often salutary to remind ourselves how much has changed since 1970.[2] For those who can remember the 60s and 70s you will probably remember some of the main areas of consensus in Old Testament / Hebrew Bible scholarship. The Documentary Hypothesis was still king of Pentateuchal research, though this began to change after

---

[2] I catalogue some of these changes with regard to the history of ancient Israel in my article, 'Writing Israel's History at the End of the Twentieth Century', in André Lemaire and Magne Saebø (eds), *Congress Volume: Oslo 1998* (VT Sup 80), Leiden 2000, 203–218.

1975 and Rolf Rendtorff's article, and especially his 1977 monograph.[3] In the end, a 'conventional' scholar like Norman Whybray–if I can so label him—rejected it.[4] The patriarchal narratives were thought to have preserved 'substantial historicity'. Some in this country may have accepted the Alt-Noth thesis of the settlement, but in North America, where I was studying, the Albright unified conquest thesis definitely reigned supreme. It is true that as a student I learned the Alt-Noth hypothesis and even about another thesis, contained in an obscure article in the *Biblical Archaeologist*, written by the Albright student George Mendenhall. But there was no question where the consensus lay.

I'll use the example of the minimalists, partly because everyone seems to want to take a whack at them. As far as I know, Thomas Thompson and Niels Peter Lemche are the only two individuals who readily accept the designation of 'minimalist', so I'll confine my remarks to them. I do not agree with the minimalists in some important areas, but I have learned a good deal from them. Sadly, they seem to have learned nothing from me! I think one of the reasons that the minimalists are so often attacked is that they seem to court trouble. In the recent SBL meeting in Boston (Massachusetts, not Lincolnshire), one of the publishers organized a session on the history of Israel that featured books by Philip Davies, Niels Peter Lemche, and myself. Oded Lipschits read a paper reviewing Niels Peter Lemche's most recent book. He pointed out in a polite but convincing way that Lemche was deliberately cutting himself off from the 'mainstream'. In a number of cases, Lemche was not that different from the 'mainstream', yet he exaggerated the differences to make himself as unrelated as possible. I think Lipschits had a good point. I myself made a related point, which is the minimalists have had more of an impact than they themselves seem to acknowledge. Almost all critical scholars agree with the minimalists in some crucial areas. Thus, in some areas of Israelite history we are all minimalists.

---

[3] See R. Rendtorff, 'Der "Jahwist" als Theologe? Zum Dilemma der Pentateuchkritik', in *Edinburgh Congress Volume* (VTSup 28), Leiden 1975, 158–166; ET 'The "Yahwist" as Theologian? The Dilemma of Pentateuchal Criticism', *JSOT* 3 (1977) 2–10 (plus responses, pp. 11–42); R. Rendtorff, *Das überlieferungsgeschichtliche Problem des Pentateuch* (BZAW 147), Berlin, New York 1977; ET *The Problem of the Process of Transmission in the Pentateuch* (transl. J.J. Scullion; JSOTSup 89), Sheffield 1990.

[4] R.N. Whybray, *The Making of the Pentateuch: A Methodological Study* (JSOT Sup 53), Sheffield 1987.

Yet we should not stop at this new consensus. In my opinion, we are minimalists by default. That is, we simply have not found enough information to say much. But I believe that with time and effort, we can find some things to say. There is room for new hypotheses to make sense of the few data we have. Many of us have doubts about the United Monarchy, but we should not allow ourselves to see the default positions as, yes, there was a United Monarchy or, no, there was not a United Monarchy. A number of possibilities present themselves, and we should avoid allowing a consensus to develop—except for one that allows for a number of possible scenarios. What we must avoid starting from is a position that accepts the biblical picture unless we can refute it; equally, we should avoid one that rejects the biblical picture yet says that we do not know anything.

One side effect of a consensus is to make us begin to think—or at least talk—in clichés. To give one small example, back in the early days of the feminist analysis of biblical texts, someone used the adjective 'feisty' to describe a female character. It was a good word and no doubt original when first used. But then use began to expand exponentially, and suddenly every female figure of antiquity is discussed only a short time before being referred to as 'feisty'. It reminds me of how I first learned the word and its meaning. I grew up on a farm, and periodically you have orphan lambs or calves. In many cases, they are not genuine orphans because the mother is still alive, but somehow the process of the mother establishing the scent trail that makes her know the calf is hers has not taken place. Moderns might say that they have not bonded—the more practical farmers simply stated that the mother did not 'claim' it. If you knew who the mother was and intervened quickly enough, you could often get the mother to recognize the calf, but this was not always possible. The result was that at any one time we might have one or two calves or lambs being bottle fed until they could look after themselves. We often gave these animals names and treated them like pets until they could survive on their own. When I was about 9 or10 years old, I remember my mother naming a female orphan calf 'Feisty'. This was a new word for me. Surprisingly, for a farmhouse we had quite a collection of books, including a copy of the Merriam-Webster unabridged dictionary of American English.[5] So I looked up 'feisty' and

---

[5] This was apparently the so-called 'Second Edition': William Allen Neilson and Thomas A. Knott (eds), *The Merriam-Webster New International Dictionary of the English Language*, Springfield MA 1934.

agreed that my mother had chosen an appropriate name for the heifer calf. The result is that to this day, whenever I see the word 'feisty', I always think of a little cow.

I work a good deal in the Persian period and remember in an academic discussion at a meeting, I mentioned as a part of my argument that the Gadatas Inscription, supposedly from the Persian period, may not be genuine. A subsequent speaker was a friend of mine. At one point in his paper he ad-libbed, 'Most people think the Gadatas Inscription is genuine.' Now, the number of people with sufficient expertise to pronounce on the matter can probably be counted on the fingers of one hand. That number does not include me, though I had done a thorough study of scholarship on the inscription and found that learned and expert voices had taken both positions for well over a century of study.[6] The fact is that most people—including scholars of the Persian period—have no right to an opinion on the Gadatas Inscription, because they do not have enough knowledge to pronounce one way or the other. To appeal to a consensus in this case was nonsense. As a footnote, a couple of years after the incident, Pierre Briant, a scholar highly respected by both my friend and me, did a thorough examination of the inscription and concluded that it was a later forgery of the Roman period.[7]

In working on the Persian period I have two frustrations. The first frustration is that so many scholars seem to have access to a source that I have not been able to find. This is the Big Red Book of Persian Policies. Now, Professor Williamson may be as surprised to hear about this source as I am, but it must exist—because I keep hearing or reading, 'The Persians had a policy on this' or 'The Persian policy on that was such and such'. Now, surely these scholars must have a good source: they would not just be extrapolating from an obscure biblical verse or a tattered piece of barely legible papyrus, would they? Hence, there must be a Big Red Book of Persian Policies from which they are quoting—even though Briant,

---

[6] I discussed the question in L.L. Grabbe, *Judaism from Cyrus to Hadrian: Vol. I: Persian and Greek Periods; Vol. II: Roman Period*, Minneapolis 1992; British edition in one-volume, London 1994, 59.

[7] See P. Briant, 'Histoire et archéologie d'un texte: La *Lettre de Darius à Gadatas* entre Perses, Grecs et Romains', in: M. Giorgieri, M. Salvini, M.-C. Trémouille, P. Vannicelli (eds.), *Licia e Lidia prima dell'Ellenizzazione: Atti del Convegno internazionale—Roma 11–12 ottobre 1999* (Monografie Scientifiche, Serie Scienze umane e sociali Consiglio Nazionale delle Ricerche), Rome 2003, 107–144.

who has an encyclopaedic knowledge and a wonderful critical sense of the Persian empire, seems to know nothing of these policies.

My second frustration with regard to the Persian period is that every new monograph on the period seems to require us to completely rewrite Persian history. Again, I think they should thoroughly digest Briant first.[8] Yet the Persian period is a problematic one, and all the new suggestions are a necessary by-product of trying to make sense of it. They are the price we pay for progress. I may disagree with many other researchers, but some will also disagree with some of my interpretations—at least, from among the three people who have read my book.[9] I firmly believe that, in spite of some of our frustrations, in a hundred years' time the present situation will have led to a better understanding of the Jews under Persian rule.

To return to my main point, a consensus may have come about for a variety of reasons. Sometimes, an argument is presented that is so cogent and so irrefutable that the whole field changes fairly quickly. This happened in the mid-1970s with regard to the patriarchal period. Two books, one by Thomas Thompson and one by John Van Seters, appeared about the same time but independently.[10] There was no unified view about when the traditions originated: Van Seters plumped for the Neo-Babylonian period, while Thompson put them several centuries earlier. What they agreed on was that the parallels, data, and arguments confining the patriarch traditions to the early 2nd millennium BCE had no basis. Some theories erode away; others go with a crash. The patriarchal thesis had the rug pulled out from under it. Here and there a rearguard defence was raised, but such actions had a habit of backfiring on the defenders. Claiming to draw on the newly discovered Ebla texts, the late David Noel Freedman argued that the patriarch traditions reflected an even earlier period, the late 3rd millennium BCE. Unfortunately, he was not relying on a personal knowledge of the texts but the claims of the epigrapher Giovanni Pettinato. Just as a rather smug article—it seemed smug to me,

---

[8] See P. Briant, *From Cyrus to Alexander: A History of the Persian Empire* (transl. Peter T. Daniels), Winona Lake IN 2002; ET of *Histoire de l'empire perse de Cyrus à Alexandre: Volumes I–II* (Achaemenid History 10), Leiden 1996 [originally published by Librairie Arthème Fayard, Paris].

[9] L.L. Grabbe, *A History of the Jews and Judaism in the Second Temple Period 1: Yehud: A History of the Persian Province of Judah*, London, New York 2004.

[10] Th.L. Thompson, *The Historicity of the Patriarchal Narratives: The Quest for the Historical Abraham* (BZAW 133), Berlin 1974; J. van Seters, *Abraham in History and Tradition*, New Haven 1975.

though I'm no doubt prejudiced—on the subject was about to go press in the *Biblical Archaeology Review*, Pettinato repudiated his earlier interpretation. Freedman only had time to pen a rather confused prefacing note to the article before the issue went to press and subsequently had egg on his face.[11]

Now, before we laugh too much, it is the sort of thing that could happen to any of us. It is a proclivity of scholars to focus too much on failures rather than successes. I have heard it said that the difference between British and Americans in the business world is that the British focus on failure and the Americans focus on success, accepting that failure is the price you pay for success. Now, I do not know whether that is true or not, but I do know that as scholars we tend to pay a disproportionate attention to scholarly failures. There was nothing inherently bad about Freedman's being wrong in this instance. What was bad was the way he ridiculed others who disagreed, which is a different matter: I heard him give a lecture at Claremont where he dismissed Van Seters in scornful terms. When it comes to being wrong, George Mendenhall (as perhaps one of the most original members of the Albright school) came up with a number of theories, all of which most of us now reject. These include the view that Deuteronomy was modelled on the 13th century Hittite treaty form.[12] Another was the authenticity of the called 'Philistine scrolls'. I know something of this since my own teacher William Brownlee was involved in this.[13] I remember that he told us students a bit about it before going to the SBL conference about 1971. But he returned disappointed because someone had pointed out a section of the Siloam inscription in the text. But he accepted that they were fakes, whereas Mendenhall apparently did not. Finally, there was his theory already alluded to that the Israelite settlement was the result of an internal revolt, an idea developed into a full thesis by Norman Gottwald.[14] Few would now accept this

---

[11] D.N. Freedman, 'The Real Story of the Ebla Tablets: Ebla and the Cities of the Plain', *BA* 41/6 (Dec. 1978), 143–164.

[12] G.E. Mendenhall, 'Ancient Oriental and Biblical Law', *BA* 17 (1954), 26–46; G.E. Mendenhall, 'Covenant Forms in Israelite Tradition', *BA* 17 (1954), 50–76.

[13] 'An Announcement Published by The Department of Antiquities of Jordan and the Archaeologists Dr. William H. Brownlee and Dr. George E. Mendenhall Regarding the Decipherment of Carian Leather Manuscripts Found in 1966 in the Hebron Area, the Hashemite Kingdom of Jordan', *ADAJ* 15 (1970), 39–40, with 3 plates (pp. 73–75); W.H. Brownlee, G.E. Mendenhall, J. Oweis, 'Philistine Manuscripts from Palestine?' *Kadmos* 10 (1971), 102–104; G.E. Mendenhall, 'The "Philistine" Documents from the Hebron Area: A Supplementary Note', *ADAJ* 16 (1971), 99–102.

[14] G.E. Mendenhall, 'The Hebrew Conquest of Palestine', *BA* 25 (1962), 66–87; N.K.

as the explanation of the settlement, yet it has been very influential and most theories now incorporate aspects of this thesis in some form. The point is that Mendenhall's theories became a point of debate and development, and he gave significant stimulus to the field and helped it advance, even if these theories have mostly been rejected by now. It is no disgrace to be wrong.

It is, however, especially difficult to critique a consensus if we have helped to establish it. That is why advances are often made by the new generation, because they are more willing to reject the consensus of the previous generation. They say that mathematicians do their best work before they are 25. Likewise, other scientists often make their greatest original contributions to the field at an early age. In some sense, those of us in the arts / humanities lack this stimulus, because we are often gray-beards before we finally reach a position of being able to make an impact on the field.

The ideal of scholarship is that all theories are evaluated on their merits, but it does not work that way in practice, as we all know. Once a consensus has been established, it develops a momentum that is hard to stop. It is not so much that we examine carefully and then reject a new idea. It is that if the new idea cannot be proved beyond a reasonable doubt, the old consensus is assumed to be confirmed. Unfortunately, that ignores how a consensus becomes established. Sometimes a consensus is established because someone comes up with a brilliant argument, for example, as noted with the patriarchal narratives above. But often a consensus develops for very nebulous reasons—because a noted authority once expressed an opinion or even because nothing better has been advanced. Unfortunately, the consensus starts to assert a powerful influence simply because it has been around a while. People will use the consensus as a weapon against new ideas. Instead of using weighty and valid arguments against the new thesis, they trot out the position that the existence of a consensus shows the other idea must be erroneous. It is not usually stated so blatantly as, 'everyone knows', but that is really the gist of the argument. So when someone says, 'I do not think this new theory stands up', the unspoken correlation is usually, 'so we can go back to the consensus'. The default position is assumed to be that of the consensus; the burden of proof is placed on the new idea. Few theories are put forward with all the loose ends tied up. You can almost always find some flaw in it. The

Gottwald, *The Tribes of Yahweh: A Sociology of the religion of Liberated Israel, 1250–1050 B.C.E.*, Maryknoll 1979; reprinted with new Preface: Biblical Seminar 66, Sheffield 1999.

trouble is that flaws in a new theory are used as a reason for rejecting it, but the consensus position is not evaluated on the same grounds. It will usually have just as many flaws or loose ends, but it is not scrutinized and critiqued, only the new idea.

In conclusion, one of the greatest dangers to scholarship is the comfortable consensus.[15] No one wants to be the underdog. Thus, when certain topics came up for academic discussion, it is easy to let it be known that you agree with the majority. In academic circles there is nothing that quite equals the sound of bandwagons being hastily boarded—it is hard to describe but is sort of a pusillanimous sound. Never forget, though, what a consensus is: it is like a stick picked up to help you in climbing the trail. Use it as long as you find it useful, but discard it without a second thought as soon as it has served its purpose. A consensus is not for life; it is not even just for Christmas. It is not to be worshipped; it is not even to be revered. On the contrary, my appeal to you is, next time you meet a consensus, do not shake its hand. Stare at it. Give it a good sniff, poke it, sneer at it, threaten it, and if it does not look you in the eye, attack it.

---

[15] This was wonderfully expounded by S. Sandmel, 'Palestinian and Hellenistic Judaism and Christianity: The Question of the Comfortable Theory', *HUCA* 50 (1979), 137–148.

# THREE HASIDISMS AND THEIR MILITANT IDEOLOGIES: 1 AND 2 MACCABEES, PSALMS 144 AND 149

HARM VAN GROL

*Tilburg—The Netherlands*

## 1. INTRODUCTION

Biblical history has a rough time nowadays. First of all, there are reasons enough to criticize traditional history writing and its modern equivalents. Fundamentalist readings and non-hermeneutical theologies are a real danger in ecclesiastical environments and beyond. Our research in the history of Israel and Judah, therefore, must come up to contemporary academic standards.[1] Further, the study of biblical history has matured, or, from another perspective, has become secularized. Biblical history is now the subject of historians (even if they are theologians), and they (we) tend to be straight in drawing a distinction between faith and fact, evidence and ideology, and sometimes, maybe, too neurotic.

The most important result of this evidence—ideology project is the loss of most of biblical history, redefined as proto-history, a world anachronistically controlled by myth, theology, and ideology. The discussion is not about this fact but its limits. Does the history of ancient Israel start with (king?) David, or does David still belong to proto-history, and should evidence based history writing begin two centuries later?[2]

Finally, according to contemporary historiography, 'history' does not exist, and what we know as 'history', is a personal or collective construct. This fundamental insight could paralyse our research if we take it as the

---

[1] The Pontifical Biblical Commission is promoting the historical-critical method as an instrument against fundamentalism, in its document, *The Interpretation of the Bible in the Church*, 1993 (see e.g. http://catholic-resources.org/ChurchDocs).

[2] My personal choice of studies that discuss this subject: J.A. Soggin, *An Introduction to the History of Israel and Judah*, London 1993, K.L. Noll, *Canaan and Israel in Antiquity: An Introduction* (The Biblical Seminar, 83), London 2001, and I. Finkelstein, N.A. Silberman, *The Bible Unearthed: Archaeology's New Vision of Ancient Israel and the Origin of its Sacred Texts*, New York NY 2001.

backdrop to our practical history writing. In fact, it presupposes the existence of (the illusion of) truth and understanding. A fundamental motive
for research is the will to know and to understand. It is a hermeneutical
fallacy to consider the results of our research as *just* a personal construct.
We should take our reenactments very seriously. It will be only a matter of time before someone deconstructs them, but precisely the play of
constructing and deconstructing is research in progress.[3] 'Go to, let us
construct!'

The subject of this paper will be the Hasidim of the second century BCE. These 'mighty warriors' have captivated the scholarly world
for more than a century. Most of the time, they were giving cause for
mighty fantasies about the ancestors of the Essenes and the Pharizees and
about the authors of apocalypses as 1 Enoch and Daniel. Lately, these theories have become an easy victim for deconstructing historians like Lester
Grabbe:[4]

> The paradoxical nature of focusing on sects, in spite of our limited evi-
> dence, is illustrated by the so-called *Hasidim*. These have been elevated to
> central catalysts for major events in Jewish history. They are supposed to
> have been the ancestors of both the Essenes and the Pharisees. Yet even
> their name is problematic: it is a scholarly invention and not found in the
> sources, which are all in Greek and call them *Asidaioi*. We know next to
> nothing about them, but this has not prevented major theories from being
> built on assumptions about who they were and what they did.

I will argue that Grabbes great clause 'We know next to nothing about
them' is beside the truth, *excusez le mot*, and that there is no reason to
ban the Hasidim from history. Grabbe mentions two arguments against
the existence of the Hasidim as a well defined group:

> The Greek translator [of 1 Maccabees] undoubtedly understood this [the
> Hebrew word *hâsîdîm*] to be a name, but this does not mean that the
> original Hebrew text of 1 Maccabees pointed to anything more than a

---

[3] B. Becking, 'The Hellenistic Period and Ancient Israel: Three Preliminary Statements', in: L.L. Grabbe (ed.), *Did Moses Speak Attic? Jewish Historiography and Scripture
in the Hellenistic Period* (JSOT SupS, 317; European Seminar in Historical Methodology,
3), Sheffield 2001, 78–90 (82), argues in favour of a balance between trust and distrust:
'the historical trade asks for distrust, while the art of reconstruction asks for trust.'

[4] L.L. Grabbe, 'Second Temple Judaism: Challenges, Controversies, and Quibbles in
the Next Decade', *Henoch* 27 (2005), 13–19 (15). Cf. Idem, *Judaic Religion in the Second
Temple Period: Belief and Practice from the Exile to Yavneh*, London 2000, 184–185.
É. Nodet, '*Asidaioi* and Essenes', in: A. Hilhorst et al. (eds), *Flores Florentino: FS Florentino
García Martínez* (Sup JSJ, 122), Leiden 2007, 63–87, offers an example of fundamental
mistrust.

miscellaneous group of 'pious individuals' (Davies; Lightstone: 38–39; Saldarini 1988:252–253; contra Kampen). That is, because *hâsîdîm* was ambiguous in the Hebrew text of 1 Maccabees, it may well be that to read this as an organized group is a misunderstanding.[5]

and

> We do not know for certain that the Hasidim were a definite, organized group; perhaps the authors of 1 and 2 Maccabees used the name only generally, to apply to a variety of groups.[6]

Because the second argument is only relevant, at least in respect of the author of 1 Maccabees, if the first one is not valid, we may summarize the arguments as follows:

1. קהל חסידים in the reconstructed Hebrew text of 1 Maccabees 2:42 meant 'a group of pious people';
2. the author of 2 Maccabees used the name Ασιδαίοι generally.

It is argued in this contribution that the Hasidim are found in at least three, and probably four, independent sources: (Psalm 144–145,) Psalm 149, 2 Maccabees, and 1 Maccabees (in historical sequence). They were a well defined religious movement, characterized by piety and militancy, and participated in the revolt against the Jewish Hellenists and the Seleucids (167–161 BCE). Of a hypothetical nature is the theory that they were scribes and belonged to the leading citizens of Jerusalem. Their role in the revolt will remain open for speculation.

The result of the following deconstruction of ideologically motivated sources and search for evidence has surprised me. I came upon three groups of Hasidim, each occupied by militant ideologies or activities, and found in that militancy a key to understanding and a reason for a new theory.

---

[5] L.L. Grabbe, *Judaism from Cyrus to Hadrian*, Minneapolis MN 1992, 466. He refers to P.R. Davies, '*Hasidim* in the Maccabean Period', *JJS* 28 (1977), 127–140; J.N. Lightstone, 'Judaism of the Second Commonwealth: Toward a Reform of the Scholarly Tradition', in: H. Joseph et al. (eds), *Truth and Compassion: Essays on Judaism and Religion in Memory of Rabbi Dr. Solomon Frank* (SR Supplements, 12), Waterloo ON 1983, 31–40; A.J. Saldarini, *Pharisees, Scribes and Sadducees in Palestinian Society: A Sociological Approach*, Wilmington DE 1988; J. Kampen, *The Hasideans and the Origin of Pharisaism: A Study in 1 and 2 Maccabees* (SCS, 24), Atlanta GA 1988.

[6] Grabbe, *Judaism from Cyrus*, 467.

## 2. 2 Maccabees: Those Jews Called *Asidaioi*

The speech of Alcimus before the Seleucid king Demetrius in 2 Maccabees 14:6–10 is a nice piece of work. It opens with the sentence: 'Those
Jews called Hasideans, led by Judas Maccabeus, are warmongers, who stir
up sedition and keep the kingdom from enjoying peace and quiet', and
closes as follows: 'As long as Judas is around, it is impossible for the state
to enjoy peace' (NAB). In between, Alcimus presents the good people:
'my countrymen', 'our entire nation', and 'our country and its hard-pressed
people'.

The writer of 2 Maccabees does not introduce the Asidaioi. He just
mentions them, without any explanation: Οἱ λεγόμενοι τῶν Ιουδαίων
Ασιδαῖοι. Clearly, he supposes that his readers are familiar with this
group, otherwise the passage would make no sense. We may conclude
that the Asidaioi are no fictional character.

Does the author of 2 Maccabees use the name Asidaioi 'only generally,
to apply to a variety of groups'?[7] The syntax of the phrase does not
allow this interpretation. The writer uses the name Asidaioi to point at
a well defined group of Judeans. Moreover, if we would think of 'a variety
of groups', we would spoil Alcimus's argument. Why does he mention
the Asidaioi? He prefers to see the Maccabean revolt as the war of the
Asidaioi, Judas being their leader. In fact, he needs a name, a well defined
group, to draw a distinction between those evil persons and the rest of the
population, which are obviously good people. Of course, at the end of his
speech he mentions only Judas. He needs a group to blame, but his main
concern is Judas.

Who are 'those Judeans called Asidaioi'? The name and the speech
tell us that they are pious people who are engaging in military activities. The name Ασιδαῖοι will be a transcription of חסידים or its Aramaic equivalent, meaning 'The Pious'. As an aside, the writer may have
a hidden agenda, construing his main hero Judas as a pious man by
associating him with this pious people.[8] The Asidaioi played a military role in the revolt of the Sixties, but there is no way to confirm

---

[7] One of the arguments of Grabbe, see the Introduction.

[8] In this suggestion, we make a distinction between the internal logic of the speech
of Alcimus, and thereby Alcimus's perspective, and the perspective of the writer, com-
bining two diametrically opposed purposes, blaming the Hasidim and using them to
glorify Judas. For more discussion about the perspective of the writer see Kampen, *The
Hasideans*, 135–148.

Alcimus's statement that they made up the army of Judas the Maccabee, and that they were warmongers (πολεμοτροφοῦσιν) and rebels (στασιάζουσιν).

2 Maccabees is based on a five volume history by Jason of Cyrene, written in Greek not too long after the events. It is an *epitome*, a summary of and selection from this work, and may be dated around 124 BCE.[9] This makes the book an important source for our inquiry. The original material dates from only ten or twenty years after the events and the book from fourty years, at most. The book is closing in on the events still further, if Jerusalem is its place of origin, and not Alexandria.[10]

### 3. 1 MACCABEES: MIGHTY WARRIORS

Some twenty years after the epitomist did his work, around 100 BCE, another historian composed his own Maccabean history. He wrote his book in Hebrew, a text now lost. We will therefore quote the Greek version and add the supposed original Hebrew.

Again the Asidaioi play a part in the first stage of the revolt, between 167 and 161 BCE,[11] but their presentation in 1 Maccabees differs a lot from that in 2 Maccabees. Now, some sixty years after the events, the Asidaioi get a proper introduction: 'Then a group of Asidaioi joined them, mighty warriors, each of them zealously devoted to the law' (1 Macc 2:42). Moreover, the army in 2 Maccabees 14 was made up of Asidaioi and Judas the Maccabee was 'just' their leader. Now the Maccabees are joined by the

---

[9] 2 Macc. covers the time span from 175 (Seleucus IV) until 161 BCE (Demetrius I). Jason of Cyrene may have been a contemporary of Judah or was possibly dependent upon earlier sources (Kampen, *The Hasideans*, 62). 2 Macc. starts with a cover letter (1:1–10a), to which a second letter (1:10b–2:18) and the *epitome* of the work of Jason (2:19–15:39) are added. According to Kampen, *The Hasideans*, 59–60, the date of the cover letter is the *terminus ad quem*, 124 BCE (2 Macc. 1:10: 188 SE). According to other scholars, this date is the *terminus post quem* (e.g. H. Lichtenberger, 'History-writing and History-telling in First and Second Maccabees', in: S.C. Barton et al. (eds), *Memory in the Bible and Antiquity* (WUNT, 212), Tübingen 2007, 95–110 [103–105]). There is no reason to date the book much later than 124 BCE.

[10] Cf. Lichtenberger, 'History-writing', 105.

[11] 1 Macc. covers the time span from 333 (Alexander the Great) until 104 BCE (the death of John Hyrcanus). The *terminus ad quem* is the Roman intervention in 63 BCE. There is no reason to date the book much later than 104 BCE. Van der Kooij dates the Greek version around the same time (A. van der Kooij, 'The Septuagint of Psalms and the First Book of Maccabees', in: R.J.V. Hiebert et al. [eds], *The Old Greek Psalter: Studies in Honour of Albert Pietersma* [Sup JSOT, 332], Sheffield 2001, 229–247 [229 note 1]).

Asidaioi. Apparently the writer is far more interested in political and military history than the writer of 2 Maccabees and construes the history of the Sixties and after as a *Maccabean* history. Finally, he not only gives the Asidaioi a proper introduction, but also an exit-story. In both passages the group is used to legitimate the military and political choices of the Maccabees. They enter the story shortly after the start of the rebellion by Mattathias. They are the only *group* that joins him and his friends, and their combination of law-oriented piety and militancy legitimates Mattathias's fundamental choice to rise in rebellion. In chapter 7 the Asidaioi leave the story dead or alive at a moment that could have been the end of the war. They enter peace talks with Alcimus, but, in their attempt, sixty of them or of a larger group of scribes they belong to are massacred. These martyrs are praised as the 'pious of Yhwh' (ὅσιοι σου: חֲסִידֶיךָ) by quoting Psalm 79:2–3. But the writer gives us second thoughts and styles them as naive (1 Macc. 7:10–11). Their martyrdom proves that the Maccabees were right to refuse any peace talks. In a strange way, they are used to legitimate the second part of the Maccabean war.

The story may suggest that the writer could not ignore the Asidaioi. He made the best of the situation and more, but the group is nowhere essential to the storyline. The main characters of chapter 2 are Mattathias and his group and those of chapter 7 (vv. 12–17) a group of scribes. Would we have missed the Asidaioi? The contemporary readers would, apparently. We may conclude that the group was not only a fictional character and was still known to have participated in the revolt, sixty years earlier.[12]

At the same time, we know next to nothing about their role in that revolt. How did they enter the rebellion, as followers of Mattathias or as initiators?[13] And what happened in 161 BCE around the coup of Alcimus? Were they unprofessional naives, or pragmatic peace negotiators, or did Judas push his rebellion?[14] It will remain unclear.

---

[12] 250 years after the events the situation has changed. Josephus was in no way interested in the Asidaioi and banned them from history (*De bello Judaico* 1:37; *Antiquitates Judaicae* 12:272 and 275; cf. Kampen, *The Hasideans*, 55–56).

[13] V. Tcherikover, *Hellenistic Civilization and the Jews*, Philadelphia PA 1959, among others, views 'the Hasidim-scribes as the initiators and leaders of the forces of national resistance who rose up against the decrees of Antiochus IV' (Kampen, *The Hasideans*, 117).

[14] Kampen, *The Hasideans*, views the Asidaioi both as pragmatics (121–122: 'Both verses [1 Macc. 7:12–13] reflect a pragmatic response to the fact that Bacchides and Alcimus were marching into Judah with a large force and that Judah Maccabee refused to talk peace terms with them'), and as naives (128–130). A rather different story is

After this evaluation of the story plot and of some motives and biases of the writer, we will now concentrate on the description of the Asidaioi in 1 Maccabees 2:42 and 7:12–13. The first text runs as follows:

| | |
|---|---|
| συναγωγὴ Ἀσιδαίων | קהל חסידים |
| ἰσχυροὶ δυνάμει ἀπὸ Ἰσραηλ | גברי חיל מישראל |
| πᾶς ὁ ἑκουσιαζόμενοσ τῷ νόμῳ | כל המתנדב לתורה |

The translation of קהל חסידים by συναγωγὴ Ἀσιδαίων, 'a community of Asidaioi', may well have been a misunderstanding, according to some scholars.[15] It should have been συναγωγὴ ὁσίων, 'a group of pious people'. But the translation is correct. The next section, about Psalm 149, will show that the Hebrew phrase does not have a general meaning. The word קהל refers to 'a religious congregation or community' and חסידים is a name in this phrase (and in Ps. 149:5).

Some aspects of the text of 1 Maccabees 2 point in the same direction. The author would have introduced 'a miscellaneous group of pious individuals' in a rather different way. The introductions in verses 29 and 43 use πολλοὶ and πάντες instead of συναγωγή. Moreover, if קהל / συναγωγὴ would mean 'a miscellaneous group', why would the author / translator have individualised this קהל / συναγωγὴ in a clause with כל ה־ / πᾶσ ὁ?! Further, why would the writer have introduced his mighty warriors as 'a miscellaneous group of pious individuals'? Nobody would have missed such a phrase. Besides, חסיד, 'pious', is not a Maccabean word, and the writer may have borrowed the phrase קהל חסידים from Psalm 149:1 or some other source (oral history?). Finally, why would the author have taken the trouble to write an exit-story for some individuals?

The words ἐκκλησία and συναγωγὴ—LXX translations of עדה and קהל—are used in 1 Maccabees, among other things, to signify a distinct group within Israel who have some common bond or purpose, a

---

told by K.-D. Schunck, 'Der Makkabäeraufstand—Entstehung, Verlauf, Bedeutung', in: H.M. Niemann, M. Augustin (eds), *Altes Testament und Heiliges Land* (BEATAJ, 50), Frankfurt am Main 2002, 73–79 (Gastvorlesung Oldenburg 1994), esp. 76: 'das ursprüngliche Ziel des Makkabäeraufstand [war] eigentlich erreicht (...) Doch Judas und seine Anhänger beschlossen, den Kampf fortzuführen.'

B. Nongbri, 'The Motivations of the Maccabees and Judean Rhetoric of Ancestral Tradition', in: C. Bakhos (ed.), *Ancient Judaism in its Hellenistic Context* (Sup JSJ, 95), Leiden 2005, 85–111, gives a new analysis of the motivations of the Maccabees from the perspective of their rhetorics.

[15] See the Introduction.

'company' or 'congregation'.[16] The words have a religious flavor, express-
ing that the designated groups are religiously inspired or together for
religious purposes. The religious inspiration has been made explicit in
1 Maccabees 2:42 (συναγωγὴ Ασιδαίων) and is implicit in 3:13 (ἐκκ-
λησίαν πιστῶν). The company in 3:44 (συναγωγὴ) is together to prepare
itself for war, according to cultic usages (vv. 44–54). The company in 7:12
(συναγωγὴ γραμματέων) could be an arbitrary group, but the occupation of these scribes is a religious one. We may conclude that the Asidaioi
are a well defined group, religiously inspired.

Since Julius Wellhausen interpreted the second phrase, ἰσχυροὶ δυνάμει ἀπὸ Ισραηλ, as 'leading citizens in Israel' (1874),[17] there exists a stale-
mate. One half of the scholarly world, traditionally the Germans, will follow Wellhausen, the other half, especially the Dominicans, like Roland de
Vaux, and his fellow French, will read 'brave warriors'.[18] At the moment,
John Kampen is the advocate of the 'leading citizens'.[19] I will follow his
argument and then reject it.

Kampen's analysis of the phrase ἰσχυροὶ δυνάμει does not lead to an
obvious conclusion:

> It is not clear to this writer that the use of the term in 1 Macc. 2:42 should
> be limited to the military definition. ( . . . ) It may be that 'leading citizens' is
> as appropriate a translation as 'mighty warriors'. As noted by Kosmala, the
> use of this phrase is diverse enough that its meaning must be determined
> from the immediate context.[20]

After a discussion of the phrase that follows ἰσχυροὶ δυνάμει in the text,
'each one willingly devoted to the law', Kampen admits that 'most of the
other places where this phrase [ἰσχυροὶ δυνάμει] appears in the work do
suggest the military definition.' He then continues:

> In these cases, however, the context is clearly a military one. With regard to
> v. 42, we already demonstrated that it is constructed in such a manner as to
> contrast the Hasideans who are 'devoted to the law' with the lawless and the
> sinners who go against the law in chapter 1. In this case, the significance of
> this verse could well be that there were 'leading citizens devoted to the law'

---

[16] Cf. Kampen, *The Hasideans*, 81–87.

[17] According to J.T. Nelis, *1 Makkabeeën* (BOT, 6), Roermond 1972, 84: J. Wellhausen,
*Die Pharisäer und die Sadducäer: Eine Untersuchung zur inneren jüdischen Geschichte*,
Greifswald 1874, 82. See *HAL* 299.

[18] R. de Vaux, *Ancient Israel. Volume 1: Social Institutions*, New York 1965, 70.

[19] Kampen, *The Hasideans*, 95–107, 113–114 and 121.

[20] Kampen, *The Hasideans*, 107. He refers to H. Kosmala, 'Gabar', in: *TDOT* 2:373–377
(374).

who supported the Maccabean efforts. (...) While we should not totally exclude the military component from this definition, we also need not make it the exclusive meaning of the term.[21]

In a last step, Kampen identifies the Asidaioi with the scribes of 1 Maccabees 7:12 and reads πρῶτοι in 7:13 as meaning 'leading citizens', which closes his argument: 'The Hasideans according to 1 Maccabees were scribes who were leading citizens'.[22]

I will take some time to criticize Kampen's analysis because it has been accepted by many (e.g. Rainer Albertz).[23] The argument that the meaning of πρῶτοι in 1 Maccabees 7:13 should define the meaning of ἰσχυροὶ δυνάμει in 2:42, is a strange one. Why then did the writer use another word?

The second comment is about the context. In a way, Kampen states that the context of 1 Maccabees 2:42 is *not* a military one, the real context being the first chapter and not the second, but even if this is correct concerning the phrase 'each one willingly devoted to the law', what does that say about the context of the other phrase, ἰσχυροὶ δυνάμει ἀπὸ Ισραηλ? The context of 2:42 is, of course, 'clearly a military one'. Verses 15–28 tell us about the violent revolt of Mattathias, and in verses 29–41 he and his comrades take the 'halachic' decision to defend themselves on Sabbath, after a cruel and massive slaughter on that day. Verses 42 and 43, which report that the Asidaioi and many refugees joined Mattathias, are the introduction to a passage in which a guerilla army is formed and has its violent successes (vv. 44–48).

Thirdly, Kampen confuses meaning and reference. The meaning of the phrase ἰσχυροὶ δυνάμει is by definition 'mighty warriors' or the like, but in a non-military context it may refer to rich people or leaders. In a military context this metaphorical use is not the most natural.

Finally, the writer of the book tries to traditionalize the Maccabees by comparing them with the heros of the past and by alluding to biblical texts and traditions.[24] The phrase ἰσχυροὶ δυνάμει may be used as an allusion to ancient times, especially to that of David. We may conclude

---

[21] Kampen, *The Hasideans*, 113–114.

[22] Kampen, *The Hasideans*, 120–121.

[23] R. Albertz, *Religionsgeschichte Israels in alttestamentlicher Zeit. Teil 2: Vom Exil bis zu den Makkabäern* (GAT, 8/2), Göttingen 1992, 598.

[24] According to Lichtenberger, 'History-writing', 100–102, 1 Maccabees 'draws on biblical historiography', 'describes the reign [of the first generation of Hasmoneans] by means of a biblical typology' (see S. von Dobbeler, *Die Bücher 1/2 Makkabäer* [NSK, AT 11], Stuttgart 1997, 44–46), contains 'numerous allusions (...) to and citations of biblical

that the writer presents the Asidaioi as mighty warriors, which clearly has a military connotation in the given context and may allude to the elite troops of David.

At the end of this discussion—there is no need for a comment on the third phrase, πᾶς ὁ ἑκουσιαζόμενοσ τῷ νόμῳ—we arrive at an interesting question. If the writer is using the Asidaioi to legitimate Mattathias's choice to rise in revolt, how can he be trusted in his description of the community? Did he create a militant identity, ἰσχυροὶ δυνάμει ἀπὸ Ισραηλ, to legitimate Judas Maccabeus's militancy (1 Macc. 2:66: ἰσχυρὸς δυνάμει)? And did he choose the clause πᾶς ὁ ἑκουσιαζόμενος τῷ νόμῳ to draw a parallel with Mattathias's zeal for the Torah (1 Macc. 2:27: πᾶς ὁ ζηλῶν τῷ νόμῳ; 2:26–27, 50, 54, 58, 64)? Did he create his Asidaioi in the image of the Maccabees, after their likeness? Or is it conceivable that the spirituality and practical choices of the Asidaioi actually parallelled those of Mattathias? Not every detail is in favour of the new creation. Why did the writer use the word ἑκουσιαζόμενοσ if he elsewhere chose the word ζηλῶν? And, of course, there is a parallel between the militancy of the Asidaioi and that of Judas, but the writer had been better drawing a parallel between the Asidaioi and Matthatias. These details may suggest that, in his choice of words, the writer largely kept to the self-definition of the Asidaioi and the way they were known.[25]

We will now turn to the second description of the Asidaioi, in 1 Maccabees 7:12–13: 'A group of scribes, however, gathered about Alcimus and Bacchides to ask for a just agreement. The Hasideans were the first among the Israelites to seek peace with them' (NAB). How do the Asidaioi relate to the scribes? Are both groups identical, or are the Asidaioi part of a larger group of scribes, or do they not relate at all? One could, of course, consider the sequence of verses 12 and 13 to be clumsy writing and try

tradition' (a 'royal typology'), and incorporates interpretative poetic insertions, linking the book with biblical traditions (see G.O. Neuhaus, *Studien zu den poetischen Stücken im 1. Makkabäerbuch* [FzB, 12], Würzburg 1974).

[25] Maybe a through analysis of 1 Maccabees 2 will throw more light on this question. Cf. O. Keel, '1 Makk 2—Rechtfertigung, Programm und Denkmal für die Erhebung der Hasmonäer: Eine Skizze', in: O. Keel, U. Staub, *Hellenismus und Judentum: Vier Studien zu Daniel 7 und zur Religionsnot unter Antiochus IV.* (OBO, 178), Freiburg 2000, 123–133; Th. Hieke, 'The Role of "Scripture" in the Last Words of Mattathias (1 Macc 2:49–70)', in: G.G. Xeravits, J. Zsengellér (eds), *The Books of the Maccabees: History, Theology, Ideology* (Sup JSJ, 118), Leiden 2007, 61–74; F.V. Reiterer, 'Die Vergangenheit als Basis für die Zukunft Mattatias' Lehre für seine Söhne aus der Geschichte in 1 Makk 2:52–60', in: Xeravits, Zsengellér, *The Books of the Maccabees*, 75–100.

to find an original text,[26] but if one accepts the given text, one must take two facts into account:

1. The writer repeats words from 1 Maccabees 2:42 in verse 12:

2:42 συνήχθησαν πρὸσ            (...) συναγωγὴ Ασιδαίων
7:12 ἐπισυνήχθησαν πρὸσ         (...) συναγωγὴ γραμματέων

2. The verses 12 and 13 are parallel to a certain degree:[27]

| 12 | 13 |
|---|---|
| A congregation of scribes | The Asidaioi |
| gathered about Alcimus and Bacchides | were leaders among the Israelites |
| to ask for just terms (ἐκζητῆσαι δίκαια) | and they were seeking peace from them (ἐπεζήτουν [...] εἰρήνην) |

The repetition from 1 Maccabees 2:42 draws a parallel between both congregations, equating the Asidaioi and the scribes. Within the parallelism of 1 Maccabees 7:12 and 13, the second verse elaborates the first, in renominalising the actors and defining the status of the peace negotiators. Both groups are one and the same.

May we trust the writer in this exit-story? Didn't he equate the Asidaioi and the scribes to disqualify the Asidaioi as warriors? Didn't he observe—in the traditional interpretation of πρῶτοι—that they were the first to start peace talks, and didn't he finish them off as the martyrs of Psalm 79? Could there be a more efficient way of removing them from the story?! There are some problems with this deconstruction. The first argument could say more about the self image of the author of this contribution than about the Judean world of the second century BCE ... The third reading is probably too cynical. Certainly, the writer characterizes the Asidaioi as naive, but his use of Psalm 79 will be based on an already known application of that psalm to the massacre of 161 BCE. He did not invent it.[28]

---

[26] E.g. Nodet, 'Asidaioi and Essenes', 77–79.

[27] I adopt the reading of verse 13 by Kampen, The Hasideans, 118–120. He reads πρῶτοι in 7:13 as meaning 'leading citizens among the Israelites'—elsewhere it is read as 'the first' among the Israelites'. In fact, more details of my argument about verse 13 have been provided by his book (115–122).

[28] Van der Kooij, 'Septuagint of Psalms', 232–238, offers a detailed study of the relation between the Hebrew version of Psalm 79, its Greek version, and the quote in 1 Macc. 7.

The result of our inquiry in 1 Maccabees may be summarized: The Asidaioi were a religiously motivated group of scribes, known for their piety. They were voluntarily devoted to the law and were known as mighty warriors. They participated in the revolt against the Hellenists and the Seleucids, at least until the confrontation with Alcimus in 161 BCE.

## 4. Psalm 149: A Two-edged Sword

Having read two sources that speak about the Hasidim, we will now analyse a spiritual text of the Hasidim themselves, Psalm 149. The psalm is written between 200 and 175 BCE. Dating psalms can only be hypothetical and the proposed date is based on two presuppositions, the date and the character of the final redaction of the Book of Psalms. The *terminus ad quem* for this redaction is 175 BCE. The defilement of the temple and the Maccabean war are reflected nowhere in the Psalter. The *terminus post quem* is difficult to determine, but the final redaction will have taken place in the Hellenistic period. Because I suppose anti-Hellenistic sentiments in Psalms 137–145, possibly an earlier stage in the development of the proto-Masoretic Psalter, I prefer a rather late date for the final redaction, somewhere between 200 and 175 BCE, the time of Ben Sira.[29] Psalm 149, written to be a part of Psalms 146–150,[30] belongs to this final redaction.

Psalm 149 consists of two parts, a hymn (vv. 1–4) and a victory song (vv. 5–9).[31] The subject of praise and, later, of the victory song is 'the congregation of the pious'. What does the psalm say about this קהל חסידים? First of all, are these חסידים 'the pious' in general or a well defined group, 'the Pious', *casu quo* 'the Hasidim'? The phrase קהל חסידים

---

[29] The period Hossfeld and Zenger propose is far too broad: 'Die Datierung dieser Redaktion ist zwischen 200 und 150 v.Chr., im Kontext des antiseleukidischen Kampfes, vorstellbar; sie könnte aber auch bereits im 3. Jh. stattgefunden haben' (F.-L. Hossfeld, E. Zenger, *Psalmen 101–150* (HTKAT), Freiburg 2008, 26).

[30] Hossfeld, Zenger, *Psalmen 101–150*, 861.

[31] The second half of Ps. 149 is a victory song. Vv. 5–6 look like a hymnic call to praise but in fact are a call to celebrate victory (compare the hymnic call to praise in vv. 1–3). The song has a virtual character: the victory has not yet taken place, but the psalm celebrates it *as if* it has taken place already. In this way, history and eschatology meet. Both are considered separarely in the discussion about the genre of the psalm (cf. the commentaries, e.g. L.C. Allen, *Psalms 101–150* [WBC, 21], Waco TX 1983, 319–320 and J.P.M. van der Ploeg, *Psalmen, Deel II: Psalm 76 t/m 150* [BOT, 7b], Roermond, 1974, 502–503).

is unique in the Old Testament and not in conformity with the use of
קהל in the Psalms. The community which comes together in the temple to
praise God, is called קהל as such, or קהל רב, or קהל עם, 'the congregation',
'the great congregation', or 'the congregation of the people'.[32] The cultic
community in the Psalms is the whole people, whereas the phrase קהל
חסידים confines it to a part of that people. Such a limitation is only
conceivable if the separate part has a clear identity. The phrase קהל חסידים
refers to a well defined group, 'the congregation of the Pious'. The use of
the word חסידים is as remarkable as that of קהל. Elsewhere in the Old
Testament the 'pious' are always related to another person, so that the
plural noun has a suffix, 'my', 'your', 'his' and 'her' pious.[33] This suffix is
missing only in Psalm 149, in the phrase קהל חסידים but also in the subject
חסידים of verse 5. This does not mean, of course, that the pious of Psalm
149 are less defined than the pious elsewhere. The noun חסידים in Psalm
149 can do without a suffix, because it is used as an 'intrinsically definite
noun', i.e. a name.[34] We may conclude from these idiomatic and syntactic
observations that the חסידים of Psalm 149 are a well defined group known
by that name.

| verses | beginning | end | middle |
|--------|-----------|-----|--------|
| 1 | קהל חסידים | | |
| 2a | | | ישראל + עשיו |
| 2b | | | בני־ציון + מלכם |
| 4a | | | יהוה + עמו |
| 4b | | ענוים | |
| 5a | חסידים | | |
| 9b | | כל־חסידיו | |

Who are these Hasidim according to the psalm? The text reveals their sectarian identity, their militancy and their messianic ideology. We have the
special character of this song to thank for these revelations. Rather than
just praising God the psalm presents their self-definition. The Hasidim
are found throughout the psalm. Their name is at the beginning of

---

[32] קהל: Ps. 22:23; קהל רב: Pss. 22:26; 35:18; 40:10.11; קהל עם: Ps. 107:32. The heavenly
congregation is called קהל קדשים: Ps. 89:6.

[33] חסידי: Ps. 50:5; חסידיך: Pss. 52:11; 79:2; 89:20; 132:9; 145:10; 2 Chron. 6:41; חסידיו:
1 Sam. 2:9; Pss. 30:5; 31:24; 37:28; 85:9; 97:10; 116:15; 148:14; 149:9; Prov. 2:8; חסידיה:
Ps. 132:16.

[34] For intrinsically definite nouns, see B.K. Waltke, M. O'Connor, *An Introduction to
Biblical Hebrew Syntax*, Winona Lake IN 1990, § 13.4b.

both parts (vv. 1, 5; see the table). At the end of both parts, they are
defined as עֲנָוִים, 'the afflicted/humble', and related to Yhwh, 'all his
pious/Hasidim', כָּל־חֲסִידָיו (vv. 4, 9). These two inclusions provide the
horizon for our interpretation. The first part of the psalm defines the
relationship between the Hasidim and ɴʜᴡʜ: Israel and its maker, the
sons of Zion and their king, and—in chiasm to close this short series—
Yhwh and his people (vv. 2a, 2b, 4a). The interpretive horizon clarifies
that these names are not extensions (from the in-group to all Judeans) but
self-definitions. The Hasidim see themselves as the pre-eminent people
of ʏʜᴡʜ. This may be a deepening of the particularism which shows itself
in the suffixes of verse 2: 'his maker' instead of 'the maker of heaven
and earth' and 'their king' instead of 'king of all the earth'. This way
of thinking meets one of the three major criteria for sectarianism: 'the
tendency to view oneself as uniquely legitimate', 'the tension with the
socio-cultural environment', and 'the tendency to establish boundaries
against another'.[35] The Hasidim of this psalm foster a sectarian identity.[36]

The militancy of the Hasidim comes up in the second part of the psalm.
The first strophe is a call to celebrate victory and the second describes the
celebrated victory.

> 5 Let the Hasidim (חֲסִידִים) exult in triumph,
>     let them shout for joy upon their couches,
> 6 with paeans to God in their throat,
>     and a two-edged sword in their hand.
>
> 7 To impose retribution upon the nations,
>     punishment upon the peoples,
> 8 to bind their kings with shackles,
>     their nobles with chains of iron,
> 9 to execute upon them the judgment written:
>     this is the glory of all his Hasidim (חֲסִידָיו).

---

[35] For a discussion of sectarianism see J. Kampen, 'The Books of the Maccabees
and Sectarianism in Second Temple Judaism', in: Xeravits, Zsengellér, *The Books of
the Maccabees*, 11–30 (19–20). For the delineated criteria, he refers to J.M. Jokiranta,
'"Sectarianism" of the Qumran "sect": Sociological Notes', *RevQ* 20 (2001), 223–239
(228–230 and 236–239).

[36] J. Blenkinsopp, 'The Development of Jewish Sectarianism from Nehemiah to the
Hasidim', in: O. Lipschits et al. (eds), *Judah and the Judeans in the Fourth Century B.C.E.*,
Winona Lake IN 2007, 385–404 (402), comments: '(...) allusion in several psalms to
'ăbādîm, ḥăsîdîm, and saddîqîm as a collectivity, as forming a qāhāl or an 'ēdâ (Ps 1:5,
89:6, 111:1, 149:1), could reflect the existence of pietistic conventicles and therefore an
incipient form of sectarianism.'

The Hasidim celebrate victory, throughout the night, with two attributes: 'with paeans to God in their throat, / and a two-edged sword in
their hand.' These unique and enigmatic expressions catch our attention
because they characterize the movement as pious and militant at the same
time. The militancy is expressed in the image of a two-edged sword, חרב
פיפיות, of which the word פיפיות may allude to the other text in the Old
Testament where it is found, Isaiah 41:15–16:

> 15  Look, I am making you into a threshing sledge,
>       a new sledge, two-edged (בעל פיפיות).
>       You will thresh the mountains and crush them,
>       the hills, you will make (them) like straw.
> 16  You will winnow them and the wind will blow them away,
>       the storm will scatter them.
>       And you, you will exult in Yhwh,
>       in the Holy One of Israel you will boast.

In this passage, Israel gets an important and aggressive role in its own
deliverance. Isaiah 41 does not specify what is symbolised by the mountains and hills,[37] but Psalm 149 does. They are the hostile nations of the
world, to be mentioned in the next verse.

The victory over the nations is described in the last strophe (vv. 7–9).
The actions are put in a series of infinitives, which are taken up by the last
colon: הדר הוא לכל חסידיו, 'this is the glory of all his Hasidim'. The strophe
is an extreme example of a classifying clause with a nominal predicate
(הדר) followed by an independent personal pronoun as a subject (הוא)
and preceded by the basic subject in casus pendens (the series of infinitives).[38] This construction gives the psalm an important ambivalence. At
first sight one is inclined to link the infinitives to what precedes, so that
the Hasidim are the subject of these actions,[39] but the last colon makes
this interpretation impossible. Nowhere is it said that the Hasidim have
subjugated the nations. In colon 4b the honor goes to God … In fact,
the ambivalence belongs to the messianic role the Hasidim have in this
psalm.

According to the third infinitive clause the victory is an execution of
a written judgment. One may look for prophetic promises,[40] but within

---

[37]  See W.A.M. Beuken, *Jesaja: Deel IIA* (POT), Nijkerk 1979, 82–84.
[38]  See for this clause type Waltke, O'Connor, *Biblical Hebrew Syntax*, § 16.3.3. Besides,
the infinitive with preposition -ל 'is found in any nominal role in a clause. In a nominative
frame, it is usually used as a subject (…)' (§ 36.2.3).
[39]  Allen, *Psalms*, 318 note 7a: 'Vv. 7–9 are loosely related to what precedes (…).'
[40]  E.g. Isa. 60:12 or the vengeance of Isa. 35:4 (referring to Isa 34).

the composition of the Book of Psalms, the written judgment is found in Psalm 2. There the nations of the world start waging war against Yhwh and his anointed. The second half of the psalm consists of a programme for subjugation of the nations by Yhwh and the king of Zion, but it is not executed. The reader lives in a time of war according to the book and he has to wait for victory until the end, the second last psalm. In the execution of the programme, the Hasidim take the role the anointed one has in Psalm 2.[41]

The Hasidim as the hymnic character and implied reader of Psalm 149 may be identified as the author-group of the psalm. They fostered a sectarian identity, a spirituality that combined piety and militancy, and a messianic ideology.

## 5. Psalm 144: The Militant Royal Servant

Psalm 144 belongs to a collection of Davidic psalms, Psalms 138–145. The psalm is written by the redactor / writer of the collection, together with Psalms 138 and 145 as well as the headings and a few verses (Pss. 140:13–14; 142:8).[42] The collection is probably part of the second last redaction, which must be dated at the end of the third century BCE. The *terminus post quem* is the date of the third last redaction, Psalms 2–136, the 'Zionspsalter',[43] somewhere in the fourth century. The *terminus ad quem* is the date of the last redaction, 200–175 BCE (see above). Because of (supposed!) anti-Hellenistic sentiments in Psalms 137–145, a date at the end of this period must be preferred.

---

[41] See my lecture 'War and Peace in the Psalms: Some Compositional Explorations', held at the ISDCL conference at Kerkrade, *"A Time for War and a Time for Peace": Visions of Peace and Tales of War in Deuterocanonical and Cognate Literature*, in July 2009. It will be published by P.C. Beentjes and J. Liesen in the Yearbook of the ISDCL (Berlin, forthcoming).

[42] See M. Leuenberger, *Konzeptionen des Königtums Gottes im Psalter: Untersuchungen zu Komposition und Redaktion der theokratischen Bücher IV–V im Psalter* (AThANT, 83), Zürich 2004, 340–345.

[43] Hossfeld, Zenger, *Psalmen 101–150*, 17–26 propose the following dates:

| 500 BCE | JHWH-König-Psalter | Pss 2–100 |
| 450 BCE | Geschichtstheologisches Psalter | Pss 2–106 |
| 400 BCE | Zionspsalter | Pss 2–136 |
| 300 BCE | Davidspsalter | Pss 1–145 |
| 200–150 BCE | *Sefer Tehillim* | Pss 1–150. |

The reason to discuss Psalm 144 in a contribution about Hasidim is not obvious. The word חסידים is found only once, in the context, hidden in a large psalm (Ps. 145:10: חסידיך). I will show that some exegetical attention pays. The headings of Psalms 138–145, all containing the phrase לדוד, interpret the main character of this collection, the first person singular, as David. He is first of all a supplicant, lamenting and praying,[44] but near the end of the collection, he gets the role of the militant royal servant of Yhwh. He blesses Yhwh, his personal trainer and helper, laments and prays for divine intervention, and confronts his enemies (Ps. 144:1–8). At that point, someone else takes over. This transformation is marked by the only textual occurrence of the name of David, i.e. apart from the headings. The new hero laments and prays for divine intervention and confronts his enemies in the same words as David (Ps. 144:9–11). At that point, a second transformation is found. A new community is born, taking over the role of servant of Yhwh. The first person singular changes to a first person plural, and that congregation is linked to David as well (Ps. 144:12–15). In the preceding psalm, David calls Yhwh 'my God' (כי אתה אלוהי) and himself 'your servant' (כי אני עבדך; Ps. 143:10, 12). The same word pair is repeated now, in chiasm, עבד and אלהים, followed by third person suffixes. David is called 'his servant' (דוד עבדו) and Yhwh is called 'his God', or better, 'its God', because now the suffix refers to the new congregation, 'the people of which Yhwh is its God' (העם שיהוה אלהיו; Ps. 144:10, 15). The double transformation shows that David is role model for a community, presenting itself in the second half of this psalm.[45] In the last psalm of the collection, this community is characterized as God's pious (Ps. 145:10), again appearing in the bosom of David. He has a new role, a cultic one, praising Yhwh in the temple. He is present as such in the first part of the psalm (a first person singular in vv. 1–2, 5–6) and at the end ('my

---

[44] This role is found, of course, in the psalms themselves, but also in the headings, which almost all refer to the headings of ancient Davidic psalms in the first part of the Psalter and to that of Psalm 102. See the detailed analysis in H.W.M. van Grol, 'David and his Chasidim: Place and Function of Psalms 138–150', in: E. Zenger (ed.), *The Composition of the Book of Psalms* (BEThL, 238), Leuven (forthcoming), and in H.W.M. van Grol, 'De David code: Psalm 138–145', in: B. Becking, A. Merz (eds), *Verhaal als Identiteits-Code* (UTR, 60), Utrecht 2008, 142–149 (143–146).

[45] For a text syntactical analysis of Ps. 144:12–15 and its embedding in the context see H.W.M. van Grol, 'De weg naar geluk: Poëzie en werkelijkheid in Psalm 144', in: B. Becking et al. (eds), *Tussen Caïro en Jeruzalem: Studies over de Bijbel en haar Context* (UTR, 53), Utrecht 2006, 31–38.

mouth', v. 21). In both instances he is accompanied by a partner subject of praise of a universalistic kind, 'one generation to another' (v. 4) and 'all flesh' (v. 21).[46] In the middle of the psalm another pair of subjects of praise is found, first, in chiasm, a universalistic one, 'all your works', and then a particularistic one, 'your pious'.[47] In the bosom of David a community appears, called by him חסידיך. They participate in his third role of cultic singer. We may conclude that within the symbolic world of this collection, the phrase 'your pious' in Psalm 145 applies to the community which is presented in the previous psalm, and which considers David as a role model, being supplicant, militant royal servant, and cultic singer.

Being interested in militancy, we will now concentrate on the second role of David, that of militant royal servant. The first part of Psalm 144 is a relecture of Psalm 18, one of the most important royal psalms. It uses the word מלך only in the plural and prefers עבד to describe David (v. 10). The royal servant is trained by Yhwh for warfare: 'Blessed be YHWH, my rock, / who trains my hands for battle, / my fingers for warfare' (v. 1), and he will be confronted with the enemy (vv. 7-8). Nevertheless, the psalm pays no attention at all to the military actions of our hero. God is the one who comes into action, 'who gives victory to kings, / who rescues his servant David' (vv. 10-11). David asks YHWH to do his divine warrior act (vv. 5-8), and blesses him for his protection: 'my loyal help and my fortress, / my stronghold and my own deliverer, / my shield and the one with whom I find shelter, / who subdues peoples beneath me' (v. 2). The psalm shows a fundamental ambivalence in the description of David's military role: he is trained and he has to stand up against the enemy, but there are no offensive actions except by God, and even the defence is in God's hands. To keep things in perspective, the David of Psalm 18 is self-confident. He is the triumphant king who thanks God for the help he received in battle (vv. 21-27). The reflection in Psalm 144:3-4 serves to underline the fundamental difference between the royal servant as human being and the mighty, superior protector-God. The psalm promotes a militant spirituality, but gives all the credits to God and refuses to give attention to human efforts.

---

[46] 'The generations' are universalistic, compare the chiasm in vv. 12-13: מלכותו + דור ודור + מלכותך // בני האדם.

[47] 'Your pious' can only be understood in a particularistic way, just like the (same!) group described in vv. 14 (introduction), 18 (call for help), and 19-20 (rescue).

The militant royal servant has a part to play in a process of deliverance. The psalms of the Davidic collection are in general individual laments, and together they describe a situation of conflict (Pss. 139–143). Psalm 144 follows with a confrontation with the enemy, which may be expected to have a happy end (vv. 10–11), so that the community of militant royal servants believes that their efforts will be rewarded with *shalom* (vv. 12–15). The collection ends with a hymn to God, which focuses on the deliverance of his pious (Ps. 145:14, 18–20). The role of the servant in this sequence of conflict, war, *shalom* and praise is to confront the enemy and to pray to YHWH for help. The Davidic collection promotes the willingness of the congregation to act in that way.

Until now we moved about in the symbolic world of the Davidic collection, but time has come to hypothesize that these psalms formulated an answer to the threat of undermining identity Hellenism posed in the third century BCE and after. This hypothesis depends on an evaluation of Psalm 137.[48] This psalm moves the reader to the Babylonian exile, which is rather curious, because the rejection of the House of David and the destruction of Jerusalem were already the theme of Book III (Ps. 89), and Book IV contained prayers for the rebuilding of Jerusalem and the return from exile (Pss. 90:15; 102:13–23; 106:47), whereas the Songs of Ascents cope with the problem of diaspora.[49] The psalm is out of place, unless its topic has a contemporary relevance. What relevance could the exile have in the Hellenistic period? In fact, the topic of the psalm is not the exile but maintaining identity in an alienating situation. The psalm shows a religious conflict that touches the integrity of the people. There is a high awareness of their own and the foreign and a firm refusal to fuse them. The conflict demands a personal choice. Their own identity and the relationship with God are at stake: 'How can we sing a song of YHWH on foreign soil (עדמת נכר)?!' Psalm 137 may be read as a parable of the struggle against Hellenism.

If Psalm 137 poses the problem, the Davidic collection following may show the way to cope with it. First of all, it elaborates the maintaining of identity. Within the laments and prayers of David the concern to find the

---

[48] See on this Psalm, B. Becking, 'Does Exile Equal Suffering? A Fresh Look at Psalm 137', in: B. Becking, D. Human (eds), *Exile and Suffering: A Selection of Papers Read at the 50th Anniversary of the Old Testament Society of South Africa* (OTS 50), Leiden 2009, pp. 183–202.

[49] For this view on the Songs of Ascents see Van Grol, 'War and Peace'.

right way, the recognition of the temptation of evil, and the necessity to keep evil and evildoers at a distance are an important motif (Pss. 139; 141; 143). This prayer book goes for integrity and strengthens the identity of its readers in their struggle with the temptation of the Hellenistic world. Secondly, it promotes a willingness to confront the enemy. The enemy has mythic proportions—they are called 'the mighty waters'—and they are alienating—they are called 'foreigners', בני נכר, referring back to Psalm 137, with its עדמת נכר.[50] David is the supplicant who fights for his own integrity and stands up against the Hellenists.

Psalm 144 decodes David—the supplicant, the militant royal servant, and the cultic singer—as a role model of a religious congregation. They are the implied reader of Psalms 137–145 and may be equated with the author-group of the Davidic redaction. They promote their spirituality in the benediction of Psalm 144 and describe themselves as YHWH's pious.[51]

## 6. Conclusion

At the end of our investigation, we may summarize and evaluate our findings. Three of our sources are essential, because they refer, independently of each other, to a group of Hasidim in a rather plain way. Their characterizations are so close that the three 'Hasidisms' may be identified as one. The table shows the common elements of Psalm 149, 2 Maccabees 14, and 1 Maccabees 2 and 7.

The Hasidim were a well-defined religious movement, characterized by piety and militancy. They were active from about 200 BCE onwards, participated in the revolt against the Jewish Hellenists and the Seleucids (167–161 BCE), and disappeared from the scene after the confrontation with Alcimus (161 BCE).

---

[50] In the Book of Psalms, the word נכר is used in Pss 18:45, 46 (בני נכר; Ps. 144 borrowed the phrase from here; in Ps. 18 the foreigners are already subjugated); 81:10 (אל נכר); 137:4 (עדמת נכר); 144:7, 11. In Sir. 36:3, the phrase עם נכר / ἔθνη ἀλλότρια is found, parallel to כל הגוים / πάντα τὰ ἔθνη in verse 2 (P.C. Beentjes (ed.), *The Book of Ben Sira in Hebrew* [Sup VT, 68], Leiden 1997, 62)—a marked singular and non-biblical phrase.

[51] You may find more details and discussion pertaining to this section in Van Grol, 'David and his Chasidim', and in Van Grol, 'De David code'.

|  |  | *Ps. 149* | *2 Macc. 14* | *1 Macc. 2; 7* |
|---|---|---|---|---|
| *date* | BCE | 200–175 | 150 > 120 | 100 |
| *genre* | spiritual text | × |  |  |
|  | history-writing |  | × | × |
| *name* | קהל חסידים & חסידים | × |  |  |
|  | Ἀσιδαῖοι |  | × |  |
|  | συναγωγὴ Ἀσιδαίων |  |  | × |
| *group* | well defined | × | × | × |
|  | religious movement | × |  | × |
| *piety* |  | × | × | × |
| *militancy* | spiritual | × |  | × |
|  | active |  | × | × |

Psalms 144–145, or more broadly the redactional unit Psalms 137–145, may not be used as a primary source, because their interpretation is heavily hypothetical, but they do confirm our findings. This text is the oldest one, probably from the last part of the third century, and shows us something of the genesis of the Hasidim. The word חסידים is not yet used as a name, but is a description of the group, placed in a central position in the final psalm. The group presents itself, in this prayer book, as a well-defined religious movement with a pious and militant spirituality. The object of their violence are the Hellenistic Judeans and / or the Hellenistic rulers.

One could challenge the independency of 1 Maccabees 2. The writer could have borrowed the phrase συναγωγὴ Ἀσιδαίων from Psalm 149:1, קהל חסידים. In fact, this is not very plausible because there are no other allusions to or quotations from Psalm 149. Besides, stressing the dependency of 1 Maccabees 2 would strengthen our thesis that Psalm 149 refers to the same group as 1 and 2 Maccabees!

Around this core of findings, confirmed by our three or four independent sources, there is a circle of important details that are found only once, in one of these sources. The Hasidim were originally a group of scribes (1 Macc. 7); the Torah played an essential part in their spirituality (1 Macc. 2); their eschatology implied the subjection of the nations and a messianic role for themselves (Psalm 149). These details may only be accepted if they fit into a larger and intelligent construct.

I will not provide this construct or these constructs here, but I will close with some stimulating thoughts. 1 Maccabees 2:42 says that the Asidaioi were 'willingly devoted to the law', πᾶς ὁ ἑκουσιαζόμενοσ τῷ νόμῳ, ‎כל המתנדב לתורה‎. In the Davidic / Hasidic prayer book, Psalms 137–145, the Torah is not mentioned at all, as well as in Psalm 149. This does not mean that it was a non-item in the original movement of the Hasidim. Within the Closing Hallel, belonging as a whole to the Hasidic redaction of the Psalter, the Torah is the climax of Psalm 147:

> 19 He declares his word to Jacob,
>    his laws and rules to Israel.
> 20 He has not done this for any of the nations,
>    of such rules they know nothing.

According to this text, the Law is special and is defining the identity of Israel. This is, of course, the foundation of any zeal for the Torah, but the formulation of 1 Maccabees 2 supposes increased tensions. One could think especially of the Seleucid ban on keeping the fundamental laws of Torah: Sabbath, circumcision and *kashrut* laws.

The Hasidim of Psalm 149 thought to play the leading part in the eschatological subjugation of the nations. According to Schultz, the es-chatological war of the War Scroll (1QMilhama) has two stages, 'the day of their war against the Kittim' and 'the war of the divisions'. The first war will bring freedom and peace to Jerusalem, in the second one the twelve tribes will conquer the entire world. This two-staged eschatological war may be compared to the sequence of the two wars of Psalms 144 and 149. The first one will bring about full *shalom* in Jerusalem and Judah: beau-tiful offspring, exuberant prosperity and peace in the streets (vv. 12–15). One may compare Psalm 147:12–14, which presents peace as realised, with the same three motifs. The second war will lead to the subjugation of the nations, and thereby to universal peace.[52] The similarity between both sequences asks for further explorations, especially because there are still other textual parallels from the Second Temple Period.[53]

According to 1 Maccabees 7, the Hasidim were scribes. We may find some confirmation in Psalms 144–145 and 149. The Hasidim are not only the hymnic character of Psalm 149 but evidently the author-group as well. The same applies to Psalms 144–145: the first person community

---

[52] More about this theme in the Psalter, seen from a composition critical perspective: Van Grol, 'War and Peace'.

[53] B. Schultz, *Conquering the World: The War Scroll (1QM) Reconsidered* (STDJ 76), Leiden 2009, 236–239 and 391–402. J.J. Collins, 'Messianism in the Maccabean Period', in: J. Neusner et al. (eds), *Judaisms and Their Messiahs at the Turn of the Christian Era*, Cambridge 1987, 97–109, states 'that messianism was neither widespread nor prominent in this period' (106) and that 1 and 2 Maccabees did not see the Hasmoneans in an eschatological way (104).

of Psalm 144 is called 'your pious', the hymnic character of Psalm 145. These observations could lead to a larger construct in which the Hasidim are seen as the redactors / writers of the closing Hallel, Psalms 146–150, and, in an earlier stage, of the Davidic prayer book, Psalms 137–145. The redactional activity of the Hasidim in the Book of Psalms deserves more attention.

The attribution of other books to the Hasidim is of a more speculative nature. Within the all-inclusive construct of Albertz in his *Religionsgeschichte*, the Hasidim are the authors of apocalyptic literature, 1 Enoch 85–90 as well as Daniel 1 and 8–12.[54] However, because the Hasidim are the only scribes of their time known by name, one will be inclined to suggest further activities.[55] And then there may come a time that a new Lester Grabbe will stand up preaching in the wilderness of Judaea: 'We know next to nothing about them!'

---

[54] Albertz, *Religionsgeschichte*, 598–604 and 664–665; a more recent discussion in R. Albertz, 'The Social Setting of the Aramaic and Hebrew Book of Daniel', in: J.J. Collins et al. (eds), *The Book of Daniel: Composition and Reception* (Sup VT, 83,1; Formation and Interpretation of Old Testament Literature, 2,1), Leiden 2001, 171–204.

[55] Interesting proposals are found in R. Gmirkin, 'The War Scroll, the Hasidim, and the Maccabean Conflict', in: L.H. Schiffman et al. (eds), *The Dead Sea Scrolls: Fifty Years after their Discovery: Proceedings of the Jerusalem Congress 1997*, Jerusalem 2000, 486–496.

# THE OLD TESTAMENT AS A DIACHRONIC CORPUS

Marinus Koster
*Bathmen*

## 1. Introduction

In this year of commemoration of Charles Darwin the extremes tend to get special attention. Apparently, all evolutionists are to be considered atheists and all Christians are supposed to believe literally in the creation of heaven and earth in six days. Speaking for myself—and, I hope, for most of us—the truth may lay somewhere in between these extremes.

In the same way there are two extremist views as to the value and significance of the Old Testament. On the one hand it is considered God's own infallible Word, which has come down to us as a kind of brick from heaven, outside history as it were, without being contaminated by the literature, history, culture and religion of Israel's neighbouring 'heathen' peoples. On the other extreme it is considered to be without any (or only little) historical value, because it was the product of religious fantasy and was conceived only in a very late time, somewhere at the end of the Persian period or, preferably, still later.

In this case, too, my preference goes to the way in between: the Old Testament is for me the result of a historical process, which has gone on for centuries, of Israel's coming to terms with its religious beliefs, in constant and fruitful interaction with its neighbours on all sides.[1] As to this historical process, our Joint Meeting of 1994 in Kampen has given a balanced insight on both the synchronic and the diachronic positions, with the inevitable conclusion that the one as well as the other has its own merits.[2] Though I am choosing here the diachronic option, as will be clear already from the title of my paper, this does not mean that I would deny

---

[1] Cf. Rainer Albertz, *Religionsgeschichte Israels in alttestamentlicher Zeit* (2 Bde; GAT, 8), Göttingen [2]1996–1997 (in particular 'Vorwort', 6); English translation: *A History of Israelite Religion in the Old Testament Period* (2 vols; OTL), Louisville (KY) 1994.

[2] Johannes C. de Moor (ed.), *Synchronic or Diachronic? A Debate on Method in Old Testament Exegesis* (OTS, 34), Leiden 1995.

the importance of the synchronic approach or that I would not be open to the new insights which it has brought about.

My intention is to give an overview of some diachronic features of each of the main sections and subsections of TeNaKh, including, if possible, connections with the heritage of the neighbouring cultures. As I am happily aware of my lack of sufficient knowledge, in particular of the more recent publications on these subjects, I am proceeding here in a way like the proverbial 'fool rushing in where angels fear to tread'.[3]

## 2. Case Studies

### 2.1. *Primeval Stories*

To begin with the beginning: *creation stories* have been known from peoples all over the world, inclusive of Israel's neighbours. Our Bible has preserved two of them, both of supreme quality and—as far as I know—unparalleled in world literature. Generally speaking, I am an adherent of the traditional diachronic scheme of the four sources (the Documentary Hypothesis), if only because otherwise one would have to invent something similar in order to explain the various phenomena covered by it. In that view the first creation story, using אלהים, is the later one (P), which was added before the older, Yahwistic one (J; with added אלהים).[4] As it seems, there are no direct parallels from the literature

---

[3] To fill in this gap I made extensive use of Lester L. Grabbe, *Ancient Israel: What Do We Know and How Do We Know It?*, London/New York 2007, which proved to be an invaluable guide. For a more detailed discussion of relevant literature up till the end of the last century, see M.D. Koster, 'The Historicity of the Bible: Its Relevance and its Limitations in the Light of Near Eastern Archaeology—From Catalyst to Cataclysm', in: Johannes C. de Moor, Harry F. van Rooy, (eds) *Past, Present, Future: The Deuteronomistic History and the Prophets* (OTS, 44), Leiden 2000, 120–149 (Discussion of the views of Niels Peter Lemche, Thomas L. Thompson, and [in a Postscript] Philip R. Davies).

[4] So also Claus Westermann in his monumental commentary, *Genesis* (BK, 1/1 [Gen. 1–11]), Neukirchen-Vluyn 1974 (⁴1999), 271 ('... dass wir dies [addition of אלהים] statt dem Verfasser einem Redaktor zuschreiben'. N.B. the observation at the previous page that the combination יהוה אלהים occurs only once elsewhere [Exod. 9:30] holds good for the Pentateuch only; it is also to be found e.g. 2 Sam. 7:25, Jon. 4:6, Ps. 72:18, 84:12, etc., cf. *THAT*, 1, 164 [W.H. Schmidt]). In the years I was engaged with Syriac manuscripts I came across ms 13a1, which only gives parts of the text of the Peshitta, thus forming a kind of shortened edition of the Old Testament. A much later hand had begun to add the missing parts of the text in the margin, but abandoned this rather cumbersome task after having supplemented the text in a number of books (Cf. M.D. Koster, *The Peshitta of Exodus: The Development of its Text in the Course of Fifteen Centuries* [SSN, 17], Assen/Amsterdam

of the *Umwelt* for these stories as a whole.[5] However, just as in the epic of Gilgamesh, the serpent plays a role in the story of Genesis 2–3, albeit a different one; and there is the striking, almost literal agreement of the serpent's statement to the woman (Eve) with that of the hetaera to Enkidu, both arguing that 'You will be like God'.[6] The well-known agreements between the *biblical flood story* and the eleventh tablet of the Gilgamesh epic (and its Sumerian predecessor) are of a quite different order: unlike the biblical creation myths, it is firmly rooted in the literary tradition of its *Umwelt*.

### 2.2. *Israelite Law*

Leaving out the narratives of the patriarchs, as well as Moses's life-story, mentioning only in passing the similarity between the episode of Joseph and Potiphar's wife and the Egyptian tale of Anpu (Anubis) and Bata,[7] and that between Moses's birth-story and that of Sargon (and of Cyrus),[8] I am coming now to the different stages of *Israelite law* which are to be found in the Pentateuch. The first one, the Book of the Covenant (Exodus 21–23), is renowned for its analogy with Hammurabi's law, both in its general casuistic framework, and in details, like the use of the term חפשי

---

1977, 17–18). Could it likewise originally have been the intention of the (hypothetical) redactor to add אלהים after יהוה everywhere, but did he stop after having added it to יהוה in Gen. 2 and 3?

[5] To be sure, there are a great number of agreements with the Egyptian and Babylonian creation stories as to details, cf. Westermann, *Genesis*, 26–65; in particular the Atramchasis epos contains many parallels (*ibidem*, 95–97 [Nachtrag]). In the discussion following my paper Prof. Lambert pointed to the possibility of taking the first sentence of the Old Testament as a subordinate clause: 'In the beginning, as God created the heaven and the earth, the earth was ...', which brings it nearer to the opening lines of *Enuma Elish*: 'When up there the heaven had not yet got its name', etc. But, with Westermann, I prefer to see Gen. 1:1 as a main clause: the superscription of the whole chapter, which as such has no parallel in other creation myths (Westermann, *Genesis*, 131, 135).

[6] Gen. 3:5; Gilgamesh epos, 1, 4, 34; 2, 2, 15. It was also Enkidu, who had been created from clay, in the image of Anu (Gilgamesh epos 1, 2, 33–34; cf. Gen. 2:7, 1:26–27; Westermann, *Genesis*, 52).

[7] To be dated ca. 1215 BCE, cf. Donald B. Redford, *A Study of the Biblical Story of Joseph* (VTSuppl, 20), Leiden 1970, 93.

[8] For a captivating reconstruction of a possible historical Moses (Beya, the tutor of young Siptah), see Johannes C. de Moor, *The Rise of Yahwism: The Roots of Israelite Monotheism* (BEThL, 91B), Leuven ²1997. Not less compelling is John Van Seters's presentation of the Yahwist's effort to (re)construct the (hi)story of Moses in his *The Life of Moses: The Yahwist as Historian in Exodus-Numbers* (CBET, 10), Kampen / Louisville (KY) 1994.

(= Akkadian *ḫupšu*), and in shared subjects, like the liberation of slaves, hurting a pregnant woman during a quarrel and the goring ox. Some of these laws return in the later composition of Deuteronomy (such as the liberation of slaves); but in particular the *festival laws* show a fourfold development which leaves no doubt as to the diachronic nature of the composition of the Pentateuch. That of Exodus 23:14–19 is presented again, in a somewhat extended form, in Exodus 34:18–26. They were rewritten and, again, expanded in Deuteronomy 16, whereas their latest, far longer version was inserted in Leviticus (Lev. 23; P).

### 2.3. Numbers 20–24: Balaam; D, P

Another part of the Pentateuch which in my view seems to point to a much older *Vorgeschichte* are the chapters Numbers 20–24.[9] Numbers 20 starts with a second version of the story of Moses pouring water from the rock, as already known from Exodus 17, which gave birth to the legend of the 'following rock'.[10] In the next chapter (Num. 21), three songs are given, those about the river Arnon (vv. 14–15: '... and the valleys of the Arnon') and the well Beer (vv. 17–18: 'Spring up, O well!—Sing to it'), as well as the ballad singers' song on Heshbon and Moab (vv. 27–29: 'Come to Heshbon, let it be built'). The first one explicitly mentions its source: the 'Book of the Wars of the YHWH' (v. 14); probably, the second one came from the same source.[11] The third

---

[9] Cf. Horst Seebass, *Numeri* (BK, 4/2 [Num. 10:11–22:1] and 4/3 [Num. 22:2–36:13]), Neukirchen-Vluyn 2003 and 2007 respectively; H. Jagersma, *Numeri* 2 (POT [Num. 16:1–24:25]), Nijkerk 1988.

[10] Cf. E. Earle Ellis, *Paul's Use of the Old Testament*, Edinburgh/London 1957, 66–70: 'The Following Rock' (in connection with 1 Corinthians 10:4).

[11] Otherwise Seebass, *Numeri*, 4/2, 342: 'Zum Buch der Kriege Jahwes gehört es nicht' (no argumentation). In Seebass's opininion, the mention of 'The Book of the Wars of YHWH' is too isolated to permit any judgment on it (*ibid.*, 340); the songs in vv. 10–20 offer no clue as to its date, although the proposed emendation of v. 14 into a theophany of YHWH would give it considerable age (*ibid.*, 338). Jagersma states as a *communis opinio* that 'The Book of the Wars of YHWH' is the title of a book now lost; vv. 14–15b could have been written in a dialect, vv. 17b–18a form a profane song, perhaps of non-Israelite origin (*Numeri* 2, 92, 94). Van Seters mentions Num. 21:14 only once, in his Introduction, in connection with Hugo Gressmann's theory on the collections of early songs (as endorsed above by me), but in his view the distinctions made by Gunkel and Gressmann do not apply to literary works of antiquity (*Life of Moses*, 4–5, cf. n. 10[!] and p. 166). His own book is 'not a historical investigation but a literary study of the Moses tradition', though it 'will not give grounds for any optimism in such an endeavor' (i.e. a quest for the historical Moses; *ibid.*, 3–4). Num. 21:16–20 have been classified, together with vv. 10–11, as 'some

one is more vague as to its background, but the reference to the 'ballad singers' also seems to indicate an older source.[12]

Finally, new light has been thrown upon the oracles of *Balaam, the son of Be'or* in chapters 22–24 by the discovery by Henk Franken and his team of the Balaam inscription during their excavations at Deir 'Alla.[13] Here, with *bl'm brb'r*, we have the earliest individual of the Bible who is mentioned in extra-biblical literature. Balaam is presented as a seer of gods (*'š ḥzh 'lhn*), that is: with the ancient title of a prophet.[14] In Numbers (24:3.15) Balaam is called 'the man with the opened eye' (if this is the correct translation of הַגֶּבֶר שְׁתֻם הָעַיִן), and further on '(with) uncovered eyes' (גְּלוּי עֵינָיִם); his prophecy is called 'the oracle of him who hears the words of God, and knows the knowledge of the Most High (עֶלְיוֹן), who sees the vision of the Almighty (שַׁדַּי)'[15] The latter title of the god(s), *šadday*, is also found (in the plural) in the Deir 'Alla text (*šdyn*, I,8).[16] Moreover, there is the interesting parallel between Balaam's rising in the morning after God / the gods had come and spoken to him at night in Numbers 22:8–13.19–21 (... וַיֹּאמֶר [לַיְלָה] אֶל־בִּלְעָם אֱלֹהִים וַיָּבֹא וַיָּקָם בִּלְעָם בַּבֹּקֶר) and in the Deir 'Alla text (*[h']wy'tw.'lwh.'lhn.blyl*h, I,1 ... *wyqm.bl'm.mn.mḥr*, I,5). Thus both texts seem to testify to the same literary tradition. Opinions as to dating the Balaam chapters are at considerable variance with each other; much may be of later composition and there is the legendary feature of the talking ass.[17] But the

---

late erudite expansions' (*ibid.*, 163, cf. 160, where also Num. 21:15 has been mentioned; page 158 deals with Num. 20:14 and 21:4, not with 21:14 [as indicated in the Scripture Index, 500]).

[12] The parallel of this song in Jer. 48:45–46, however, where it forms an integral part of a much longer taunt song in the form of a dirge, has brought Jagersma (*Numeri 2*, 104) and Van Seters (*Life of Moses*, 398–402) to date it in the time of Jeremiah, whereas Seebasss (*Numeri*, 4/2, 359–360; with H-C. Schmitt) sees the relationship the other way round and dates it in the 8th or 7th century BC (see also K.A.D. Smelik, ' "Een vuur gaat uit van Cheshbon". Een onderzoek naar Numeri 20:14–21; 21:10–35', *ACEBT* 5 [1984], 61–109).

[13] Cf. H.J. Franken, 'Archaeological evidence relating to the interpretation of the text', in: J. Hoftijzer, G. van der Kooij (eds), *Aramaic Texts from Deir 'Alla* (DMOA, 19), Leiden 1976, 3–16; idem, 'Deir 'Alla re-visited', in: J. Hoftijzer, G. van der Kooij (eds), *The Balaam text from Deir 'Alla re-evaluated: Proceedings of the International Symposium held at Leiden 21–24 August 1989*, Leiden 1991, 3–15.

[14] Deir 'Alla text I, 1. Cf. חֹזֶה (*hozè*[h]) Isa. 30:10 (// רֹאֶה), 2 Kgs 17:13 (// נָבִיא), Mic. 3:7 (// קֹסֵם).

[15] Num. 24:4.16 (*RSV*; in v. 4 'and knows the knowledge of the Most High' is missing).

[16] Hoftijzer, van der Kooij, *Aramaic Texts*, 173, 179, 275–276 (with n. 14).

[17] Cf. M. Dijkstra, 'The Geography of the Story of Balaam: Synchronic Reading as a Help to Date a Biblical Text', in: de Moor, *Synchronic or Diachronic?* (cf. n. 2), 72–97 (see

gist of the oracles may be authentic, as, in any case, is the *name* of the 'seer of gods'—for it now has appeared as *bl'm brb'r* in the Deir 'Alla text.[18]

The books of Deuteronomy and Leviticus each show for the greater part a specific style of writing; they were included, accordingly, in the diachronic scheme of the four sources as 'D' and 'P'. The latter, also responsible, among others, for chapters 25–30 and 35–40 dealing with the project and the building of the tabernacle in Exodus, is considered the latest, post-exilic addition to the Pentateuch, which gave it its final shape.

---

73–74 for these divergent views); Dijkstra himself favours the second half of the ninth century BC as the *terminus ante quem* for the origin of the biblical as well as the extra-biblical literary Balaam texts (*ibid*, 94).

[18] According to Jagersma, who dates the Deir 'Alla texts to about 700 BC, Balaam was undoubtedly a historical figure, as is convincingly proven by these texts (*Numeri* 2, 99; cf. 124 on the talking ass); Van Seters devotes a whole chapter (16) to 'The Story of Balaam: Numbers 22–24' (*Life of Moses*, 405–435), with a special section on the Deir 'Alla texts (408–413), where he indicates the eighth century BC (to which these texts are to be dated) as the beginning of the Balaam tradition ('There is no reason to believe that there was any ⟨older⟩ Balaam tradition', 412), whereas the whole Balaam episode (Num. 22–24) is dated by him, mainly on the ground of similarities with Deutero-Isaiah, to the late exilic period (435)—both these opinions are rather contestable in my eyes. According to André Lemaire the Carbon 14 test indicates a date towards 800 BC for the Deir 'Alla texts; Balaam must have been a famous Aramaic chief-prophet (like Samuel in Israel) who for that reason was incorporated by the Israelite scribes as favouring Israel (A. Lemaire, 'Les inscriptions sur plâtre de Deir 'Alla et leur signification historique et culturelle' in: Hoftijzer, van der Kooij, *The Balaam text* … [cf. n. 13], 33–57 [34, 51–52]). Manfred Weippert also dates the texts in the early 8th century or the second half of the 9th century BC (almost contemporary with the Mesha inscription). The fact that there was already a tradition of professional writing in that region at that time contradicts 'the present tendency among Old Testament scholars to postulating very low dates for large portions of the Hebrew Bible' (M. Weippert, 'The Balaam Text from Deir 'Allā and the study of the Old Testament', in: Hoftijzer, van der Kooij, *The Balaam text* …, 151–184 [176, 177]). Seebass, in an excursus 'Zum Bileam-Text von *tell dēr 'allā*', confirms the positions of Weippert and Lemaire (*Numeri*, 4/3, 55–59); with Dijkstra he considers the second half of the ninth century BC as the *terminus ante quem* (and the beginning of the tenth century as the *terminus post quem*) for Balaam: '(es gibt) keinen Grund, seine Historizität zu bezweifeln' (*Numeri*, 4/3, 67). According to Thomas L. Thompson, however, in his contribution to the Oslo Congress, 'What we learn from this remarkable parallel is not the existence of an historical Balaam, but an ancient way of telling stories about prophets or holy men, etc.'; the same holds good for the Mesha inscription, which, 'rather than an historical text, … belongs to a substantial literary tradition of stories about kings of the past', Thompson, 'Problems of Genre and Historicity with Palestine's Inscriptions', in: A. Lemaire, M. Saebø (eds), *Congress Volume Oslo 1998* (VTSuppl, 80), Leiden 2000, 321–326 (323, 324). See also n. 33 (R. Albertz).

## 2.4. *Former Prophets*

As we turn now to the *former prophets*, there too we come across a reference to an earlier source: the Book of the Upright (ספר הישר) is mentioned twice, in Joshua 10:12–13 (Joshua's saying: 'Sun, stand thou still at Gibeon, and thou Moon in the valley of Aijalon'), as well as in 2 Samuel 1:18–27 (David's lamentation on Saul and Jonathan). Moreover, there is no better example of the use of an old song as the core of a later narration than *the Song of Deborah* in Judges 5 (though in this case no mention has been made of the source-book from which it was taken). What makes it exceptional is that not only the later text in prose has been preserved, in Judges 4, but also the song from which it probably originated, in chapter 5. As Dirksen states: 'There is no reason to doubt the historicity of the event'.[19] The differences between the original song and the prose story show either that considerable freedom was allowed in composing the latter, or that smaller and larger irregularities could slip in during the process of transmission.

Still another diachronic feature in Joshua-Judges should be mentioned: the twofold conception of the conquest of the promised land: on the one side the idealistic view of total occupation, inclusive of Jerusalem (Judg. 1:8), on the other hand the realistic and undoubtedly more orig-inal tradition represented by the list of unconquered cities in Judges 1 (among which Jerusalem, 1:21), which is reflected in loose notes scattered throughout Joshua 15–17. Of some places the former name is mentioned, such as Luz for the later Bethel.[20]

Passing over the enigmatic stories of Judg. 17–18 and 19–21, we now arrive at the impressive figure of Samuel, judge, priest and prophet, who stands at the transition of the period of legend to more historic times. In 1 Samuel 9:9 the old name for נביא 'prophet' is given as ראה 'seer'. The genuineness of this statement has been confirmed now by the indication of Balaam, the son of Beor, as *'š ḥzh 'lhn*, as we saw above.

From the books of Samuel I mention the case of the slaying of Goliath. According to the list of David's heroes in 2 Samuel 21 (v. 19) it was Elchanan who killed Goliath, in sheer contradiction with the well-known

---

[19] P.B. Dirksen, *Richteren: Een praktische bijbelverklaring* (Tekst en Toelichting), Kampen 1990, 38 [my translation of the Dutch], cf. 39–45 for the differences between Judg. 4 and 5, and 18 for further literature.

[20] Judg. 1:23 (as in Gen. 28:19, 35:6 etc.); cf. Hebron (formerly Kiryath-'arba'), and Debir (formerly Kiryath-sepher), Judg. 1:10.11; also Dan (formerly Laish) Judg. 18:29.

story about young David killing Goliath in 1 Sam. 17. This remarkable contradiction proves on the one hand, that at least some of these lists were genuine, but it shows on the other hand how a legendary story could be woven around a historical fact in connection with a historical figure.[21] The already much discussed 'Beth David' inscription from Tel Dan seems at last to anchor the biblical king David to outer-biblical history.[22]

The diachronic character of the books of Kings is shown by their Deuteronomistic framework, within which facts and fiction of very different origin have been brought together. Moreover they repeatedly make mention of their own sources, like the Book of the Acts of Solomon (1 Kgs 11:41), the Book of the Chronicles of the Kings of Judah (1 Kgs 14:29 etc.), and the Book of the Chronicles of the Kings of Israel (1 Kgs 14:19 etc.), which in my view should not be mistaken for our books of Chronicles. From the Mesha Stela onwards, with its mention of the Tetragram, the first one in history, there is a number of texts from the *Umwelt* which seem to corroborate the general outline of some of the names and events mentioned in Kings, like the black obelisk and other texts of Shalmaneser III and the prism-texts of Sennacherib.[23]

Of special interest are the chapters 1 Kings 6 and 7 dealing with the building of the temple and Solomon's palace. As they are devoid of every kind of smooth Deuteronomistic language, I suggest that much older archival material has been included in these chapters by the author(s), which may have been damaged in the process of transmission.

## 2.5. Latter Prophets

As to the *latter prophets*, the well-known division of the book of Isaiah into first, second and third Isaiah shows that there was a long tradition of several centuries of Isaianic prophecy.[24] The longevity of this Isaianic scroll is matched by that of the minor prophets, which covers a still longer period, from Hosea in the eighth until Zechariah and Malachi

---

[21] Cf. Graeme Auld, 'The Deuteronomists between History and Theology', in: Lemaire, Saebø (eds), *Congress Volume Oslo1998*, 353–367 (364). In his opinion, however, these *data* are not necessarily *facta*: 'We have little or no reliable information to deduce from Saul and the Judges before him' (*ibid.*).

[22] Grabbe, *Ancient Israel* (cf. n. 3), 129–130.

[23] For Thomas L. Thompson's view on the Mesha inscription see above, n. 18.

[24] For the relationship of Israelite prophecy with that of its neighbours, see the dissertation of Matthijs J. de Jong, *Isaiah among the Ancient Near Eastern Prophets. A Comparative Study of the Earliest Stages of the Isaiah Tradition and the Neo-Assyrian Prophecies* (VTSuppl, 117), Leiden / Boston 2007.

in the sixth and fifth centuries. But also internally many of them seem to be composite texts, like the books of Amos,[25] Micah (which could be divided into first and second Micah),[26] and Zechariah (also: first and second Zechariah). At the Joint Meeting in Kampen (1994) Wim Beuken showed, by means of the analysis of one chapter (Isaiah 28), how its diachronic provenance and its synchronic structure could be reconciled with each other.[27] For the diachronic element in Jeremiah it suffices to mention its Deuteronomistic redaction and its double textual tradition in a longer and a shorter version.

## 2.6. *Writings*

As the temple in Jerusalem, already mentioned in connection with its building story in Kings, had become the centre of devotion for the people of Judah / Israel, *the Psalms* could be called their hymnal: the Book of Psalms is the hymn-book of the temple.[28] Although their collection opens the third and latest part of the Hebrew Bible, they contain a number of ancient features, like the Ugaritic parallels of Psalm 29 and the strong likeness of part of Psalm 104 to Ichnaton's hymn to the sun. On the other hand, many Psalms, like the alphabetical ones, give the impression of being from a rather late date. Although a more specific dating of most of the Psalms seems impossible, I have the impression that here too, in the

---

[25] Cf., e.g., R.G. Kratz, 'Die Worte des Amos von Tekoa', in: M. Köckert, M. Nissinen (eds), *Propheten in Mari, Assyrien und Israel* (FRLANT, 201), Göttingen 2003, 54–89 (with thanks to Dr. M.J. de Jong for this reference).

[26] Thus A.S. van der Woude, *Micha* (POT), Nijkerk 1976, 14–15, 195–199.

[27] W.A.M. Beuken, 'Isaiah 28: Is It Only Schismatics That Drink Heavily? Beyond the Synchronic Versus Diachronic Controversy', in: de Moor, *Synchronic or Diachronic?* (cf. n. 2), 15–38 (38).

[28] According to Erich Zenger, 'Psalmenforschung nach Hermann Gunkel und Sigmund Mowinckel', in: Lemaire, Saebø (eds), *Congress Volume Oslo 1998*, 399–435, the *Sitz im Leben* of our Psalter in its present form has to be sought in the wisdom milieu (430–434). However, a) he, too, does not deny that the origin of the *Hauptgattungen* of the biblical psalms lies in the cult, or that earlier collections of psalms existed in that milieu (430); b) the supposed influence of the later wisdom books on the language of the psalms could also have been the other way round; c) in my opinion the hymnal, liturgical character of the closing psalms 146–150 is as manifest as one could wish; Cas Labuschagne, in his new, numerical analysis of the composition of the Psalms (recently presented to the OTW and soon to be published) calls Pss. 146–150 'Closing Hallel: 5 Hallelujah Psalms'. See also Harm van Grol's lecture at the Joint Meeting 'Visions of the *Chasidim*' in the present volume, on the (קהל) חסידים in Ps. 149:1.5.9.

Psalms, we have a collection of writings which represents the outcome of a long history of composition, that went on for many centuries—just like most of our present hymn-books.

Not only hymns and lamentations have a timeless character, but also *Wisdom literature*. Yet it was when reading in the excellent volume on *Wisdom in ancient Israel. Essays in honour of J.A. Emerton*, edited by John Day, Robert P. Gordon and H.G.M. Williamson, that I came upon the idea for this lecture. For biblical wisdom literature in general, and the book of Proverbs in particular, testify to a clear diachronic pattern. As to Proverbs there is the striking agreement of chapters 22–24 with the Egyptian Instruction of Amenemope, dating from the twelfth or eleventh century.[29] There are more short collections of proverbs, like those of Agur and of Lemuel (chapters 30 and 31:1–9 respectively), which give an impression of antiquity, while others, like the didactic chapters 1–9 at the beginning, and perhaps also the alphabetical 'Praise of a Worthy Woman' at the end, seem to belong to a much younger, post-exilic period. In between these two periods there is the collection of 'Proverbs of Solomon copied by the men of Hezekiah king of Judah' (Prov. 25:1).

And then, finally, what seems to me the major example of diachronic procedure in the Old Testament, there are the *books of Chronicles* as an evident attempt at rewriting most of 2 Samuel and 1–2 Kings (which date from the time before or during the Exile) from the scope and religious needs of *post-exilic* Yehud. Almost all negative stories concerning king David have been left out, as well as (almost) the whole history of the northern kingdom;[30] the books of Ezra and Nehemiah form its logical continuation, relating the history of their own time.[31] The use of אלהים instead of יהוה for the divine name need not indicate priority in time for Chronicles: the substitution of the Tetragram in 2 Samuel 24:1 by 'Satan' in 1 Chronicles 21:1 seems to me to point definitely to the Persian era as

---

[29] Prov. 22:17–24:22, cf. J.D. Ray, 'Egyptian wisdom literature', and G.I. Davies, 'Were there schools in ancient Israel?', in: John Day et al., *Wisdom in ancient Israel: Essays in honour of J.A. Emerton*, Cambridge 1995, 17–29 (23–24) and 199–211 (203–204) respectively.

[30] However, there is the unexpectedly critical note that David was not allowed to build the temple because of the many wars he had waged: 'You have shed much blood' (1 Chron. 22:8, cf. 28:3); in 1 Kgs 5:17 (3) a similar motivation is given to David in a different, more favourable way.

[31] See, however, S. Japhet, "The supposed common Authorship of Chronicles and Ezra—Nehemiah investigated Anew", *VT* 18 (1968), pp. 330–371; H.G.M. Williamson, *Israel in the Book of Chronicles*, Oxford 1977.

the time of the composition of the books of Chronicles.[32] As from time to time whole sections from 2 Sam – 2 Kings have been copied almost literally this seems to preclude the possibility that both may have gone back to a common source.

## 3. Conclusion

With this survey I hope to have established that the Old Testament bears, in all its branches, a diachronic character and could be called a diachronic corpus. Not least is this shown by the *diversity* of style, theme, form, and moral and religious outlook to which it testifies. Moreover, this 'diachronicity' of the Old Testament has to tell us also something about its *historicity*. Through an uninterrupted chain of oral and, subsequently, scribal transmission, traditions from almost a millennium about the vicissitudes of the people of Israel, its history, its culture and its belief, have come to us. As, in its present form, it still witnesses to this long, complicated and, at times, frustrating process, it should not be degraded to a secondary source: it has a specific *longue durée* of its own, which makes it a primary source for writing its own history, the history of ancient Israel.[33]

---

[32] Otherwise Auld, 'Deuteronomists', in: *Congress Volume Oslo*, 357, cf. 358–360. N.B. On the last day of the EABS Congress that was held at Lincoln alongside the Joint Meeting, Mrs. Yairah Amit from Tel Aviv gave a very illuminating lecture on the literary devices used in 1 Chron. 21:16–22:1 to accommodate the rather loosely connected appendix about the threshing floor of Araunah / Ornan at the end of 2 Samuel (24:16b–25a) in order to link its contents firmly to those of the preceding and following chapters and the building of the temple (2 Chron. 3:1), thus establishing at the same time further proof for the priority of Sam.-Kgs.

[33] Cf. Rainer Albertz, 'Die Exilszeit als Ernstfall für eine historische Rekonstruktion ohne biblische Texte: Die neubabylonischen Königsinschriften als "Primärquelle"', in: L.L. Grabbe (ed.), *Leading Captivity Captive: 'The Exile' as History and Ideology* (JSOTSuppl, 278), Sheffield 1998, 22–39; Albertz criticizes 'Die Entgegensetzung von späten, tendenziösen und darum historisch wertlosen biblischen "Sekundärquellen" und zeitgenössischen und darum historisch zuverlässigen auszerbiblischen "Primärquellen"' (26), as it is founded on 'das Vorurteil ... im Unterschied zu den theologisch aufgeladenen Bibeltexten seien die auszerbiblischen "Primärquellen" viel profaner, weniger tendenziös und darum historisch glaubwürdiger. Das ist aber ein falscher Eindruck ...' (*ibid.*, 27). Similarly to Thompson (in a way, cf. n. 18), he points to the religious language of the Mesha-Stele and the Deir 'Alla text—without the implication, however, that this aspect would make these texts less historical (with which I agree; his main proof are the Neo-Babylonian royal inscriptions). Otherwise Grabbe, *Ancient Israel*, 35 (1.3.3, *ad* 2.).

Essentially—that is not counting the creation myths and most of the patriarchal sagas—its character is that of *story-like history*, however many examples of history-like story may also be found in it (like the story of David and Goliath). The *book of Daniel* is there to show us, as a contrast, what would have been the appearance and the contents of our Old Testament, had it been the product of scribal activity during a very short late period: then indeed it would have been essentially *history-like story* in character.[34]

One needs a certain amount of knowledge of basic details, and of basic experiences and convictions in order to build up one's basic perception of a complicated subject such as the Old Testament. Thenceforth one is inclined to gather all other details, experiences and convictions one meets into this one basic perception. But it is with these as with the wonderful red and white cattle grazing in the meadows near our home: almost all of them move their heads in the same direction, but there are always two or three looking the opposite way. However that may be, the foregoing is my basic perception, which I wanted to share with you.[*]

---

[34] For this distinction between story-like history and history-like story see C.J. Labuschagne, *Zin en onzin over God: Een kritische beschouwing van gangbare godsvoorstellingen*, Zoetermeer 1994, 58–59; cf. J. Barr, 'Story and History in Biblical Theology', in J. Barr (ed.), *The scope and authority of the Bible* (EIT, 7), London 1980, 1–17. See further 'The Historicity of the Bible,' n. 60 on page 146(-7); 'The *veracity* of the OT is at stake' (*ibid.*, p. 123); B. Becking, *From David to Gedaliah: the Book of Kings as Story and History* (OBO 228), Fribourg, Göttingen 2007, 1–22; H.M. Barstad, *History and the Hebrew Bible: Studies in Ancient Israelite and Ancient near Eastern Historiography* (FAT 61), Tübingen 2008.

[*] I want to thank Gillian Greenberg for a number of last-minute corrections in my English text, and Bob Becking for adding a few suggestions as to literature, for providing the lay-out, and in general for meeting my requests with cheerful magnanimity.

# PHARAOH SHISHAK'S INVASION OF
# PALESTINE AND THE EXODUS FROM EGYPT

ANDREW D.H. MAYES
*University of Dublin—Ireland*

## 1. INTRODUCTION

Shishak's invasion of Palestine in the fifth year of Rehoboam, King of Judah, is recorded in 1 Kgs 14:15–28, a record which, while not excluding an Egyptian interest in Palestine more generally, presents the event as an expedition against Jerusalem. The city was spared, apparently, only at the cost of Rehoboam's having handed over the treasures of both temple and palace. There is also a much more elaborate Egyptian record. This account, inscribed on a triumphal gateway, the so-called Bubastite Portal, of the great temple of Amun at Karnak, describes a campaign into Palestine on the part of Pharaoh Shoshenq I, the first ruler of the 22nd Libyan dynasty. There is no linguistic difficulty in the equation of Shoshenq with Shishak,[1] and there are few who dispute that the references in 1 Kgs 14 and in the Egyptian record are to the same event.[2] Otherwise, however, understandings and interpretations vary considerably in relation to both the date and the significance of the event. We can here only glance at the complex issue of dating. Our focus, rather, will be on the significance of the event, both of the event in itself and also in terms of its consequences. While the question of date is obviously important for that of significance, there are dimensions of the significance of this campaign which may be discussed independently of our reaching certainty on its precise date.

---

[1] In Egyptian the name is written variously with and without the *n*, and the *kethiv* of 1 Kings 14:25 attests the vowel *ô* rather than *i*; cf. K. Kitchen, *The Third Intermediate Period in Egypt (1100–650 BC)*, Warminster, 2nd ed. 1986, 73n. 356.

[2] Though cf. Bill Manley, *The Penguin Historical Atlas of Ancient Egypt*, London 1966, 102.

## 2. Date of Shishak's Campaign into Palestine

The different chronological systems proposed for the kings of Judah[3] vary
between 932 and 922 BCE for the beginning of the seventeen year reign
of Rehoboam, making his fifth year lie somewhere between 927 and 917
BCE. Egyptian chronology is also uncertain, and the commonly accepted
dates of 945–924 BCE for Shishak[4] do not fit with all the suggested Judean
royal chronologies in terms of allowing for an invasion of Palestine by
Shishak in Rehoboam's fifth year. In fact, Shishak's reign correlates more
completely with the reign of Solomon, in whose time, indeed, Jeroboam
fled for refuge from Solomon to the court of Shishak (1 Kgs 11:40). Moreover, if it is the case that the description of Rehoboam in 1 Kgs 12:1–24;
14:21–31 has been deliberately structured so as to illustrate how 'the wise,
old king [Solomon] is followed by the foolish, young king, the statesman
gives place to the tyrant',[5] and that the Egyptian invasion was attached
to Rehoboam in order to illustrate the inevitable consequence of such
a decline, then Shishak's invasion may in fact have taken place during
the reign of Solomon rather than that of Rehoboam.[6] Over against this,
however, it has been noted that 1 Kgs 14:25–26 associates this invasion
with the stripping of the treasuries of the temple and palace, an association found also in 1 Kgs 15:18; 2 Kgs 18:15–16; 24:13. This may suggest
that one of the sources used by the deuteronomist was a record of temple
income and its use, which may in turn support the historical accuracy of
the dating of this event to the reign of Rehoboam.[7] Also, it seems unlikely

---

[3] Cf. the table in J.H. Hayes, J.M. Miller, *Israelite and Judaean History*, London 1977,
682–683.

[4] Cf. e.g. A. Kuhrt, *The Ancient Near East c. 3000–330 BC*, London 1995, 624. Kuhrt's
adoption of Albright's chronology for the kings of Israel and Judah (*ibid.*, 468) means that
Rehoboam is dated 922–915 BCE, outside the period of the reign of Shishak.

[5] D.B. Redford, *Egypt, Canaan, and Israel in Ancient Times*, Princeton 1992, 315.

[6] Cf. also G. Garbini, *History and Ideology in Ancient Israel*, London 1988, 29–30;
H.M. Niemann, 'The Socio-Political Shadow Cast by the Biblical Solomon', in L.K. Handy
(ed.), *The Age of Solomon*, Leiden 1997, 296–297; E.A. Knauf, 'Le roi est mort, vive le roi!
A Biblical Argument for the Historicity of Solomon', in Handy (ed.), *Age of Solomon*, 93–
95. That the invasion belongs to the reign of Solomon rather than that of Rehoboam is a
possibility that exists whether that invasion is dated early or late in Shishak's reign.

[7] Cf J. Van Seters, *In Search of History*, New Haven 1983, 301; M.Z. Brettler, '2 Kings
24:13–14 as History', *CBQ* 53 (1991), 547–548; *id.*, 'Method in the Application of Biblical Source Material to Historical Writing (with Particular Reference to the Ninth Century BCE)', in H.G.M. Williamson (ed.), *Understanding the History of Ancient Israel*,
Oxford 2007, 320–322; N. Na'aman, 'The Northern Kingdom in the Late Tenth-Ninth
Centuries BCE', in Williamson (ed.), *Understanding the History of Ancient Israel*, 399–400.

that a deuteronomistic author who was prepared to deliver the negative account of Solomon that we have in 1 Kgs 11 would have scrupled to associate the invasion with that king if that had been what his sources related. With some uncertainty, therefore, Shishak's invasion of Palestine may be dated to the reign of Rehoboam, and set sometime around the middle of the second half of the 10th century BCE. This is, in any case, about the time of the foundation of the states of Israel and Judah, and it is this which is of importance for us here.

### 3. SIGNIFICANCE OF SHISHAK'S CAMPAIGN INTO PALESTINE

When it comes to the significance of the event, it is clear that the account of it given in 1 Kgs 14 and that provided by Shishak cannot be immediately related. The claim[8] that the Egyptian record provides 'a striking verification' of 'the stunning historical accuracy of the biblical account' is surely an egregious example of the misuse of epigraphic materials for apologetic purposes. Quite clearly, the Egyptian record cannot be held to say anything about the historical accuracy of Rehoboam's having bought off Shishak with the treasures of the temple and palace, unless, that is, one is going to go so far as to claim that Shishak's erection of the Bubastite Portal at the temple at Karnak, and indeed his other building activities, could have been possible only as a result of the wealth acquired from this raid on Jerusalem.[9] But in addition to that, it is equally clear that while Shishak's account does not necessarily contradict the record of 1 Kgs 14, the accounts are certainly different and have very different understandings of the purpose and objective of the Egyptian campaign. For 1 Kgs 14, Shishak's objective was Jerusalem, and nothing is said of any other interest in Palestine apart from that city. Even 2 Chron. 12, which expands on 1 Kgs 14 by enumerating the chariots and horsemen of Shishak's army,

---

[8] J.D. Currid, *Ancient Egypt and the Old Testament*, Grand Rapids 1997, 174.

[9] So Kitchen, 'Egyptian Intervention in the Levant in Iron Age II', in W.G. Dever, S. Gitin (eds.), *Symbiosis, Symbolism and the Power of the Past*, Winona Lake 2003, 121–125. Presumably, however, the more prosperous northern areas conquered by Shishak yielded significant resources. An alternative source of wealth at a time of external Egyptian weakness, when the booty of conquests was not available, was that accumulated in earlier royal tombs. On royal tomb robbery, particularly from the late 20th dynasty onwards, cf. J. Tyldesley, *Judgement of the Pharaoh: Crime and Punishment in Ancient Egypt*, London 2000, 127–139; B.G. Trigger, B.J. Kemp, D. O'Connor, A.B. Lloyd (eds), *Ancient Egypt: A Social History*, Cambridge 1983, 229, 247–248; I. Shaw (ed.), *The Oxford History of Ancient Egypt*, Oxford 2000, 303.

and noting the ethnic background of its composition, as well as by asserting that Shishak conquered the fortified cities of Judah, similarly under-
stands that Shishak's real objective here was Jerusalem. But this is not so
in Shishak's own account; this account fails even to mention Jerusalem, or
Israel or Judah or Rehoboam or Jeroboam for that matter. It is often suggested that Jerusalem may have featured originally among the towns in
the topographical list of Shishak's inscription, for this list has many era-
sures, and of its original approximately 175 names only 127 can now be
read.[10] But this is, in fact, improbable. It is not only reference to Jerusalem
that is missing, but also reference to cities in the highlands of Judah generally. Also, as has been noted,[11] none of the gaps in the Shishak list
has a geographical context suggesting an original reference to Jerusalem.
The closest the list comes to that city is lines 2–3, where Gibeon, Beth-
horon, Kiriath-jearim and Aijalon are mentioned, but the immediately
adjoining places at each end of the list are Mahanaim and Megiddo. It
may, of course, be claimed that Jerusalem is not mentioned by Shishak
because Jerusalem, as 1 Kgs 14 clearly implies, surrendered and was not
conquered. But this too is a weak argument. Not only is the context for
referring to Jerusalem missing, but the presupposition of such an argument is that all the other places mentioned by Shishak did not surrender
and were conquered. Shishak's inscription, however, does not make clear
what happened in relation to the places listed: some may have been conquered, others may have surrendered and been spared.[12] In any case, the
focus of Shishak's campaign, as implied in the list, was not Jerusalem.

A fresh attempt has been made to resolve the issue of the relationship between the two records by Kevin Wilson.[13] According to this, it
is not the Old Testament record that comes under historical qestion
but that of Shishak. Developing a view which has its roots already in
Wellhausen's dismissal of the historical value of the inscription,[14] Wil-

---

[10] For recent detailed studies of the inscription, see especially A.F. Rainey, R.S. Notley,
*The Sacred Bridge: Carta's Atlas of the Biblical World*, Jerusalem 2006, 186–188; K.A. Wilson, *The Campaign of Pharaoh Shoshenq I into Palestine* (FAT 2/9), Tübingen 2005.

[11] Cf. Knauf, 'Le roi est mort', 93 n. 54.

[12] Cf. the comments of J.M. Weinstein, 'The Egyptian Empire in Palestine: A Reassessment', *BASOR* 241 (1981), 10–12, on the topographical lists relating to the campaign of
Thutmoses III against Megiddo: not every place mentioned was individually conquered;
the submission of the Palestinian princes to the Pharaoh in the battle implied the surrender of all the towns opposing him.

[13] Wilson, *Campaign of Pharaoh Shoshenq I*.

[14] For this, and a robust rejection of Wellhausen, cf. Kitchen, *Third Intermediate Period
in Egypt*, 432 n. 49.

son argues that Shishak's inscription belongs to a conventional Egyptian genre to which belong also the triumphal reliefs of the New Kingdom Pharaohs Thutmose III, Seti I, Ramesses II and Ramesses III. All have a tripartite structure comprising a relief scene, a topographical list and an inscription, and all are highly conventional, and the language used is 'highly stereotypical'.[15] As far as the topographical lists are concerned these too must be judged to be conventional: besides being repetitive, they may, on occasion, be shown to be inconsistent with other royal annals which do provide a historical record. So, inscription, relief and topographical list belong together as a conventional genre, intended to present the king as the beneficiary of Amun's gift of victory over all foreign lands. They cannot be used to derive historical information relating to particular campaigns. This view of the Shishak inscription then allows Wilson to argue that the sole historical record on Shishak's campaign into Palestine is 1 Kgs 14.

The argument, however, is not wholly convincing. I have noted elsewhere[16] that, while the general self-presentation of Shishak in his inscription is highly conventional, there is sufficient to suggest that this Libyan Pharaoh is in fact consciously using a standard Egyptian genre in order to integrate his own specific achievement into the pattern of activity of traditional Egyptian Pharaohs, and so legitimate and strengthen his own royal position. Shishak refers specifically to this campaign as 'his first expedition of victory', and the places that he lists include some, such as Arad, Taanach and Rehov, that do not appear in the earlier lists. This suggests that Shishak's record may well contain significantly accurate historical information relating to his Palestinian campaign.

On the other hand, attempts to use this topographical list to plot a route march followed by Shishak through Palestine have been largely unsuccessful.[17] A more attractive alternative[18] is that the list contains clusters of place names, reflecting concerted military action in certain areas, perhaps carried out by separate military detachments sent out

---

[15] Wilson, *Campaign of Pharaoh Shoshenq I*, 18.

[16] I have argued this at greater length in another article, 'The Palestinian Campaign of Pharaoh Shishak', to be published elsewhere.

[17] Cf. the critical review in Wilson, *Campaign of Pharaoh Shoshenq I*, 2–15; Kitchen, *Third Intermediate Period in Egypt*, 442–446; and also my forthcoming article referred to above n. 16. Reference may also be made to N. Na'aman, 'Israel, Edom and Egypt in the Tenth Century BCE', in his *Ancient Israel's History and Historiography*, Winona Lake 2006, 126–133.

[18] Cf. Rainey, Notley, *Sacred Bridge*, 187.

from an Egyptian base at perhaps Gaza or Megiddo. These areas include
the Jezreel valley, the international road in the plain of Sharon, the area
of Gibeon in the highlands, the area of Penuel and Mahanaim east of
the Jordan, and the Negeb in the south. For the moment at least it can
only be concluded that Shishak's campaign 'was probably a blitzkrieg
affair intended to give status to his regime, collect booty, and perhaps
reassert Egyptian influence on Arabian trade'.[19] It is to this understanding
rather than to the Jerusalem focused invasion recorded in 1 Kgs 14 that
historical probability should be attached.

## 4. CONSEQUENCES OF SHISHAK'S CAMPAIGN INTO PALESTINE

Given its limited nature and also the lack of a follow-up invasion, either
by Shishak or his successor, it is probable that in itself the campaign is
to be seen as a large-scale raid that, apart from the Negeb, was aimed
against significant regions of the more prosperous area of the northern
kingdom of Israel rather than Judah; but this does not exhaust the question of its significance. Even if Shishak had no interests and purposes
that went beyond this, there is a realm of unintended consequences that
should not be ignored despite the uncertainty that may attach to them.
Our inability to access the motives of actors in events,[20] particularly when
it comes to historical reconstruction of this period, still leaves open significant possibilities for understanding the interconnectedness of historical phenomena. A dimension of a study by Israel Finkelstein[21] is of particular interest here. Noting that among the areas *not* threatened by Shishak
is the fertile and densely settled highland territory of northern Samaria,

---

[19] Cf. J.M. Miller, J.H. Hayes, *A History of Ancient Israel and Judah*, Louisville 2nd ed.
2006, 279.

[20] This is well illustrated, as far as the present context is concerned, by the variety
of motives ascribed to Shishak: so, for example, Wilson, *The Campaign of Pharaoh
Shoshenq I*, 97–99, believes that Shishak was acting in support of his vassal Jeroboam, who
had earlier taken refuge with him to escape Solomon (1 Kgs 11:40); B. Mazar, 'Pharaoh
Shishak's Campaign to the Land of Israel', *VTS* 4 (1957), 57–66, argues that the intention
was to punish Jeroboam as a rebellious vassal; Na'aman, in *Ancient Israel's History and
Historiography*, 131, suggests that Shishak was acceding to a request from Rehoboam,
his former ally (1 Kgs 3:1; 9:16,24), to assist in restoring order in his country, and that
Rehoboam's payment (1 Kgs 14:22) 'can be regarded as an enforced remuneration for
"services rendered"'.

[21] I. Finkelstein, 'The Campaign of Shoshenq I to Palestine. A Guide to the Tenth
Century BCE Polity', *ZDPV* 118 (2002), 109–135.

whereas, apart from the south, a significant focus of his hostile intentions was the Jezreel valley and its key site of Megiddo, Finkelstein proposes[22] that the effect of this invasion, following on the withdrawal of Shishak, was to leave the way open for those settled on the highlands of Samaria to expand into and dominate the Jezreel valley. It is out of this expansion that the later powerful northern kingdom of the Omrides emerged.[23] Much of Finkelstein's view is dependent on an understanding of material cultural development in Palestine which does not allow for a framework of history involving a united monarchy of David and Solomon which later divided into the two kingdoms of Israel and Judah; but the advantage of this element of his argument is that it still stands whatever view is taken of that larger question: it was the invasion of Shishak which was *a* if not *the* major factor in the rise of the northern kingdom. Whether the cities of the Jezreel valley in particular are viewed as still Canaanite city-states, enclosing tribal areas in the highlands, or as by now incorporated into the kingdom of the Davidides ruling from Jerusalem, their destruction by, or submission to, Shishak was the predisposing factor in the emergence of a territorial state based in the highlands and incorporating the valleys and plains. The invasion of Shishak and his subsequent withdrawal is, therefore, to be seen as having had the, unintended, consequence of the rise of the northern kingdom.[24]

---

[22] 'The Campaign of Shoshenq I to Palestine', 117–122.

[23] Cf. also M. Liverani, *Israel's History and the History of Israel*, London 2005, 101–103.

[24] N. Na'aman, 'The Northern Kingdom in the Late Tenth-Ninth Centuries BCE', in H.G.M. Williamson (ed.), *Understanding the History of Ancient Israel*, Oxford 2007, 401–402, provides a clear outline of the process which led to the rise of the northern kingdom, viz. the expansion of the highland tribes into the northern valleys in the second half of the tenth century BCE. For Na'aman, however, the destruction of the Iron I cities of Megiddo, Yokneam, Taanach, Bethshean and Chinnereth (Megiddo, Taanach and Bethshean are among the identified sites in the Shishak list) is to be attributed to raids by these highland settlers rather than to the invasion of Shishak. This is based largely on the assumption that the victory stele of Shishak was set up in the inhabited city of Megiddo VB rather than the ruined city of Megiddo VIA. The argument is tenuous: Shishak may well have set up his victory stele in a city partially destroyed by his own invasion and then re-settled. In any case, it is clear that the expansion into the plains and the invasion of Shishak are closely related: the former made possible by the latter, or the latter following closely on the former, so that the rise of the northern kingdom is intimately bound up with the invasion, and subsequent departure, of Shishak. The earliest Iron IIA strata in the valleys, including Megiddo VB, represent, according to Na'aman, the first stage of the establishment of the northern kingdom. These strata are characterized by a modest material culture with no evidence of monumental architecture. It is to the second stage of the development that monumental architecture and administrative centres belong (e.g. Megiddo VA–IVB), a stage to be dated to the time of the Omrides in the first half of the 9th century BCE.

This may be further elaborated. The development of states involves not only administrative and political arrangements, but also ideological justifications, legitimations and expressions. It is ideologies that give cohesive identity to the group organized through its administrative and political arrangements. Such ideologies are implicit in material culture, and explicit in the stories and beliefs articulated by the group. In relation to the northern kingdom of Israel the story of the exodus from Egypt is one such ideology. It has been plausibly argued to have functioned as the charter myth of the northern kingdom, that ideology which provides the foundation and expresses the identity of the nation.[25] It has also been argued, however, that in relation to the exodus tradition a distinction must be made between how it may have functioned and how it originated,[26] and much effort has been, and continues to be, expended on the problem of the origin of this tradition, with a view to tracing it back to experiences and events in the period of the Egyptian New Kingdom.[27] The stronger arguments, however, both positive and negative, point to a much later time of origin. The first fairly secure and datable references to the exodus tradition come from the eighth century prophets Amos and Hosea (Amos 2:10–11; 3:1; 9:7; Hos. 2:17 [EVV 15]; 11:1; 12:10,14 [EVV 9,13]; 13:4); these presuppose an established tradition of origins, and it may be, then, that 1 Kgs 12:28 (Jeroboam 'said to the people, "You have gone up to Jerusalem long enough. Behold your gods, O Israel, who brought you up out of the land of Egypt"') preserves a traditional doxology, deriving from around the time of the formation of the northern kingdom, praising Yahweh who brought Israel out of the land of Egypt, a doxology rooted in a cult festival context at the royal sanctuary of Bethel.[28] Pentateuchal source criticism can no longer provide access to any earlier tradition, for the Pentateuchal material *presupposes* prophetic and proto-deuteronomic forms of the tradition,[29] and there is much in

---

[25] Cf. especially K. van der Toorn, 'The Exodus as Charter Myth', in J.W. van Henten, A. Houtepen (eds.), *Religious Identity and the Invention of Tradition*, Assen 2001, 113–127.

[26] Cf. R. Albertz, 'Exodus: Liberation History against Charter Myth', in van Henten, Houtepen (eds.), *Religious Identity and the Invention of Tradition*, 128–143.

[27] Cf. e.g., G. Davies, 'Was there an Exodus?', in J. Day (ed.), *In Search of Pre-Exilic Israel* (JSOTS 406), London 2004, 23–40.

[28] Cf. K. van der Toorn, *Family Religion in Babylonia, Syria and Israel*, Leiden 1996, 289; R. Albertz, *A History of Israelite Religion in the Old Testament Period*, London 1994, 145.

[29] Cf. especially, E. Blum, *Studien zur Komposition des Pentateuch* (BZAW 189), Berlin 1990. Blum's analysis is accepted by Albertz, *A History of Israelite Religion in the Old*

the detail of the account of the exodus in the Pentateuch which links that story with later rather than earlier time.[30] The question still remains, of course, as to how much of this exodus as charter myth is in fact dependent on older traditional memories which have been given new and revitalized expression. The question is essentially this: does the exodus story demand a background and history other than what is provided by the circumstances surrounding the rise of the northern kingdom? Karel van der Toorn, to whom we owe the characterization of the exodus tradition as charter myth, has written:[31] 'We must be careful to distinguish, however, between use and origin. It is one thing to say that the exodus tradition was promoted, along with Yahweh as the national god, as a national charter myth; it is something else to say that the tradition grew out of the political need for it. The available evidence warrants the conclusion that the exodus motif was appropriated by the state religion as the national myth; there is also sufficient evidence to say that the motif was originally Ephraimite. It is hard to determine, however, in which particular segment of the early Israelite society the tradition originated and developed. Both the Egyptian background of the name Moses, and the data concerning the presence of Western Asiatic people in 13th century Egypt, argue in favour of the historicity of an exodus of some kind. The most satisfactory solution is to assume that the origin in and the flight from Egypt were

---

*Testament Period*, 469. That Albertz can nevertheless go on to draw traditional conclusions with regard to the antiquity of the exodus tradition is an inconsistency noted by J.J. Collins, 'The Development of the Exodus Tradition', in van Henten, Houtepen (eds.), *Religious Identity and the Invention of Tradition*, 144–147.

[30] Cf. J. Van Seters, 'The Geography of the Exodus', in J.A. Dearman, M.P. Graham (eds.), *The Land that I will Show You* (JSOTS 343), Sheffield 2001, 255–276. The reference to Israel having laboured in the building of Pithom and Rameses (Exod. 1:11) is often taken as a valuable historical reference linking Israelite enslavement in Egypt directly with the time of Rameses II. Rameses is indeed probably to be identified with the site Piramesse founded by Rameses II, a site that declined after the Ramesside period. But the name did not disappear and occurs in a list of place names coming from the 21st dynasty and the place had a brief revival under Shishak in the 22nd dynasty, while the name is still associated with the ruins of Piramesse in the 6th century AD. Pithom, on the other hand, has no evidence for its use as a place name in early time. It appears to be the name of Tell el-Maskhuta in the Pithom Stele from the 3rd century BCE. That site was not occupied in Ramesside times. The alternative site proposed for Pithom, Tell er-Retabah, was occupied in the Ramesside period and, moreover, inscriptions referring to Atum have been found there. But while the temple of Atum there might have been known as Per-Atum (Pithom), there is no evidence for the name having been applied to the site; cf. R.E. Gmirkin, *Berossus and Genesis, Manetho and Exodus*, London, New York 2006, 225–227.

[31] *Family Religion in Babylonia, Syria and Israel*, 301.

historical realities for a limited group of immigrants to Israel. This particular history was gradually transformed into a national past of sheerly mythical proportions.'

This, probably, represents a widespread understanding, but it is less than satisfactory. The evidence indeed demonstrates ongoing contact at various levels between Egypt and Palestine through the second millenium, contact which also involved Asiatics being brought to Egypt as prisoners of war, being enslaved in Egypt, going to Egypt in search of pasture, and indeed reaching positions of prominence and influence in Egypt,[32] but none of this supports the historicity of the exodus tradition.[33] To substitute for 'the exodus' the expression 'an exodus of some kind' is something of a sleight of hand, and as soon as any attempt is made to give substance to the proposal, in terms of demonstrating an old tradition and establishing its context of preservation and transmission, its weakness becomes clear. Albertz has indeed stated:[33] 'I cannot see any evidence that the Exodus tradition was used for defining a particular religious identity, promoting the Yahweh cult, and curbing local and family religion, before the time of Josia'. But if this is so, what possble context could there have been for the preservation and transmission of the exodus tradition before it became the charter myth of the northern kingdom?

In order to try to advance discussion, I should like to refer to a sentence from Rainer Albertz's *History of Israelite Religion*.[34] Having presented the evidence for the Exodus presentation of Moses as reflecting the figure of Jeroboam, and indeed also for detail of the exodus tradition having drawn on experience of forced labour under Solomon,[35] Albertz concludes that 'it is highly probable that the battle against Solomon's forced labour by Jeroboam and the northern tribes was fought with an

---

[32] Cf. my 'The Exodus as Ideology of the Marginalized', in W.G. Jeanrond, A.D.H. Mayes (eds), *Recognising the Margins: Developments in Biblical and Theological Studies*, Dublin 2006, 61–66; Redford, *Egypt, Canaan, and Israel in Ancient Times*, 221–227. A useful summary of the various points of relationship between the exodus story (including the plagues motif) and historical events of the second millenium BCE is given by R. Hendel, *Remembering Abraham. Culture, Myth and History in the Hebrew Bible*, Oxford 2005, 57–73.

[33] 'Exodus: Liberation History against Charter Myth', 140.

[34] Albertz, *The History of Israelite Religion*, 142.

[35] The correspondences between Moses and Jeroboam, noted by Albertz, include: both have royal connections; both identify with oppressed fellow-country-men; both rebel; both flee, following the failure of the revolt; both return after the death of the king; both negotiate with the king's successor; both lead a withdrawal from the king's sphere of power.

appeal to the liberation of their forefathers from Egyptian forced labour, and that these old religious reminiscences took their first narrative form from the contemporary experiences of Jeroboam's revolt'. The question that arises here is, of course, to do with the nature of those 'old religious reminiscences', which 'took their first narrative form' in the context of Jeroboam's revolt. What is being here suggested by Albertz is that within the (to use a term now much in vogue) cultural memory of Israel there lie at the one end the experience of liberation from Egypt, the exodus, and at the other the narrative rendition of this experience which belongs to the time of Jeroboam.

Philip Davies has written of cultural memory in these terms:[36] 'Cultural memory provides a better conceptual tool than history, myth, or tradition for classifying the biblical narratives about the past because it better reflects the ways in which the past was understood and utilized in ancient societies ... In particular, accepting that cultural memory—like personal memory—not only recalls the past but also forgets and invents it severs the notion of a necessary link between historical event and narrative account'. This is undoubtedly correct so far as it goes, though it seems to me that recent studies of memory make possible the use of certain distinctions and discriminations which hold out the promise of advancing our understanding.

The first such distinction is that between communicative and cultural memory.[37] The former, communicative memory, refers not simply to individual memories, but to such individual memories insofar as they have a social dimension.[38] Memory is a social phenomenon, growing into us from outside, and in the act of remembering the individual introduces socially conditioned order and structure into the internal life. The distinctive thing about communicative memory is also that it is the memory which is typical of communities still close to their origins, a time of eye-witnesses, of living memory.[39] Such communicative

---

[36] P.R. Davies, *Memories of Ancient Israel*, Louisville 2008, 122.

[37] Cf. especially J. Assmann, *Religion and Cultural Memory*, Stanford 2006, 1–4, 24–30.

[38] For M. Schudson, 'Dynamics of Distortion in Cultural Memory', in D.L. Schacter (ed.), *Memory Distortion: How Minds, Brains and Societies Reconstruct the Past*, Harvard 1995, 346–347, there is no such thing as individual memory. Memory is social. Even individual memories are social in that they operate through the cultural construction of language; they come into play in response to social situations, and are socially structured patterns of recall.

[39] Cf. J.D.G. Dunn, 'Social Memory and the Oral Jesus Tradition', in L.T. Stuckenbruck, S.C. Barton, B.J. Wold (eds), *Memory in the Bible and Antiquity* (WUNT 212), Tübingen 2007, 184.

memory has a limited time span of three to four generations, a maximum of probably one hundred years, the time within which living contact exists with the original generation. At this limit, if the community is not to disappear with its memory, communicative memory is replaced by more enduring forms of cultural memory, embodied in monuments, rituals, feast days and customs, within the context of which foundational stories are cultivated and performed by cultural specialists, so continually integrating the present of a society with its past.[40] Albertz's observation that Israel's memories of the exodus first took narrative form at the time of Jeroboam is important here, for this process of narrativization is not simply the linguistic rendering of stable and enduring community images already stored in the mind, but is rather a process of articulation that effectively creates memory, and does so through stereotypical patterns of communication familiar to the group.[41] Such narrativization is the means by which an enduring form of cultural memory is created, a form which cannot be seen simply as the writing down of individual reminiscences, but rather the rendering of such reminiscences in a form which can command community assent.

A second distinction to be drawn is one between a Freudian view of memory and a different approach founded in the work of the sociologist Maurice Halbwachs carried out in the 1920s. These are not necessarily mutually exclusive, but it seems to me that it is Halbwachs who is more directly relevant to our issue. Freud's work was rooted in his study of individual psychology, and his theory of trauma, repression, period of latency and the return of the repressed, a theory which he applied also to the emergence of Jewish monotheism,[42] is based on his understanding of the psychology of the individual. Freud's argument for making the transfer from individual to group psychology, an argument which, in the form in which it was presented, would not find support today,[43] was that the memory traces lodged in the individual mind are not restricted to the individual but include also 'things that were innately present in him

---

[40] Cf. Dunn, 'Social Memory and the Oral Jesus Tradition', 185.

[41] Cf. A. Le Donne, 'Theological Memory Distortion in the Jesus Tradition', in Stuckenbruck, Barton, Wold (eds.), *Memory in the Bible and Antiquity*, 169–175.

[42] S. Freud, *Moses and Monotheism* (Standard Edition of the Complete Psychological Works of Sigmund Freud, vol. XXIII), London 1964. For a discussion of this work, cf. my 'Moses and Monotheism: The Future of Freud's Illusion', in P. Esler (ed.), *Ancient Israel: The Old Testament in its Social Context*, Minneapolis 2006, 296–308, 348–351.

[43] Cf. the discussion in Y.H. Yerushalmi, *Freud's Moses*, New Haven 1991, 30–33; R.J. Bernstein, *Freud and the Legacy of Moses*, Cambridge 1998, 52–64; S.J. Gould, 'Freud's Evolutionary Fantasy', in his *I Have Landed*, London 2003, 147–158.

at his birth, elements with a phylogenetic origin—an archaic heritage', an archaic heritage which included 'memory traces of the experience of earlier generations'.[44] On such a theory, the exodus could be understood as a traumatic experience which was repressed and then, following a period of latency, was brought back to consciousness by the experience of the Shishak invasion, and was brought back in terms appropriate to that later time. In such a form, however, the theory cannot stand. Experiences are not encoded in such a way in the genetic make-up of individuals to form a collective unconscious independent of cultural expression.

Yet this does not exhaust the question of the relationship of individual and group memory. For Maurice Halbwachs,[45] coming from a structural-functionalist sociological tradition, memory is not individual but social, the past is not preserved but is reconstructed; in the act of remembering the individual does not just descend into the depths of private inner life, in order to retrieve stored images, but rather introduces a socially conditioned order and structure into that internal life. Even 'trauma' is not to be understood naturalistically as an originating event, but is a socially mediated attribution: trauma is not simply an event, as the result of which a group experiences pain and distress, but is rather the result of this pain and distress entering into the core of the group's sense of its own identity.[46] Memory is thus developed in individuals in proportion to their connection with others and their membership of a social group. Thus, the past is not an objective given but a collective reconstruction in the making of which the group acquires its identity.[47] The effect of this approach is that we can dispense with such uncertainties as the 'collective unconscious', and instead of thinking of collective memory as the past shaping the present see it as the mechanism by which the present determines and shapes what we remember from the past.

A striking instance of this, and one of which I wish to make a very limited use, is afforded by a now ten year old study, *The Holocaust and Collective Memory*, by Peter Novick.[48] The question Novick seeks to answer is how and why the Holocaust became 'the emblematic Jewish experience ... the only common denominator of American Jewish identity',[49]

---

[44] Freud, *Moses and Monotheism*, 98–99.
[45] M. Halbwachs, *On Collective Memory*, Chicago 1992.
[46] Cf. J.C. Alexander, 'Toward a Theory of Cultural Trauma', in J.C. Alexander, R. Ayerman, *et al.* (eds), *Cultural Trauma and Collective Identity*, California 2004, 10.
[47] Cf. Assmann, *Religion and Cultural Memory*, 1–4, 93–95.
[48] P. Novick, *The Holocaust and Collective Memory*, London 2001 [1999].
[49] Novick, *Holocaust and Collective Memory*, 7,10.

only from the 1970s onwards, some thirty years after the events com-
memorated. This was undoubtedly, at first, in part because of the lack
of detailed knowledge of the scale of the atrocity, but even more it was
because of the way in which that knowledge was ordered and framed.
Jews were not the only victims; the term 'holocaust' was at first used of
the totality of the destruction rather than of the specifically Jewish experience; for Americans, the Pacific conflict was of greater significance than
the European. The Holocaust, as symbol of Jewish experience, is indeed
based on documented historical events and a host of particular communicative memories; for Novick, however, it became an archetypal symbol of collective Jewish experience in the context of a late 20th century
need to forge a particular and distinct identity for American Jews: 'These
days American Jews can't define their Jewishness on the basis of distinctively Jewish religious beliefs. They can't define it by distinctively Jewish cultural traits, since most don't have any of these either. American
Jews are sometimes said to be united by their Zionism, but if so, it is
of a thin and abstract variety: most have never visited Israel; most contribute little to, and know even less about, that country .... What American Jews *do* have in common is the knowledge that but for their parents'
or (more often) grandparents' or great-grandparents' immigration, they
would have shared the fate of European Jewry. Within an increasingly
diverse and divided American Jewry, this became the historical foundation of that endlessly repeated but empirically dubious slogan "We
are one"'.[50] So Novick then argues: 'The murderous actions of the Nazi
regime, which killed between five and six million European Jews, were all
too real. But "the Holocaust" as we speak of it today, was largely a retro-
spective construction, something that would not have been recognizable
to most people at the time. To speak of "the Holocaust" as a distinct entity
... is to introduce an anachronism that stands in the way of understanding contemporary responses'.[51]

Quite obviously, there is no intention here to diminish the reality of
Jewish experience during the Nazi period in Germany; the details of this
experience are well documented. What Novick demonstrates, and it is

---

[50] Novick, *Holocaust and Collective Memory*, 7. Novick argues that the wider general American cultural context within which this concern for particular Jewish identity
emerged was marked by: the development of a particularist ethos, stressing what differ-
entiates and divides, in place of an integrationist ethos; the rise of a victim culture, which
replaced stoicism with sensitivity; the 'inward and rightward turn of American Jewry in
recent decades'.
[51] Novick, *Holocaust and Collective Memory*, 20.

this which is of significance here, is that it is within a relatively short period of time, thirty years, that the particulars of historical experience come to receive expression in terms of an archetypal symbol, a symbol that functions not only to say something of the past but rather also to preserve that past through making it the identifying marker of the community, that which marks off the community as distinctive in its history and its essential nature.

That this offers a good parallel to the collective memory of the exodus is clear. Like the Holocaust, so the exodus is an archetype, the symbol of Israelite identity, presupposing community assent to this narrativization of its communicative memories. Israel is the people whom Yahweh brought out of Egypt. The usage of this symbol is not to be traced to a time before the rise of the northern kingdom of Israel. This is not to say that the present narrative of the exodus can be traced back to this period, for this narrative, which now emphasizes the bondage of Israel in Egypt and the plagues brought by Yahweh, is an elaboration which owes much to the late connection between Passover and exodus, and is not presupposed in references to Egypt particularly in the eighth century prophets.[52] Behind the present narrative lies a first narrativization of the exodus, to be associated with the rise of the northern kingdom of Israel, which, in asserting that Yahweh brought Israel out of Egypt, conferred a distinctive identity on this people.

Insofar as it has historical roots—and such archetypes are indeed founded in history—the exodus is based on historical experiences which, arising out of the particular needs of the northern kingdom, have been given archetypal significance.[53] The historical experiences, however, which gave rise to the communicative memories of the original actors in the events, will most probably belong to a period shortly before their transformation into a mythic archetype, a cultural symbol; otherwise these memories would have disappeared.[54] In the case of the exodus

---

[52] Cf. P.A.H. de Boer, 'Egypt in the Old Testament: Some Aspects of an Ambivalent Assessment', in: C. van Dam (ed.), *Selected Studies in Old Testament Exegesis* (OTS 27), Leiden 1991, 160–161.

[53] The parallel with American Jewry of the late 20th century may extend even to this: that in both cases there was also a need to mark off in a particularist way the Israelite identity from the surrounding culture.

[54] It is striking that P.D. Miller, *The Religion of Ancient Israel*, Louisville 2000, 80–81, has to create a federation celebrating the exodus in the pre-monarchic period, in order to bridge that time between the 'exodus event' (understood to belong to the New Kingdom period) and its appearance as symbol in the prophets. No such federation existed, and the religious practice of the pre-monarchic period is adequately accounted for, as

the historical experiences to which we are pointed must include the
Shishak invasion and subsequent withdrawal. It is this which created a
context for understanding the communicative memories enshrined in
other historical experiences, significant enough in themselves, such as
Jeroboam's recorded flight to Egypt and subsequent return to assume
kingship. Behind these events we need not go in order to understand the
emergence of the exodus story as an enduring symbol of national identity.[55] If there is a Pharaoh of the exodus, therefore, that Pharaoh was
Shishak.

Miller otherwise does, by reference to family based cults and local harvest celebrations.
The connection of the exodus with Passover is demonstrably secondary and probably
deuteronomic.

[55] There is, therefore, no need to point to Jerusalem and liberation from Solomonic
slavery as the motivation behind the formulation of the exodus story. Insofar as memory
distortion is involved here, this cannot be seen as a significant weakness in the view proposed. For a good example of such distortion in a not unrelated context, cf. J. Assmann,
'Ancient Egyptian Antijudaism: A Case of Distorted Memory', in D.L. Schachter (ed.),
*Memory Distortion: How Minds, Brains and Societies Reconstruct the Past*, Harvard 1995,
365–376.

# THE GREEK ESTHERS AND THE SEARCH FOR HISTORY: SOME PRELIMINARY OBSERVATIONS

Jill Middlemas

*Faculty of Theology, Århus University—Denmark*

## 1. Introduction: Three Interpreters

The biblical book of Esther has long been recognized as a historical novel, that is, having the appearance of a history with folkloristic embellishments.[1] As such, its claim to historicity has been the source of debate.[2] On the one hand, its relation to actual historical events has been supported on the basis of a variety of arguments including that it contains details about Persia and Persian administration and customs known from other ancient sources, Aramaisms and other Persian loan words appear interspersed in the narrative, the names Artaxerxes and Mordecai are known from evidence external to the Hebrew Bible, Esther's name is evocative of that of the Babylonian Goddess Ishtar, and the events that transpire could have happened during the reign of Xerxes (the Persian king most widely recognized as being Ahasuerus). In addition, the book of Esther is presented as history, beginning as it does with the chronological *way* hî 'and it happened', typical of other historical presentations in texts from biblical Israel and it was regarded as such by personages in antiquity as well as those who put together the canon. On the other hand, there are indications that suggest it is a very good story.[3] Not only is there no

---

[1] F.S. Weiland, 'Historicity, Genre, and Narrative Design in the of Esther', *Bibliotheca Sacra* 159 (2002), 151–165, provides a helpful overview of the current state of the discussion, while arguing for the recognition of a new genre, that is heroic narrative literature.

[2] See reviews of the discussion by L.B. Paton, *A Critical and Exegetical Commentary on the Book of Esther* (ICC), Edinburgh 1908, 64–77; S.B. Berg, *The Book of Esther: Motifs, Themes and Structure* (SBLDS, 44), Missoula 1979, 1–11.

[3] See, for example, J.A. Loader, 'Esther as a Novel with Different Levels of Meaning', *ZAW* 90 (1978), 417–421.

outside confirmation of any of the events in actual Persian history,[4] but there are exaggerations that make the story of Esther bigger than any one event in the Persian empire, that is itself magnified in its retelling (to 127 provinces).

Although the account retold in the biblical book of Esther tends no longer to be accepted as factual, the story nonetheless invites a historical reading. The invitation to read or understand the story historically was first accepted within the Greek versions of the Esther scroll.[5] There are two Greek versions of Esther—the Septuagint text sometimes referred to as the B text and the Lucianic text, now more commonly regarded as the Alpha text, because Lucianic authorship is no longer accepted. I will refer to them as the Septuagint (LXX) and the Alpha text (AT). These two versions appear to stem from either the same *Vorlage* or two different *Vorlage* (the Alpha text from an otherwise unknown Proto-Alpha text and the LXX from the Masoretic text).[6]

The AT and LXX depart from the MT in a number of ways. Most obviously they contain 6 Additions[7] in the sense of large blocks of material included in, but for the most part not well integrated into the story (the exception being the so-called Addition D),[8] where the scribe has intervened to provide details not found in the MT version. Two of these Additions clearly function to buttress the historical claims of the text. These

---

[4] S. Dalley, *Esther's Revenge at Susa: From Sennacherib to Ahasuerus*, Oxford 2007, has argued for Assyrian origins in that a historical kernel, that of the Assyrian destruction of Susa in the seventh century BCE, lies at the backdrop of the biblical Esther story.

[5] I understand the story of Esther as a different entity to the Hebrew version found in the Masoretic Text, so there is neither an implicit claim here about the priority of the Hebrew version nor an implicit assumption that the scribes reworking the Esther story in Greek actively added material to a known Hebrew version.

[6] A flurry of activity exists on the relationship of the Greek versions to the Masoretic Text (MT). The AT appears to be a translation of a text very similar to that used by the MT, see K.H. Jobes, *The Alpha-Test of Esther: Its Character and Relationship to the Masoretic Text* (SBLDS, 153), Atlanta 1996. The shorter ending of the AT argued for by D.J.A. Clines, *The Esther Scroll: The Story of the Story* (JSOTSup, 30), Sheffield 1984 and M.V. Fox, *The Redaction of the Books of Esther: On Reading Composite Texts* (SBLMS, 40), Atlanta 1991, no longer appears persuasive in the light of new evidence, see Jobes, *Alpha-Text of Esther*, L.S. Fried, 'Towards the UR-Text of Esther,' JSOT 88 (2000), 49–57, and K. de Troyer, *The End of the Alpha Text of Esther: Translation and Narrative Technique in MT 8:1–17, LXX 8:1017, and AT 7:14–41* (Septuagint and Cognate Studies, 48), Atlanta 2000.

[7] The term 'Additions' as a designation for these 6 blocks of material is commonly used and reflects the general agreement that they are later than the stories in which they are embedded. See, Fox, *Redaction of the Books of Esther*, 17–30 and Jobes, *Alpha-Text of Esther*.

[8] The terminology for the Additions employed in this paper (A-F) is adopted from the editors of the Cambridge critical edition of the Greek texts.

are the B and E Additions, which provide the actual wording of two edicts, one dictated in the king's name by the antagonist Aman (Haman in the MT) and the other dictated in the king's name by the protagonist Mordecai. The edicts are legalistic in language and present two orders by the king—one calling for the eradication of the Jews and the other calling for the protection of the Jews. It is claimed that they were copied, exhibited, and even dispersed, with specific orders from the Persian king. In this respect they are reminiscent of Ezra 1–6 where Aramaic source documents and letters appear intertwined with narrative to create a story about the community returning from the Babylonian exile and its endeavors to reconstruct the temple.

Scribes in antiquity added a historical verisimilitude to the story retold in the scroll of Esther by including documents that resemble known edicts of the Persian kings. The inclusion of 'source' documents reveals an interest in history that contrasts that of contemporary interpreters of the story. Because there is general agreement that the Esther story represents a novel or novella, concerns about whether events related in the scroll actually happened rarely appear. Instead, the interest has shifted in recent years to account for the provenance or concrete social context in which the narrative or narratives arose. Although this is a regular type of question especially well suited to the task of the redaction critic, it is quite interesting to consider how scholars using a variety of approaches to the Esther Greek material nevertheless come back to this question.

The discussion that lies closest to the concerns of history stems from that of Karen Jobes, who analyzes the Alpha Text of Esther in order to ascertain its relationship to the Masoretic text.[9] Her method incorporates a complicated system of calculations developed originally by Raymond Martin, who analyzed the grammar and syntax of known Greek translations and originator texts in order to provide a means to adjudicate the relationship of a Greek manuscript to a non-Greek alternative.[10] Jobes's investigation results in an impressive statistical analysis that provides solid grounds for regarding the AT (almost in its entirety) as a translation of a Semitic *Vorlage* very similar to that used by the Masoretic text and also, eventually, the Septuagint. Although the determination of the relationship of the AT and MT to a Semitic *Vorlage* provides the results

---

[9] Jobes, *Alpha-Text of Esther*.

[10] R.A. Martin, *Syntactical Evidence of Semitic Sources in Greek Documents*, Missoula 1974, and R.A. Martin, 'Syntax Criticism of the LXX Additions to the Book of Esther', *JBL* 94 (1975), 65–72. Fried, 'Towards the UR-Text', uses Martin's approach also.

of the statistical analysis she utilizes and fulfils the concern that drove her point of departure, she concludes with a consideration of the provenance of the material.

Her conclusions include a critique of a doctoral dissertation that found 17 distinct redactional stages in the growth of the AT Esther on the basis of a lack of historical documentation, inferring too much from internal evidence, associating layers of the text with various political parties, and utilizing circular reasoning in order to identify the segments of the text that belong to different political viewpoints.[11] In her view the evidence was not conducive to the establishment of such a detailed delineation of social locations, nevertheless she provides her own reconstruction of provenance. A Semitic text of Esther (Hebrew or Aramaic) arrived in Egypt possibly via the Elephantine community and circulated independently of a similar text that was brought back to Judah / Jerusalem from exile. This text and its story circulated among the Jews of Egypt and eventually gave rise to the AT. During the Hasmonean period the need was felt to send an authoritative version of a Greek Esther text to the Alexandrian Jews to promote the observance of Purim. The LXX text supplanted the AT, to which an attempt to harmonize it with the LXX led to mixed results. Afterwards it failed to be authoritative for the majority of the population and circulated in smaller circles, possibly even redacted by and for a Christian audience. As evidence for the last, she finds some affinity between Mordecai's dream and the Christian apocalypse of Revelations. A careful statistical analysis of the syntactical and grammatical relationship of the AT to the MT that provides evidence of the mutual dependence on a common Semitic *Vorlage*, clearly from an overriding concern with the development of the text, has led to conclusions that speculate about the communities and the socio-historical circumstances in which the traditions circulated. It may be that Jobes's point of departure about how the texts developed leads to the incorporation of an additional historical discussion, that of provenance, but the goal of her analysis does not naturally include this type of question.

In a somewhat different vein, Linda Day presents a literary study of the Esther scroll with particular attention to the characterization of Esther.[12] In her review of scholarship she observes that the overriding concern

---

[11] Jobes, *Alpha-Text of Esther*, 228.

[12] L. Day, *Three Faces of a Queen: Characterization in the Books of Esther* (JSOTSup, 186), Sheffield 1995.

has been on the origins and textual history of the story, which although important, has left many other areas as yet unexplored.[13] She regards her consideration of the character of Esther in the MT as well as in the Greek texts as more of a literary endeavor, 'This present study will look closely at the textual variations among the versions of the Esther story, but with literary objectives rather than redactional'.[14] Nevertheless, after a very considered and thoughtful study of literary issues, she concludes her analysis by returning to questions that tend to form the final thoughts of the redaction critic by suggesting the social contexts that produced the different versions of Esther.

In her view the AT contains features that suggest it would be the product of a Jewish community in Diaspora that was more integrated with non-Jews and more Hellenized in thought and behavior. In contrast, the LXX text presents Esther as having greater affinity with the Jewish community and being more concerned about proper religious observance. Thus its origin would be more consistent with a setting in Palestine or at the least within the Diaspora by a community who retained more of its traditional practices and who may have experienced increased tension or discrimination at the hands of non-Jews. Meanwhile, the MT lies somewhere in between the AT and the LXX texts and reflects a situation in which the Jews have a 'professional relationship' with the Persians, but who seek to retain a strong Jewish identity based upon religious observance. Day concludes a fine literary study of Esther as a character in a history-like novel by focusing on questions that place more stress on assertions about history rather than those of literature as she considers the socio-historical background in which the texts were produced. Although she is not alone in this, perhaps it is all the more striking because of the literary framework on which she embarks.

The final interpreter to be considered is Charles Dorothy, who like Jobes provides a rather meticulous study of the LXX and the AT Esther with the Additions, but his focus lies on generating a structural analysis rather than establishing the text basis.[15] Dorothy utilizes methods that stem from structuralist studies that aim in the main to define the system, rather than provide meaning. Nevertheless, he concludes his detailed study with a view to the socio-historical settings in which the two Greek

---

[13] Day, *Three Faces of a Queen*, 17.
[14] Day, *Three Faces of a Queen*, 18.
[15] C.V. Dorothy, *The Books of Esther: Structure, Genre and Textual Integrity* (JSOTSup, 187), Sheffield 1997.

versions arose. His conclusions reflect the exact opposite position to those outlined by Day. In his view the AT is more insular and probably from the homeland, while the LXX text is more open and from the Diaspora. The evidence he adduces to support the character of the communities that produced the texts or for whom the texts were written tends to be based on his understanding of the nature of each. The LXX, for example, is written more as an objective account, whereas the AT comes from a writer who gives him the impression of being more personally involved in the story and thus commends it as 'our story' to a Jewish community. Again, the fact that Dorothy concludes with assertions about the socio-historical circumstances that gave rise to the Greek versions of Esther is somewhat out of place given that his point of departure is a structuralist study of the material.

What is striking about the three interpreters mentioned here is how their analyses conclude with the establishment of social contexts from which sacred literature arose in spite of the fact that the methods employed do not necessitate such conclusions. Jobes, Day, and Dorothy thus reveal an interest in history, but their questions related to provenance rather than whether an account is true or has elements in it that can be taken as true (e.g. as with the inclusion of Persian monarchical edicts). Moreover, it is equally clear that not one of the interpreters mentioned here arrives at the same assessment of the communities underlying the texts. Their ascribed social locations vary dramatically, even seem mutually exclusive. There is an ambiguity or openness to the literature that invites a variety of viewpoints, thus the lack of agreement among the interpreters. What each of them has not done is to approach the versions of Esther as source documents from antiquity and to ask questions about how history is recounted in the text and what light that might shed on how much we can know about the circumstances that gave rise to the narratives as we have them. Given that the Greek versions of the Esther scroll present themselves as authentic history through the inclusion of two Persian documents, a query could be raised about what is history to those writing and transmitting the Greek Esthers and the elements understood to be operative in their telling. Attending to these types of questions should reveal how a study of the Greek Esthers contributes to an understanding of what history entails to writers in antiquity.

## 2. Unique Material in the Greek Versions of the Esther Story

The MT of Esther is different from the two Greek versions. One of the major differences has to do with the appearance of 6 blocks of material, the Additions, included in the AT and LXX. Two of them, the edicts B and E, have already been introduced. The others include a dream of Mordecai with apocalyptic elements and the discovery of a plot against the king's life in A, prayers of Mordecai and Esther in response to the looming death sentence pronounced by Haman in C, a greatly dramatized scene of Esther's approach to the king to seek his favour in D, and the interpretation of Mordecai's dream (in A) as the conclusion in F.

In addition to the appearance of 6 blocks of material in the Greek version, there are other textual details and narrative interjections not found in the MT. Unlike the MT which is well known for its lack of reference to the deity of ancient Israel as well as religious details of any kind, in the AT and LXX God in the sense of the deity active within the traditions of ancient Israel is mentioned over 50 times and reference is made to pagan gods as well (the latter moreso in the AT than the LXX). A question remains about whether references to the god of ancient Israel and other gods were deleted by the authors of the MT version of the Esther story or whether they were added to the Greek versions. David Clines argued originally that the authors of the MT deleted references to the divine considering them too sacrilegious[16] and others have suggested that religious language was added to the Greek versions rather than deleted from the MT.[17] There seems to be a middle ground. Lawrence Wills has argued that the earliest layer of the Esther scroll appears to be the court tale of the wise courtier who triumphs over a foolish one known more widely in the ANE (see also the Joseph story).[18] Deities appear in ANE versions of the story. If this (or some similar tale) were part of an original layer of the Esther scroll that formed the basis of the MT and AT, it seems that the scribes working on the AT maintained references to other deities and included details about their deity, Yahweh, while those of the MT simply deleted references to other deities and refrained from including details about Yahweh. That the inclusion of the god of ancient

---

[16] Clines, *Esther Scroll*.

[17] Fox, *Redaction of the Books of Esther*, 120; Jobes, *Alpha-Text of Esther* 213.

[18] L.M. Wills, *The Jew in the Court of the Foreign King* (Harvard Dissertations in Religion, 26) Minneapolis 1990.

Israel in the Greek texts appears in the main stories of the AT and LXX, but becomes more pronounced in the Additions suggests that there was a concerted effort at a later stage to emphasize the deity's role in the story. This would suggest that the *Vorlage* of the MT and AT contained some references to deities other than Yahweh and the two textual traditions diverged in their inclusion of the deity of ancient Israel. A counter-study to the one presented here could consider the lack of the inclusion of the deity in the MT in an analysis of what it contributes to the understanding of history or religion in the MT, but that would take us too far afield from the present task.

More than adding God as a character and actor within the story or even fashioning the story of Esther to appear more historically authentic, the material found in the Greek scrolls of Esther, but not the MT, provides information on how some scribes in antiquity dealt with history and historical questions.[19] There are three main ways they contribute to an understanding of history in the ancient world: the events of history are divine in origin and continuation, the biblical story provides the basis for the understanding the story of the Jewish people, and its message resonates in contemporary circumstances.

## 2.1. *The Events of History are Divine in Origin and Continuation*

The largest chunk of material divergent to the MT, both in the Additions, but also elsewhere in the main body of the Esther scroll where the Greek texts differ from the MT, contributes a sense of the divine acting in and guiding history. There is a general belief in the ability of the gods (Yahwistic and non-Yahwistic) to effect affairs in the human realm. This is apparent already among the non-Jews in the main story of the AT (but not the LXX). The narrator reports that non-Jews consult their gods about events to take place. For example, Aman seeks guidance in

---

[19] This discussion verges on the boundary of that found in rewritten bible / scripture circles. Rewritten Bible, originally defined by G. Vermes, *Scripture and Tradition in Judaism* (StPB, 4), Leiden 1961, is understood as a phenomena whereby scribes in late Second Temple Judaism, intervened in scriptural texts to revise or recast inherited traditions to explain them to a new generation (exegesis in antiquity). For a brief overview to the current state of the discussion, see S.W. Crawford, *Rewriting Scripture in Second Temple Times*, Grand Rapids 2008. The present study departs from Rewritten Bible / Scripture discussions in failing to assert that the Greek Esthers were self-consciously adapting the Hebrew version of the Esther story. Scribes were re-working the Esther story as authors and editors, but it is not clear that they were doing so with a received and authoritative text.

order to determine the time to strike against the Jewish community, καὶ ἐπορεύθη Αμαν πρὸς τοὺς θεοὺς αὐτοῦ τοῦ ἐπιγνῶναι ἡμέραν θανάτου αὐτῶν 'Haman went to his gods to learn the day of [the Jews] death' (AT 4:12, compare MT 3:7) and his wife asserts that the deities have granted him a fixed time, καὶ ἔδωκάν σοι οἱ θεοὶ εἰς ἐκδίκησιη αὐτῶν ἡμέραν ὀλέθριον 'and (as) the gods have given you a day of destruction for taking revenge on them' (AT 6:23, compare MT 5:14).

This type of belief in the divine is also apparent among Jews in the main story of the AT and to some extent the LXX, especially in connection with Esther and Mordecai who express a belief in God working in the human realm and the efficacy of prayer.

### 2.1.1. Belief in the Activity of the Divine

There is a general belief that the deity of the Jews can act within historical time. The expression for this belief comes from the Jews (Mordecai) and non-Jews (Aman's wife). Mordecai exemplifies this understanding when he says to Esther, Ἐὰν ὑπερίδης τοῦ ἔθνους σου τοῦ μὴ βοηθῆσαι αὐτοῖς, ἀλλ᾽ ὁ θεὸς ἔσται αὐτοῖς βοηθὸς καὶ σωτηρία 'If you reject your people by not helping them, God will be their helper and salvation' (AT 5:9, compare MT 4:14). Similarly, Mordecai recognizes the activity of the divine when Aman elevates him and clothes him in a royal garment, καὶ ἐδόκει Μαρδοχαῖος τέρασ θεωρεῖν, καὶ ἡ καρδία αὐτοῦ πρὸς τὸν κύριον 'And Mordecai thought he saw a miracle, and his heart was toward the Lord' (AT 7:15–17, compare MT 6:11 and LXX 5:11–12). Alternatively, the efficacy of the god of Jews to effect change in the human realm is acknowledged by Aman's wife in both Greek versions. She says in response to Aman's account of his humiliation before Mordecai that, καὶ εἶπεν ἡ γυνὴ αὐτοῦ καὶ οἱ σοφοὶ αὐτοῦ ᾿Αφ᾽ ὅτε λαλεῖς περὶ αὐτοῦ κακὰ, προσπορεύεταί σοι τὰ κακά ησυχαζε, ὅτι ὁ θεὸς ἐν αὐτοῖς 'And the time you spoke evil about him, evil has come upon you. Be quiet! For God is among them' (AT 7:22, no MT equivalent) and οὐ μὴ δύνῃ αὐτὸν ἀμύνασθαι ὅτι θεὸς ζῶν μετ᾽ αὐτοῦ 'you will not succeed against him because the Living God is with him' (LXX 6:13).

### 2.1.2. Belief in the Efficacy of Prayer

In addition to the inclusion of a general belief that the deity of the Jews can effect change in history, the main text of the Greek versions includes occasions when the characters express belief in the efficacy of ritual

observance and prayer to the deity. The inclusion of prayer is particularly striking with regards to the main characters Esther and Mordecai. When Esther agrees to Mordecai's request to intercede with the
king on behalf of the Jewish community, she tells him to, Παραγγεί-
λατε θεραπείαν καὶ δεήθητε τοῦ θεοῦ ἐκτενῶς 'Announce an assem-
bly and pray earnestly to God' (AT 5:11, compare MT and LXX 4:15–
16). Similarly, Esther calls upon the deity in a moment of weakness
(AT 8:2, dealt with more fully below). Also, Mordecai expresses such
a belief when correlating intercession with divine deliverance, ἐπικαλεσαμένη οὖν τὸν θεὸν λάλησον περὶ ἡμῶν τῷ βασιλεῖ, καὶ ῥῦσαι ἡμᾶς
ἐκ θανάτου 'after calling upon God, speak to the king concerning us,
and deliver us from death'. (AT 5:5, compare MT 4:8) and ἐπικάλε-
σαι τὸν κύριον καὶ λάλησον τῷ βασιλεῖ περὶ ἡμῶν καὶ ῥῦσαι ἡμᾶς
ἐκ θανάτου 'call upon God and speak to the king so that we should
be saved from death' (LXX 4:8). The belief in the ability of the deity
to answer prayer is substantiated when the narrator intervenes in the
story to attribute divine support for Esther at a point when she becomes
afraid and calls for divine assistance, καὶ ἠγωνίασεν Εσθηρ…,καὶ ὁ
θεὸς ἔδωκεν αὐτῇ θάρσος ἐν τῷ αὐτὴν ἐπικαλεῖσθαι αὐτόν 'And Esther
was anxious …, and God gave her courage when she called upon him'
(AT 8:2).

### 2.1.3. Belief in Divine Determinism

In general the plot of the Esther story as found in the MT, AT, and LXX is
an extensive reversal of fortune: danger is transformed into deliverance,
humble beginnings to success.[20] In the Greek versions, it is made clear
that the actor behind the reversal is the deity of the Jews. There are
hints of divine determination already in the main body of the story,
but this aspect of the presentation becomes more clear in the Additions.
Hints appear when the narrator attributes critical events to direct divine
intervention. For example, the king's insomnia will eventually lead to
the realization of the importance of Mordecai, but it does not stem from
natural causes, rather, ὁ δὲ δυνατός ἀπέστησε τὸν ὕπνον τοῦ βασιλέως
τὴν νύκτα ἐκείνην 'The Almighty took away the king's sleep that night'
(AT 7:1, compare MT 6:1) and ὁ δὲ κύριος ἀπέστησεν τὸν ὕπνον ἀπὸ

---

[20] Clines, *Esther Scroll*, 155.

τοῦ βασιλέως τὴν νύκτα ἐκείνην 'But the Lord removed sleep from the king that night' (LXX 6:1).

These features provide examples in which the narrator expressed a belief that the God of the Jews engages in history and the efficacy of human communication with the deity. They also provide examples for behaviour to emulate in that Mordecai and Esther represent role models who believe in the Jewish God as an actor in history, appeal to the deity when in need, and recognize divine intervention. The belief of non-Jews in deities is also represented in the story. In the Additions, the role of the God of the Jews becomes more pronounced, perhaps even transforming Yahweh into the hero of the Greek stories as Moore has suggested.[21]

### 2.1.4. *The Additions: Belief in the Efficacy of Prayer*

Just as there were two Additions included to provide details of the edicts issued by Aman and Mordecai on behalf of the Persian king, there are two Additions that offer a more detailed look at the religious life of the characters Mordecai and Esther. In Addition C, Mordecai fasts and prays. Esther prays and observes other ritual observances in Additions C and D. The prayer of Mordecai is the shorter of the two and follows a structure well known from the psalms: an invocation is followed by praise and protestations of innocence, and an address and petition conclude.[22] Esther's prayer, in contrast, has a lengthy introduction detailing her assumption of mourning attire and the rituals she observes followed by a lengthy prayer consisting of an invocation, a cry of distress, a communal confession, and petition. Queen Esther concludes her prayers by focusing on how she has acted worthily in her service in the Persian court and as the wife of a Gentile king as well as with a more general interest in petitioning the deity for the well being of the community and herself. In a highly fictionalized account, Esther approaches the king in Addition D. After Esther arrays herself in clothing fit for a Queen, she begins her approach to the king, but importantly only after appealing to the deity, καὶ ἐπικαλεσαμένη τὸν πάντων γνώστην καὶ σωτῆρα θεὸν 'and she invoked the aid of the all-knowing and Savior God' (AT Add D 2) (compare 'the all seeing God and Saviour' in the LXX).

---

[21] C.A. Moore, *Daniel, Esther and Jeremiah: The Additions* (AB, 44), Garden City 1977, 8.

[22] So, also, Dorothy, *Books of Esther*.

As found elsewhere in the main body of literature, the Additions present pious individuals, whose faith offers them sustenance in the midst of crisis. In so doing, the Additions include the deity of the Jews as an actor in the story who is understood to intervene, decisively and determinatively.

### 2.1.5. *The Additions: Divine Determinism*

Additions A and F serve as the prologue and epilogue to the Greek stories of Esther and thus provide the lens through which to read the Esther story and the conclusion with which to understand it. They exert no influence on the narrative itself, but function instead to place the triumph of Mordecai and Esther within a more cosmic realm, as part of an apocalyptic story. They show that the God of the Jews is in control of events that transpire on a cosmic level rather than just a local one. Moreover, they reveal a prophetic understanding to history in that the deity's universal plans are revealed to certain individuals.

Through the Additions, the author of the Greek version of the Esther scroll reinforces the impression given in the main body of the material: a powerful deity engages in history on behalf of select individuals, prayer and religious observance activate divine intervention, and there is an overarching divine plan for historical events. This material functions on another level to highlight pious Jewish individuals who serve as role models for how to maintain Jewish faith in a non-Jewish, even threatening, environment.

### 2.2. *Traditional Stories from Biblical Israel Provide the Basis for Understanding the Story of the Jewish People*

A significant amount of research on the versions of the Esther story (the MT, AT, and LXX) has focused on its relationship to literature stemming from the biblical period.[23] Results of intertextual analysis of this nature has not tended to be utilized in more general discussions about what evidence it provides for understanding categories of history in antiquity.

---

[23] James Aitken has drawn attention to an equally important issue regarding how the Greek Esthers relate to literature commonly dated to the Intertestamental period. So far, there has been less published on this question (although there has been some degree of interest in the Greek Esthers and their relationship to the book of Judith and 3 Maccabees, for example). A full length consideration of the Greek Esthers alongside other material from the Greco-Roman world would be most welcome. Because the present study is

I will briefly summarize some of the more applicable findings in order to clarify what they contribute to the task at hand. Briefly, they indicate an interest in associating the story of Esther with the traditions of ancient Israel.

Clines has noted this to a certain extent already in that he has argued that 'the primary effect of the LXX expansions as a whole is … to *assimilate the book of Esther to a scriptural norm*, especially as found in Ezra, Nehemiah, and Daniel'.[24] The scriptural norm of which he speaks is in reality a historical norm, that is, history as understood to be true and/or operative for the people who inherited the traditions found collected in the Hebrew Bible/Old Testament. This principle is found not only in the LXX of the Esther scroll, but also in the AT. One of the more obvious ways that the story of Esther is fashioned to be more scripture-like is by the inclusion of the two edicts, Additions B and E. In addition, one of the chief effects of the inclusion of elements of religiosity in the Greek versions (the AT moreso than the LXX) is to align Esther and Mordecai with characters in the biblical story elsewhere and with commandments made through Scripture.[25] A clear indication of this feature occurs when Mordecai advises Esther φοβεῖσθαι τὸν θεὸν καὶ ποιεῖν τὰ προστάγματα αὐτοῦ 'to fear God and do his commandments' (LXX 2:20).

Otherwise, the story of Esther has been found to echo the Pentateuch through similarity to the story of the Exodus, although it is not persuasive to argue that the details of the Exodus account underlie its composition[26] and this commonality is also found with regards to the story that appears in the MT. There is a resonance with the Exodus traditions that is further reinforced when Egypt is mentioned in conjunction with the inheritance of Israel in the Additions (LXX Add C 8–10; AT Add C 16–17). Moreover, Jobes has found language consistent with the Exodus narrative elsewhere in the LXX (e.g. the consistency of the Greek translation of 'God's mighty hand', see Exod. 3:19; 6:1; 13:3, 9, 14, 16; Deut. 3:24; 4:34; 5:15; 6:21; 7:8,

---

interested in what evidence can be adduced for the use of prior traditions as a way of understanding conceptions of history among the scribes of the Greek Esthers, it will not deal with this otherwise interesting question.

[24] Clines, *Esther Scroll*, 169, see also 170–174.

[25] Also observed by Clines, *Esther Scroll*, 169–171.

[26] Contra G. Gerleman, *Studien zu Esther: Stoff—Struktur—Stil—Sinn* (Biblische Studien, 48), Neukirchen-Vluyn 1966. Also see, C.A. Moore, 'Esther Revisited: An Examination of Esther Studies over the Past Decade', in: A. Kort, S. Morschauser (eds), *Biblical and Related Studies Presented to Samuel Iwry*, Winona Lake 1985, 163–172.

19; 9:26; 11:2; 26:8; 34:12). Otherwise Pentateuchal references appear
in the mention of 'the covenant with Abraham' in AT (Add C 16) and
'the covenant to Abraham' in LXX (Add C 8). Likewise, Jobes finds faint
echoes or metalepsis of the LXX version of Moses's prayer in Deut. 9 in
LXX Add C 2, 23[27] that suggest to her that the story of Esther is drawn
into the mainstream tradition of the Pentateuch.[28]

It has long been recognized that the story of Esther in the Greek
versions also shares commonality with the stories of Joseph and Daniel.[29]
Apocalyptic elements in the Additions A and F certainly reinforce a
strong connection to the Daniel tale, while the emphasis on Mordecai's
dream and its fulfilment suggest commonality with Joseph the dreamer.
Jobes also sees some degree of overlap with the Septuagint of Jeremiah
28, the Oracle against Babylon. The echo of Jeremiah 28 is found in Add
A through the imagery of the dragon, fountain, battle, and the contrast
of darkness and light. Based on this overlap, Jobes suggests that the
imagery in Esther refers to the fulfilment of Jeremiah's condemnation
and thereby suggests an end to the punishment of the exile. If seen in this
way, referencing provides a means of circling back to situations left open
in the scriptural[30] history (the exile never truly ended because Diaspora
existence continued well beyond the advent of Cyrus). Allusions to the
LXX Oracle against Babylon reveal that the scriptural interpretation of
history is still operative and that the Greek Esthers are part of that history.

These examples show that a wide variety of scriptural literature seems
to be influential to the scribes reworking the Greek story of Esther. What
is important about this apparent sea of ideas is that it suggests that
there was an attempt to make Esther more traditional, especially when
compared to the lack of religious activity among the heroes in the MT
version. These allusions function both to align the characters in the story
of Esther with other scriptural figures recognized as leaders appointed
by Yahweh and to place the story itself within an interpretive continuum.
The scribes narrating the Greek versions of Esther understood history as

---

[27] Jobes, *Alpha-Text of Esther*, 188.

[28] Jobes, *Alpha-Text of Esther*, 176–180.

[29] L.A. Rosenthal, 'Die Josephsgeschichte mit den Büchern Ester und Daniel ver-
glichen', *ZAW* 15 (1895), 278–284, and L.A. Rosenthal, 'Nochmals der Vergleich Ester,
Joseph, Daniel', *ZAW* 17 (1897), 125–128.

[30] Nomenclature for material circulating in antiquity that would eventually become
biblical texts is quite a contentious area. I have chosen to use scriptural (as is consistent
with some of the current literature on the topic of Rewritten Bible) as a way to indicate
that there are authoritative texts circulating that are not yet incorporated into a canon as
we come to understand the Old Testament / Hebrew Bible.

a direct descendent of scriptural traditions. Esther's story was part of and in line with scriptural history. As such, it would share a degree of overlap with traditions and figures from those narratives.

## 2.3. Contemporizing the Message

A final type of historical approach is found among the writers of the Greek scroll of Esther. There are examples where the details of the story differ between the LXX and the AT such that they appear to relate information to a specific target audience contemporaneous with the author / editor of the material. These provide examples of contemporizing the story to appropriate an historical event. History or the reconstructed story is not just referred to as occurring in the past, but generates new meaning for a contemporary audience.

Updating the story takes place on a number of levels. The first of which is clearly related to clarifying details of the story to make them more understandable to its audience. For example, the narrator of the AT combines the dating of the events according to the Hebrew calendar with Macedonian dates, 'In the second year of the reign of Ahasuerus the Great, on the first day of the month Adar-Nisan, that is Dystros-Xanthicus' (AT Add A 1).[31] This has the effect of making the story understood by its contemporary audience, who were presumably more used to the Macedonian calendar and less familiar with the Hebrew one. Another interesting feature of the Greek versions is that Aman is called both a Bagaion (LXX A:17; 3:1; 9:10; AT 3:1; E:10; 9:10) and a Macedonian (LXX E:10; AT A:17). The MT introduces Haman as an Agagite (3:1) seemingly appealing to the tradition of the sparing of the lives of the Amalekites after their defeat by Saul. The use of the terms in the Greek versions is thought to be some type of reproach. Of them Moore observes, 'Thus, just as the MT (3:1) used "Agagite" (Josephus *amalekiten*) as a name representing the implacable arch enemy of the Israelites, so Greek editors of Esther used equally meaningful contemporary terms for their Hellenistic readers'.[32] Jobes considers this in more detail and speculates that there is an identifiable person behind the term Bagaion.[33] What her suggestions would illustrate is the alignment of a figure known to the audience from stories circulating at the time with the Aman of the biblical tale.

---

[31] See Moore, *Additions*, 175, n. 1.
[32] Moore, *Additions*, 178, n. 17.
[33] Jobes, *Alpha-Text of Esther*, 125–126.

There are other examples that seem to relate more to issues (religious in the main) experienced by the contemporary community. One of the striking examples of this type occurs in the AT, where the story concludes with the Jews circumcising themselves (Add 8:41). The LXX version has the more expected ending in that the Gentiles acknowledge the God of the Jews and are circumcised (LXX 8:17). The difference in the AT version must be related to the community in which the texts were received. Under Hellenism the practice of circumcision fell out of favour among certain Jews in the homeland and in Diaspora. Its appearance in the AT Esther clearly sends a message about the importance of ritual observance to the present generation. Similarly, the AT appropriates Mordecai's entreaty to the current generation in that his prayer in Addition C concludes with a chorus of the Jewish people from the current generation. Although Mordecai's intercession had been in the first person singular (Add C 13–16), he is joined by another group speaking in the first common plural, 'Hear our prayer, and have mercy upon your inheritance; turn our mourning into rejoicing, that we may live and sing praise to you; do not destroy the mouth of those who praise you' (C 17). This contrasts remarkably to the LXX version, where the use of the third masculine plural indicates that Mordecai's generation alone is involved, 'And all Israel cried out as loud as they could because their end was near'. In the AT, the danger threatening Mordecai was not a past event, but one that the contemporary audience could claim also to be theirs.

Another way of contemporizing the story is that it appears to serve apologetic purposes. The inclusion of the second edict (Add E) in which the king issues a command to protect the Jews presents the Jewish religion and its deity in a positive light. The fact that this comes from not just any foreigner, but the Persian king, suggests that the edict also functions as a defence of Judaism to a Gentile audience or at least to a Jewish audience concerned about Gentile perceptions. A similar effect is achieved by the Aramaic documents in Ezra 1–6 (1:2; 4:20; 5:12; 6:8–10) and by the Persian imperial statements in Daniel (3:29, 31–34:34; 6:26–27) as Clines has noted.[34] Further, the alignment of the imperial edict in Daniel

---

[34] Clines, *Esther Scroll*, 173, writes, 'we find that they witness to such effects of the Jewish faith: to Cyrus's conviction that Yahweh has given him world dominion and a special responsibility to rebuild the Jerusalem temple (Ezra 1:2), to Artaxerxes' realization that Jerusalem is an ancient city and former capital of a great empire (4:20), to Tattenai's understanding that the exile of the Jews was due to the anger of their God (5:12), to Darius's desire that the Jerusalem temple cult be supported from satrapal revenues and that prayers should be made by its priests for the life of the king and his successors (6:8–

lies close to that found in the Greek Esther as Clines states, 'Especially worthy of note is the letter of Nebuchadnezzar in the form of a 'confession of faith', sent to all peoples, nations, and languages' (Dan 3:31–34.34 [ET 4:1–37]) because of its similarity to Artaxerxes' second decree in the LXX Esther'. It can also be seen that the *apologia* is established already within the first edict promulgated by Haman (Add B) in that it gives a standardized negative evaluation of Judaism that is to be overturned (see also Ezra 4:11–16).[35]

These examples provide some indication that the historical presentation of the writers / editors of the Esther scroll was not just about the past, but also about the present of the community. The story of Esther was being reworked in order to appropriate it to a contemporary audience with its own concerns.

There are three ways the scribes involved with the Esther story diverge from the account in the MT with regards to the inclusion of historical categories: (1) the deity engages in history, even determines it, (2) the story of Esther, Mordecai, and their Diaspora community is part of scriptural history, and (3) history is unfolding in the present time. These three facets of the construction of the story show that the scribes were interested in historical questions in quite a different way than modern interpreters. The Greek versions of Esther (often the AT moreso than the LXX) evidence that history is understood to include a category including divine activity and intervention, to be related to and even determined by the traditions of ancient Israel, and related to the present experiences of the community.

### 3. Summary and Conclusions

There are five main types of historical questions that can be brought to bear in the analysis of scripture:

(1) to question the historical presentation with a view towards ascertaining the reliability of the scriptural story with concerns about whether it portrays actual historical events as they happened or whether they belong to a later time and are retrojections onto an

---

10), to Nebuchadnezzar's assurance that there is no other god who is able to deliver as the God of Daniel's three friends has done (Dan. 3:29), to Darius's intention that throughout his empire citizens should tremble and fear before the God of Daniel (6:26–27)'.

[35] Clines, *Esther Scroll*, 174.

earlier time, thereby serving ideological purposes. These are two sides of the same coin, as it were,

(2) to question the history of the literary development with particular attention to how the texts took shape over time and their relationship to each other. This is an historical inquiry in spite of the fact that it concentrates on reconstructing sources and textual development rather than dealing with the question of whether an event transpired as recounted,

(3) to question the social and historical settings that produced different material. The fundamental historical concern here is to ascertain provenance,

(4) to question the history of reception in the sense of how were the stories transmitted through time (examples include the concerns of those engaged in the Rewritten Bible / Scripture discussion as well as those interested in how sacred stories appear in the Church Fathers or in Medieval commentaries, literature, and cartography),

(5) and to question historical presentations in antiquity with a view towards the historical presuppositions of the story itself, to take seriously what the scribes writing and rewriting stories understand to be operative and what they take to be true.

John Barton has already shown how very early on biblical criticism included many of these types of historical concerns.[36] What contributes to a discussion of the use of historical categories within a method of analysis is the acknowledgement that a traditional (in the sense of inherited story) understanding of history was operative for scribes working with sacred traditions. In order to be more critically aware, an interpreter should take this aspect into account when approaching sacred (not necessarily biblical) texts with historical questions.

The understanding of history in antiquity as revealed in the Greek stories of Esther certainly does not equate to a real history in the sense of an objective chronicle of actual events that took place in the past as they occurred. Rather, they represent an interpretation of history that scribes either understood to be true or sought to promote as true. With this understanding of representations of historical events it becomes more difficult to ascertain the actual events that underlie the presentation at our disposal. This holds true equally for attempts to capture a sense of the events experienced by the communities in which the texts circulated.

---

[36] J. Barton, *The Nature of Biblical Criticism*, Louisville 2007.

Philip Davies has been instrumental in alerting interpreters that there is a biblical Israel that is represented in a way that makes it difficult to ascertain the actual events that took place in biblical times.[37] This is clear in the Greek Esthers, but the awareness that writers in antiquity were operating with different categories for what comprises history is a necessary addition to thoughts about these questions at the current time.

What the evidence of the Greek texts of Esther contributes to the discussion is that the scribes seem to have had different types of historical categories operative for them. They were interested in adding a religious dimension to the inherited story of Esther. For them, the God of ancient Israel fashions history and engages in the lived experiences of people through time. In addition, they were keen to show that the story of Esther, Mordecai, and the Persian Jews were part of a scriptural story, in what was becoming at the time authoritative literature. There is a scriptural historical representation of events that is taken as a given. Indeed, scriptural representations of historical events were understood to be authoritative and true enough to supply the background for the scribes working with the story of Esther. Finally, the events surrounding the salvation of the Jews and the establishment of the celebration of Purim were made relevant for the current generation. Scriptural history, therefore, has a fluid quality—capturing in one moment the far distant past, the past, and the present. It is an aspect of historical representation that we miss when we only ask questions related to the veracity or the objectivity of the account.

There is a limitation to using the term history in English that is not found when speaking of *Geschichte* in German or *historie* in Danish. In English parlance history refers to the (objective) representation of events as they took place in the past, whereas the terms in German and Danish include this definition as well as that of a story or a portrait of events not necessarily objectifiable and verifiable. The latter is clearly representative of the events retold in the Greek Esthers. History as found here is a people's reconstruction of their past and their categories for what history could include are different from what modern/postmodern interpreters would accept. The Greek Esthers reveal through story the importance of history to those in antiquity. Ultimately, it is an awareness of differences in definitions of history that contributes to the objective and critical analysis of textual representations of the past.

---

[37] P.R. Davies, *In Search of 'Ancient Israel'* (second edition; JSOTSup, 148), Sheffield 1995.

# DOES ARCHAEOLOGY REALLY DESERVE THE STATUS OF A 'HIGH COURT' IN BIBLICAL HISTORICAL RESEARCH?

NADAV NA'AMAN
*Tel Aviv University*

## 1. INTRODUCTION

From its earliest days, modern research archaeology has played an important role in biblical-historical studies. Many of the places mentioned in
the Bible were identified in the early stage of research, and it was assumed
that excavating them would complement the limited information con-
veyed in the Bible. In those years, archaeology was seen as an important
instrument in the struggle against the 'higher criticism'—the approach
that questioned the historicity of some parts of biblical historiography.
Since archaeology is an external, 'objective' scientific tool, it was believed
that it could disprove the modern literary critical approach. These hopes
were shared by fundamentalist Christians and orthodox Jews, and so
archaeology gained a highly favourite place in the early biblical historical research.[1]

Since the late nineteenth century, major biblical sites—such as Jerusalem, Gezer, Taanach, Megiddo, Samaria and Jericho—have been excavated. However, the technical skills and pottery knowledge of the early
excavators was very limited, and it took many years before archaeology
developed a proper methodology for excavating the ancient mounds.
Likewise, the accurate sequence of pottery and its chronology were only
gradually established, and today these are the key to all modern excavations and the point of departure for discussing the results of the excavations.

In addition to site excavations, archaeology has developed other research tools. These include surveys, in which beside the urban centres,

---

[1] Y. Shavit, M. Eran, *The Hebrew Bible Reborn: From Holy Scripture to the Book of
Books. A History of Biblical Culture and the Battles over the Bible in Modern Judaism*
(Studia Judaica, 38), Berlin / New York 2007, 17–191.

the surrounding hinterland as well as the peripheral zones are systematically studied. The material remains of the societies that inhabited Palestine became the key for reconstructing the history of settlement throughout the country. In addition, scientists in various fields (such as nuclear physics, archaeozoology, archaeobotany, geomorphology, etc.) became increasingly involved in the archaeological research. An example of the usefulness of these new scientific tools is the growing application of radiocarbon measures to the results of the archaeological excavations. Compared to the dates obtained by the traditional pottery analysis, radiocarbon supplies much more accurate dating for the destroyed strata, and helps refine the date of the pottery. The increasing use of scientific tools in archaeology has given it an aura of exact science and increased the trust in its results.

By contrast with the progress made in the field of archaeology, the study of the Bible as an historical source has lost many of its former safe anchors. For example, for many years scholars believed that biblical historiography was written as early as the time of the United Monarchy; and that two generations after the establishment of the monarchy, the history of the United Monarchy, and even works of the early history of Israel, were put in writing. Today, however, there is a fairly broad consensus that biblical historiography did not emerge before the eighth century BCE, and that the extensive historiographical works were written at the earliest in the seventh century BCE, while most of the biblical literature was composed during the Babylonian exile and the Persian period. Thus it is evident that biblical historiography was written hundreds of years after many of the events it describes. Scholars also grew more aware of the many other difficulties of treating the Bible as historical source—such as its literary nature, its marked ideological and theological nature, and the central part played by God in the events described.

We see then that biblical history and archaeology moved in different, almost opposite, directions. Whereas archaeology gained the status of quasi-scientific research, dealing in solid scientific evidence, biblical history has been increasingly considered an unreliable field, full of uncertainties and question-marks. No wonder that many biblical scholars tend to accept the conclusions drawn from archaeology, and in light of these conclusions dismiss the historicity of many biblical descriptions.

But is archaeology such an accurate scientific discipline that its conclusions must always be preferred to those of the written sources? This is the opinion of the archaeologist David Ussishkin who, upon discussing the excavations of Jerusalem, wrote as follows:[2]

> The corpus of archaeological data should be the starting-point for the study of Jerusalem, its borders, history, and material culture in the biblical period. This source of information should take preference, whenever possible, over the written sources, which are largely biased, incomplete, and open to different interpretations.

The artificial contrast that this statement poses between the written sources, which are 'open to different interpretations', and the results of the archaeological research, which by inference are free from such problems, is doubtful. Like the written sources, the results of the archaeological excavations are open to different, sometimes even contradictory, interpretations. The archaeological literature is replete with controversies on endless number of issues, including stratigraphy and pottery typology, the function of the excavated buildings and artefacts, settlement hierarchy, population estimate, among many others. Archaeological data do not speak for themselves and its interpretation is fraught with difficulties.[3]

It goes without saying that in many cases, archaeology is an excellent research tool and supplies solid evidence. But is archaeology as accurate as some archaeologists claims it to be? Should we always prefer the results of the archaeological research over the biblical evidence? In what follows I will examine a series of test-cases in which the documentary evidence disagrees with the results of the archaeological research. In the light of this comparison, I will point out the circumstances in which the archaeological research is quite limited and should be treated with great caution.

## 2. ARCHAEOLOGY AND THE AMARNA LETTERS

Let me start with the Amarna letters. The great advantage of the Amarna period (the fourteenth century BCE) for examining the potential and the limitations of the archaeological research is that here we have the

---

[2] D. Ussishkin, 'The Borders and De Facto Size of Jerusalem in the Persian Period', in: O. Lipschits, M. Oeming (eds.), *Judah and the Judeans in the Persian period*, Winona Lake 2006, 147–148.

[3] For the issue of text and archaeology, see D.V. Edelman (ed.), *The Fabric of History. Text, Artifact and Israel's Past* (JSOTSup, 127), Sheffield 1991.

evidence of both the archaeological excavations and surveys and of primary written sources. Amarna was a time of great decline in urban culture in Canaan, hence an ideal case for comparing text and archaeology. Since I have discussed this problem in detail elsewhere,[4] I will summarize the results of my research of four sites, two in the highlands (Jerusalem and Shechem), and two in the lowlands (Gezer and Lachish).

There is a striking discrepancy between the testimony of the Amarna letters concerning these four cities, which present them as strong and flourishing kingdoms, playing important role in the affairs in southern and central Canaan and having considerable influence over other city-states near and far, and the finding of the archaeological excavations at their sites. To illustrate it, we need only ask what kind of picture would the archaeologists have visualised if the settlement strata and the findings dated to the Amarna period were associated with a time for which we had no written documentation? In that case they would have concluded that in the entire mountain region between the Jezreel Valley and the Beersheba Valley there was only one ruling centre, that of Shechem, which controlled the northern part of the hill country; the rest was a kind of no-man's-land. Jerusalem would have been thought of as a village in a sparsely-inhabited highland region. Sites like Gezer and Lachish would have been defined as either unimportant city-states, or as provincial towns in the territories of the neighbouring kingdoms. Some scholars might even have suggested that at that time the enormous, strong and prosperous kingdom of Hazor ruled over most of the inner regions of Canaan, and that all the cities in this vast area were secondary centres in its territory.

How can we explain the discrepancy between the documentary and archaeological evidence? Following the utter destruction of the prosperous Middle Bronze III urban culture, the country underwent a serious decline, and this is indicated in the excavations and surveys of the Late Bronze Age I–II. When urban culture is at a low ebb, structures of lesser

---

[4] N. Naʾaman, 'The Contribution of the Amarna Letters to the Debate on Jerusalem's Political Position in the Tenth Century BCE', *BASOR* 304 (1996), 17–27; N. Naʾaman, 'The Trowel vs. the Text: How the Amarna Letters Challenge Archaeology', *BARev* 35/1 (2009), 52–56, 70–71; N. Naʾaman, 'Text and Archaeology in a Period of Great Decline: The Contribution of the Amarna Letters to the Debate on the Historicity of Nehemiah's Wall', in: P.R. Davies (ed.), *The Historian and the Bible: Essays in Honour of Lester L. Grabbe* (forthcoming).

strength and quality are often built on the foundations of solid structures from an earlier time. In multi-strata tells, these feeble structures are easily obliterated by later building operations. This is especially true of highland sites, where the bedrock is high and late construction and levelling can remove almost all traces of the earlier buildings and artefacts. Archaeological research can identify the fragmented remains and establish their date and function. Yet often the erosion and obliteration of much of the evidence by later operations, the fragmented state of the structures and the dispersal of the artefacts, hinder the reconstruction of the ancient reality. In this situation, only the documentary evidence can indicate the political situation in a broader territory and the relative status of cities *vis à vis* their neighbours.

## 3. JERUSALEM IN THE IRON AGE IIA

In the Amarna period the results of the archaeological research can be checked against the written sources, but the situation is quite different in other periods of urban culture decline, such as the times of the so-called United Monarchy (tenth century BCE) and the Persian period. There are no primary written sources for those periods, and the Bible, the single written text available for comparison with the results of the archaeological excavations, has well-known limitations. Given the many problems inherent in the historical study of the biblical texts, biblical scholars tend to accept uncritically the conclusions drawn from archaeological research. However, as we have noted, in periods of decline, the archaeological research, particularly in highland mounds, also suffers from severe limitations. This is especially true of Jerusalem, which was continuously inhabited for thousands years and many of the ancient remains disappeared completely over time.

To illustrate the problems entailed in the excavations of Jerusalem, let me present a recent discovery from the excavations of the City of David.[5] A few scattered and fragmented pottery vessels from Iron Age IIA, and hardly any pictorial artefact have been found in 150 years of excavations at Jerusalem; our archaeological knowledge of ninth century BCE Jerusalem was severely limited. Recently, however, Ronny Reich and Eli

---

[5] R. Reich, E. Shukron, O. Lernau, 'Recent Discoveries in the City of David, Jerusalem', *IEJ* 47 (2007), 153–160.

Shukron excavated a rock-cut pool near the spring, and in the fill they found a large number of pottery vessels from Iron Age IIA, dated to the late ninth century BCE. When sifting the earth of the fill, they found ten seals and scarabs, about 170 broken clay bullae bearing seal impressions with different motifs, and s large amount of fish bones. None of the seals, scarabs or bullae found bears any alphabetical writing, but the reverse side of some of the bullae bears the imprint of papyrus, indicating that they were used to seal letters. Other bullae bear imprints of woven fabrics, straw and canes, indicating that they sealed packaged commodities. An analysis of the fish bones showed that the bulk originated in the Mediterranean, but some were from the Nile.

This accidental find makes it possible to re-evaluate the society, economy and culture of Jerusalem in the ninth century BCE. The importation of a large amount of fish from the Mediterranean and the Nile testifies that a network of commerce with the coast of Philistia was already developed at that time. The papyrus imprints on the bullae indicate extensive writing, though it may have been used only by the royal palace and the elite. The many different designs on the bullae, each representing the seal's owner, show that seals were used by many court officials and private citizens. The absence of writing on the seal impressions shows that the fashion of inscribing the owner's name on a seal was introduced later, in the second half of the eighth century BCE. The sealed artefacts must have been commercial commodities, or taxes, brought to the court from the surrounding districts.

In sum, this accidental discovery shows how little we still know about Jerusalem in the early first millennium, after 150 years of excavations, and how risky it is to draw conclusions from negative evidence (namely, the not-found = never-existed dictum). The reconstruction of tenth-ninth century Jerusalem made on the basis of the archaeological evidence alone, while ignoring the biblical text, might be misleading, because it fails to take into account the great limitation of the archaeological research while ignoring the historical potential of the biblical text.

### 4. JERUSALEM'S WALLS IN THE LATE NINTH-EIGHTH CENTURIES BCE

Almost all the scholars who discussed the description of the wall built by Nehemiah in Jerusalem (Neh. 3:1–32) assumed that it surrounded only the City of David, but a few argued that it surrounded both the

Western Hill and the City of David.[6] The latter position was recently defended by my colleague, Prof. David Ussishkin, on the basis of the archaeological evidence alone.[7] His discussion rests on the finding of the archaeological excavations conducted along the western slope of the City of David. No city wall was discovered along this line. He thus concluded that during the First Temple period, the City of David was not fortified along its western slope.[8] It led him to the conclusion that Iron Age Jerusalem was fortified for the first time in the late eighth century, when the wall surrounding the Western Hill was built. Since there was no Iron Age wall along the western slope of the City of David, and Nehemiah restored the destroyed Iron Age city wall, he suggested that Nehemiah's wall surrounded both the Western Hill and the City of David.

This bold reconstruction has many flaws. First, all Syro-Palestinian capital cities and all the major Judahite cities were fortified during the ninth century BCE (e.g., Beth-shemesh, Lachish, Tel Beersheba). It is highly unlikely that Jerusalem alone was left unfortified until the late eighth century. Second, according to 2 Kgs. 14:13, following his victory in the battle of Beth-shemesh, King Joash of Israel conquered Jerusalem, 'and he made a breach of four hundred cubits in the wall of Jerusalem, from the Ephraim Gate to the Corner Gate'. Also, when Rezin, king of Aram, and Pekah ben Remaliah advanced on Jerusalem, 'They besieged Ahaz, but they were not able to attack' (2 Kgs. 16:5; see Isa. 7:1). The two accounts show that Jerusalem was already fortified throughout the eighth century BCE. Third, Neh. 3:8b reads as follows: 'and they left out Jerusalem as far as the broad wall'. As noted by Williamson,[9] 'Taking the words at face value, the clause will offer further evidence for the view that Nehemiah's wall cut inside part of the pre-exilic city'. According to Neh. 12:38–39, the second procession marched on the wall, 'above the Tower of Ovens to the Broad Wall; and above the Gate of Ephraim.' The 'Broad Wall' can safely be identified as the 'wall outside it', whose construction is attributed to Hezekiah according to 2 Chr. 32:5.[10] Thus

---

[6] See the list of references in Ussishkin, 'De Facto Size of Jerusalem', 147.

[7] Ussishkin, 'De Facto Size of Jerusalem', 147–166.

[8] Ussishkin, 'De Facto Size of Jerusalem', 153.

[9] H.G.M. Williamson, *Ezra, Nehemiah* (WBC, 16), Waco 1985, 205.

[10] N. Na'aman, 'When and How Did Jerusalem Become a Great City? The Rise of Jerusalem as Judah's Premier City in the Eighth-Seventh Centuries BCE', *BASOR* 347 (2007), 44–45.

the description of the building of Nehemiah's wall suggests that 'the Broad Wall' surrounding the Western Hill was left out of the fortifications built by Nehemiah.

Although the remains of the western wall of the City of David have never been found, we may safely assume that Jerusalem was fortified along its western side in the early eighth century, probably earlier. The wall must have been removed or eroded in the course of time, so that no fragment of it was discovered until now in the excavations. Nehemiah's wall must have surrounded the City of David, whereas the Western Hill remained unfortified and deserted in the Persian and early Hellenistic period, and was first fortified in the Hasmonaean period.

## 5. JERUSALEM IN THE PERSIAN PERIOD

No wall dated to the Persian period has ever been found, and very few remains from this period have been assembled in the many excavations conducted in the City of David. The number of sites with archaeological remains in the immediate environs of Jerusalem is very small, and there is a drastic demographic depletion in the area of the province of Yehud in the Persian period.[11] Based on this and other negative evidence, my colleague Prof. Israel Finkelstein rejected the authenticity of the detailed description of Nehemiah's building of a city wall.[12] In his opinion,

> 'The finds indicate that in the Persian and early Hellenistic periods Jerusalem was a small unfortified village that stretched over an area of about twenty dunams, with a population of a few hundred people—that is, not much more than one hundred adult men. This population—and the depleted population of the Jerusalem countryside in particular and the entire territory of Yehud in general—could not have supported a major reconstruction effort of the ruined Iron II fortifications of the city'.

The earliest Second Temple city wall unearthed in the excavations of Jerusalem is dated to the Hasmonaean period. Many buildings, too, as well as substantial quantities of pottery and other artefacts uncovered in the excavations, are dated to this period.[13] Finkelstein therefore suggests that the description of the building of Nehemiah's wall was written in

---

[11] I. Finkelstein, 'Jerusalem in the Persian (and Early Hellenistic) Period and the Wall of Nehemiah', *JSOT* 32 (2008), 504–507.

[12] Finkelstein, 'Jerusalem in the Persian Period', 501–520.

[13] Finkelstein, 'Jerusalem in the Persian Period', 510–514.

the second century BCE and was inspired by the construction of the Hasmonaean city-wall.[14]

Wolfgang Zwickel calculated the population of the province of Yehud in the Persian period to about 2000–4000 men. On this basis he estimated the population of Jerusalem to about 200–400 or 400–600 men, 10 % to 15 % of the overall population of the province.[15] Zwickel's rough estimation of the population of Jerusalem is close to Finkelstein's calculation, as against Hillel Geva, who estimated the number of inhabitants in the late Persian period to about 1000 men.[16]

Was fifth century BCE Jerusalem so small, and was its population so tiny as Finkelstein and Zwickel suggest on the basis of the archaeological evidence? A letter from Elephantine addressed by Jedaniah, the priests, and all the Jews of Elephantine, to Bagavahya, governor of Judah in the late fifth century, includes the following passage:[17]

> Moreover, before this, at the time that this evil was done to us, a letter we sent to our lord [namely, Bagavahya], and to Jehohanan the High Priest and his colleagues the priests who are in Jerusalem, and to Avastana the brother of Anani and the nobles of the Jews. A letter they did not send us.

The original letter was sent by the community of Elephantine to the heads of the religious and civil institutions of Jerusalem, asking them to intervene on their behalf to the Persian authorities of the 'Satrapy Beyond the River'. The picture of an established city with its local institutions that emerges from this late fifth century letter stands in marked contrast to the image of Jerusalem, as a small unfortified village that stretched over an area of about twenty dunams, with a population of not much more than one hundred adult men.

Calculating the inhabited area and the size of the population in multi-layered mounds, on the basis of the distribution and quantity of pottery, is always problematic. We should recall that Jerusalem was continuously

---

[14] We may question Finkelstein's assumption that biblical authors were free to manipulate the evidence even when it contradicted the reality of their own time. It is inconceivable that scribes, who lived in the Hasmonaean period and knew very well that the wall was built at that time, ignored it altogether and attributed the building to Nehemiah, who lived three hundred years before their time.

[15] W. Zwickel, 'Jerusalem und Samaria zur Zeit Nehemias—Ein Vergleich', *BZ* 52 (2008), 204–218.

[16] H. Geva, 'Estimating Jerusalem's Population in Antiquity: A Minimalist View', *Eretz Israel* 28 (2007), 56–57 (Hebrew).

[17] B. Porten, 'Request for Letter of Recommendation', in: W.W. Hallo, K.L. Younger (eds.), *The Context of Scripture*, III: *Archival Documents from the Biblical World*. Leiden/Boston 2003, 128.

inhabited from the late sixth – early fifth century BCE down to the Roman conquest and destruction of 70 CE, and that in the course of these centuries the fragile buildings of the Persian period were destroyed and obliterated and the pottery broken and dispersed. Estimating the inhabited area and the size of the population in the fifth century BCE on the basis of the archaeological evidence alone is highly uncertain. In my opinion, it cannot be used as a premise for judging the authenticity of the description of Nehemiah's building operations.

Taking into account the relatively small number of people who built the wall, and that it took only fifty-two days to build (Neh. 6:15), Nehemiah's wall must have been thin, an enclosure rather than a city wall. On three sides it was built on the foundations of the First Temple city wall, so these upper courses on top of the early wall simply could not have survived. I agree with scholars who have suggested—on the basis of the description—that on the eastern side Nehemiah deviated from the line of the early wall and constructed a new wall near the eastern edge of the city.[18] This must have been a thin, fragmentary wall, rising on top of a steep slope. Such a thin wall could hardly survive the erosion and extensive building operations that took place on that slope in later years. It is therefore unlikely that the enclosure wall built by Nehemiah in the City of David would last, and it is not surprising that it has not been found.

## 6. GIBEAH OF BENJAMIN

Another case in point is biblical Gibeah (Tell el-Fûl). The site was first excavated by Albright (1922–1923, 1933)[19] and later by Paul Lapp (1964).[20] The destruction of the Iron Age I fortress (Stratum II) was fol-

---

[18] H.G.M. Williamson, 'Nehemiah's Walls Revisited', *PEQ* 116 (1977), 82; H.G.M. Williamson, *Ezra, Nehemiah*, 200, 208; J. Blenkinsopp, *Ezra-Nehemiah—A Commentary* (OTL), London 1989, 231–232, 237; H. Eshel, 'Jerusalem under Persian Rule: The City's Layout and the Historic Background', in: S. Ahituv, A. Mazar (eds.), *The History of Jerusalem in the First Temple Period*, Jerusalem 2000, 339 (Hebrew).

[19] W.F. Albright, *Excavation and Results at Tell el-Fûl (Gibeah of Saul)* (AASOR, 4), New Haven 1924; W.F. Albright, 'A New Campaign of Excavations at Gibeah of Saul', *BASOR* 52 (1933), 6–12. See L.A. Sinclair, 'An Archaeological Study of Gibeah (Tell el-Ful)', *AASOR* 34–35 (1960), 1–52; L.A. Sinclair, 'An Archaeological Study of Gibeah (Tell el-Ful)', *BA* 27 (1964), 52–64.

[20] P.W. Lapp, 'Tell el-Fûl', *BA* 28 (1965), 2–10; N. Lapp, 'Casemate Walls in Palestine and the Late Iron II Casemate at Tell el-Fûl (Gibeah)', *BASOR* 223 (1976), 25, 36–42; N. Lapp, *The Third Campaign at Tell el-Fûl: The Excavations of 1964* (AASOR, 45),

lowed by a long gap in the site's occupation. Only late Iron II pottery was found in the excavations (Stratum IIIA). Lapp therefore suggested that the late Iron site, with its casemate walls, was built no earlier than the second half of the seventh century BCE.[21] He thus corrected the earlier, eighth century date, proposed by Albright for the foundation of this stratum.

However, fourteen *lmlk* seal impressions were discovered in the site.[22] The impressions are dated to the late eighth and early seventh century BCE, indicating that stratum IIIA was founded no later than the early seventh century. Moreover, Gibeah is mentioned three times in the Book of Hosea: once in the call, 'Blow the horn in Gibeah, the trumpet in Ramah' (Hos. 5:8), which may possibly be dated to the Syro-Ephraimite war;[23] and twice in the combination 'the days of Gibeah' (Hos. 9:9; 10:9). Gibeah of Saul is also mentioned in the prophecy of Isaiah (10:28–32) side by side with Ramah. These four prophetic texts seem to indicate that Gibeah was inhabited in the second half of the eighth century BCE. There is thus a marked discrepancy between the biblical evidence and the results of the archaeological excavations at Tell el-Fûl. It brings us to the question, which set of evidence should be preferred?

Whereas fixing the date of the destruction of archaeological strata is relatively easy, as it is based on the pottery unearthed on the floors, establishing the date of strata's foundations is notoriously difficult. I have already mentioned the problem of detecting pottery of intermediate stages in multi-layered highlands sites, which existed uninterruptedly

---

Cambridge, Mass. 1981; N. Lapp, 'Fûl, Tell el-', in: E. Stern (ed.), *The New Encyclopedia of Archaeological Excavations in the Holy Land*, vol. 2, Jerusalem 1993, 445–448, with earlier literature.

[21] P. Lapp, 'Tell el-Fûl', 3; N. Lapp, 'Casemate Walls', 40; P. Lapp, 'Fûl, Tell el-', 446.

[22] A.G. Vaughn, *Theology, History and Archaeology in the Chronicler's Account of Hezekiah* (SBL, Archaeology and Biblical Studies, 4), Atlanta 1999, 192.

[23] A. Alt, 'Hosea 5,8–6,6: Ein Krieg und seine Folgen in prophetischer Beleuchten', *Kleine Schriften zur Geschichte des Volkes Israel*, II, München 1953, 163–174 (originally published in *Neue kirchliche Zeitschrift* 30 [1919], 537–568). Alt's analysis was accepted by many scholars; see the list of literature cited in H.W. Wolff, *Hosea. A Commentary on the Book of the Prophet Hosea* (Hermeneia), Philadelphia 1982, 110–114 (original publication: *Dodekapropheton. 1: Hosea* [BKAT, 14/1], Neukirchen-Vluyn 1965); H. Donner, *Israel unter den Völkern: die Stellung der klassischen Propheten des 8. Jahrhunderts v. Chr. zur Aussenpolitik der Könige von Israel und Juda* (SVT, 11), Leiden 1964, 47–48; W. Rudolph, *Hosea* (KAT, 13/1), Gütersloh 1966, 122–129; J.L. Mays, *Hosea—A Commentary* (OTL), Philadelphia 1969, 85–90; F.I. Andersen and D.N. Freedman, *Hosea* (AB, 24), New York 1980, 399–416; J. Jeremias, *Der Prophet Hosea übersetzt und erklärt* (ATD, 24/1), Göttingen 1983, 78–81; G.I. Davies, *Hosea*, (NCBC), Grand Rapids 1992, 145–148.

for long time. Stratum IIIA at Tel el-Fûl was settled from its foundation
down to the Babylonian destruction of 587, and resettled in the sixth –
early fifth century BCE (stratum IIIB). Detecting the pottery of the earliest
stage of this stratum is difficult, as the bedrock is high and there is little
accumulation of strata on top of it. Moreover, the site was settled in
the Hellenistic period, and the late settlement must have damaged the
underlying strata. The pottery of the earliest stage of Stratum IIIA must
have been scattered and most of it completely disappeared.

Some years ago I discussed a similar contradiction in the excavations
of Tel Miqne (Ekron), where the cuneiform documents demonstrate that
it was already an important city in the late eighth century BCE, though
only pottery of the seventh century has been discovered in the excavations of the lower city.[24] I believe that the case of Tell el-Fûl is similar.
Stratum IIIA was probably founded in the second half of the eighth century, as indicated by the prophecies of Hosea and Isaiah, whereas the
unearthed pottery indicate only the date of the site's destruction, not that
of its foundation.

## 7. BETHEL IN THE SIXTH CENTURY BCE

The city of Bethel is well attested in biblical historiography and prophetic
books of the eighth-seventh centuries.[25] A settlement at Bethel in the
sixth century is not mentioned explicitly in the Bible,[26] but a fifth century

---

[24] N. Na'aman, 'Ekron under the Assyrian and Egyptian Empires', *BASOR* 332 (2003),
81–91. For a similar date reached on the basis of the archaeological evidence, see D. Ussishkin, 'The Fortifications of Philistine Ekron', *IEJ* 55 (2005), 35–65.

[25] Four monographs devoted to the history and archaeology of Bethel have been
published in the last decade. See H. Pfeiffer, *Das Heiligtum von Bethel im Spiegel des
Hoseabuches* (FRLANT, 183), Göttingen 1999; K. Koenen, *Bethel: Geschichte, Kult und
Theologie* (OBO, 192), Freiburg / Göttingen 2003; J.F. Gomes, *The Sanctuary of Bethel and
the Configuration of Israelite Identity* (BZAW, 368), Berlin / New York 2006; M. Köhlmoos,
*Bet-El—Erinnerungen an eine Stadt. Perspektiven der alttestamentlichen Bet-El-Überlie-
ferung* (FAT, 49), Tübingen 2006 (the book of Köhlmoos is not available to me).

[26] The interpretation of Zech 7:2 is debated among scholars. Some understand 'Bethel'
as the destination ('had sent to Bethel'), others as the subject of the sentence, either as part
of a composite proper name (Bethel-sharezer) or as a personified place name ('Bethel sent
Sharezer'). In addition to the commentaries see: J.P. Hyatt, 'A Neo-Babylonian Parallel to
Bethel-sar-eser, Zech. 7:2', *JBL* 56 (1937), 387–394; P.R. Ackroyd, *Exile and Restoration,
A Study of Hebrew Thought of the Sixth Century BC*, London 1968, 206–208; T. Veijola,
*Verheissung in der Krise. Studien zur Literatur und Theologie der Exilzeit anhand des 89.
Psalms*, Helsinki 1982, 194–196; J. Blenkinsopp, 'The Judaean Priesthood during the Neo-
Babylonian ans Achaemenid Periods: A Hypothetical Reconstruction', *CBQ* 60 (1998),

settlement is presupposed by the lists of returnees in Ezra (2:28) and Nehemiah (7:31; see 11:31). However, Finkelstein, who systematically examined the sites named in these lists, suggested that they reflected the reality of the Hasmonaean period, and that Bethel was deserted in the Persian period.[27]

Four seasons of excavations were carried at Bethel (in the years 1934, 1954, 1957 and 1960) and the final results of the excavations were published by James Kelso.[28] In the historical chapter he concluded that 'Bethel was destroyed in a great conflagration either at the hands of the Babylonian Nabonidus or shortly afterwards at the hands of the Persians, perhaps in the chaotic period preceding Darius'.[29] Lawrence Sinclair, who analyzed the pottery unearthed at Bethel, suggested that there was continuity in the site from the early Iron Age down to the second half of the sixth century.[30] Yet John Holladay, who examined the published pottery, claimed that pottery of the sixth century was missing from the archaeological reports and that the site was deserted at that time.[31] Recently, Finkelstein and Singer-Avitz published a detailed article in which they examined the results of the excavations at Bethel.[32] They analysed the published pottery of the sixth-fourth centuries BCE and concluded that material evidence for activity at Bethel in the Babylonian, Persian and early Hellenistic period is very meagre, if it exits at all. They thus dismissed the idea that Bethel served as a prominent cult place in the

32–33; E.A. Knauf, 'Bethel: The Israelite Impact on Judean Language and Literature', in: Lipschits, Oeming (eds.), *Judah and the Judeans*, 306 n. 77; Y. Hoffmann, 'The Fasts in the Book of Zechariah and the Fashioning of National Identity', in: O. Lipschits and J. Blenkinsopp (ed.), *Judah and the Judeans in the Neo-Babylonian Period*, Winona Lake 2003, 200–202; Koenen, *Bethel*, 62–64; J. Middlemas, *The Troubles of Templeless Judah* (Oxford Theological Monographs), Oxford / New York 2005, 134–136.

[27] I. Finkelstein, 'Archaeology and the List of Returnees in the Books of Ezra and Nehemiah', *PEQ* 140 (2008), 1–10.

[28] J.L. Kelso, *The Excavation of Bethel (1934–1960)* (AASOR, 39), Cambridge, Mass. 1968.

[29] Kelso, *Excavation of Bethel.*, 51; cf. p. 37.

[30] L.A. Sinclair suggested that there was a substantial continuity of occupation in Bethel in the 6th century BCE. See L.A. Sinclair, 'Bethel Pottery of the Sixth Century BC', in Kelso, *Excavation of Bethel*, 70–76; cf. O. Lipschits, 'The History of the Benjamin Region under Babylonian Rule', *Tel Aviv* 26 (1999), 171–172, with earlier literature.

[31] J.S. Holladay, in W.G. Dever, 'Archaeological Methods and Results: A Review of Two Recent Publications', *Or* 40 (1971), 468–469.

[32] I. Finkelstein, L. Singer-Avitz, 'Reevaluating Bethel', *ZDPV* 125 (2009), 33–48.

Babylonian period, and that significant scribal activity at Bethel in this
time is not a viable option.[33]

In spite of the scanty archaeological evidence of the sixth century BCE,
some scholars recently suggested that after the destruction of Jerusalem,
the administrative centre moved to Mizpah, and Bethel became the central cult place of either the Babylonian province of Yehud, or the southern district of the province of Samerina.[34] According to this assumption,
Bethel, in particular the temple, continued to be inhabited in the sixth
century. These scholars further suggested that part of the biblical historiography was composed at Bethel, which served as a crossroad for Israelite
and Judahite literature and literary traditions. Later, when Jerusalem was
rebuilt and restored as the capital of the province of Yehud, the scrolls
produced at Bethel were transferred to the new capital and formed the
nucleus of the growing corpus of scrolls assembled in the temple.

Richard Steiner suggested that Papyrus Amherst 63 is a liturgy of a
New Year's Akitu festival and was written by people deported by Ashurbanipal from the land of Rashi, on the Babylonian-Elamite border, and
settled in Bethel.[35] In his opinion, this is the deportation that is mentioned in Ezra 4:9–10. The deportees lived in Bethel for an unknown
period, but severe drought forced them to leave the place, and they
migrated to Syene, on the southern border of Egypt and settled there.
However, his interpretation of the papyrus is controversial and remains
uncertain.[36]

---

[33] Finkelstein, Singer-Avitz, 'Reevaluating Bethel', 47–48.

[34] For the suggestion that Bethel was an important cult and scribal centre in the exilic
and early post-exilic periods, see Veijola, *Verheissung*, 176–210; J. Schwartz, 'Jubilees,
Bethel and the Temple of Jacob', *HUCA* 56 (1985), 74–81; Blenkinsopp, 'Judaean Priesthood', 25–43; Blenkinsopp, 'Bethel in the Neo-Babylonian Period', in: Lipschits, Blenkinsopp (eds.), *Judah and the Judeans*, 93–107; A. de Pury, 'Le cycle de Jacob comme
légende autonome des origines d'Israël', *SVT* 43 (1991), 237–241; A. Rofé, 'The History of
Israelite Religion and the Biblical Text. Corrections Due to the Unification of Worship', in:
S.M. Paul, R.A., Kraft, L.H. Schiffman (eds.), *Emanuel. Studies in Hebrew Bible, Septuagint
and Dead Sea Scrolls in Honor of Emanuel Tov*, Leiden 2003, 781–793; Gomes, *Sanctuary of Bethel*, 185–223; Knauf, 'Bethel', 291–349; Middlemas, *Templeless Judah*, 133–144;
P.R. Davies, *The Origins of Biblical Israel* (Library of Hebrew Bible / Old Testament Studies, 485), New York, London 2007, 159–171, with earlier literature.

[35] R.C. Steiner, 'The Aramaic Text in Demotic Script: The Liturgy of a New Year's
Festival Imported from Bethel to Syene by Exiles from Rash', *JAOS* 111 (1991), 362–363;
R.C. Steiner, 'Papyrus Amherst 63: A New Source for the Language, Literature, Religion,
and History of the Aramaeans', in: M.J. Geller, J.C. Greenfield, M.P. Weitzman (eds.),
*Studia Aramaica. New Sources and New Approaches* (JSS Supplement 4). Oxford 1995,
204–207.

[36] For discussions, see e.g., R.C. Steiner, C.F. Nimms, 'You Can't Offer Your Sacri-

The documentary evidence proposed by these scholars for the rise of Bethel as a cult centre after the downfall of Jerusalem is of varying strength and nature, but remains inconclusive. To this evidence I would like to add new, and in my opinion crucial, data. Scholars have long realized that elements in the story of Jacob's dream at Luz (Gen. 28:10–22) have remarkable Babylonian comparisons.[37] In a recently published article, Victor Hurowitz compared the story of Jacob's dream at Bethel to Mesopotamian sources connected specifically with Babylon, in particular Nabopolassar's construction of the wall Imgur Enlil at Babylon and the fifth tablet of the Babylonian Epic of Creation (*Enūma Eliš*).[38] By meticulous examinations of these compositions he demonstrated that 'the account of Jacob's dream contains hardly a detail without some prominent linguistic or thematic parallel to Babylon in general and the myth of its primeval foundation in particular'. On this basis he concluded that the Bethel legend is a clear example of appropriating traditions of one city and applying them to another.[39] Hurowitz logically dated the composition of Jacob's dream to the time when the Babylonian empire dominated the ancient Near East, and Babylon, with Marduk's temple of

fice and Eat It Too: A Polemical Poem from the Aramaic Text in Demotic Script', *JNES* 43 (1984), 89–114; R.C. Steiner, C.F. Nimms, 'Ashurbanipal and Shamash-shum-ukin: A Tale of Two Brothers from the Aramaic Text in Demotic Script', *RB* 92 (1985), 60–81; S.P. Vleeming, J.W. Wesselius, *Studies in Papyrus Amherst 63. Essays on the Aramaic Texts in Aramaic/Demotic Papyrus Amherst 63*, vol. I, Amsterdam 1985; Steiner, 'The Aramaic Text', 362–363; Steiner, 'Papyrus Amherst 63', 199–207; R.C. Steiner, 'The Aramaic Text in Demotic Script (1.99)', in: W.W. Hallo, K.L. Younger (eds.), *The Context of Scripture*, I: *Canonical Compositions from the Biblical World*. Leiden/Boston 2003, 309–327; I. Kottsieper, 'Anmerkungen zu Pap. Amherst 63 Teil II–V', *UF* 29 (1997), 385–434; I. Kottsieper, 'Zum Hintergrund des Schriftsystems im Pap. Amherst 63', *Dutch Studies* 5/1–2 (2003), 89–115; N. Na'aman, R. Zadok, 'Assyrian Deportations to the Province of Samerina in the Light of Two Cuneiform Tablets from Tel Hadid', *Tel Aviv* 27 (2000), 179.

[37] C. Houtman, 'What Did Jacob see in His Dream at Bethel? Some Remarks on Genesis xxviii 10–22', *VT* 27 (1977), 337–351, with earlier literature; M. Weinfeld, 'Zion and Jerusalem as Religious and Political Capital: Ideology and Utopia', in: R.E. Friedman (ed.), *The Poet and the Historian. Essays in Literary and Historical Biblical Criticism* (HSS, 26), Chico 1983, 104–108; F.E. Greenspahn, 'A Mesopotamian Proverb and Its Biblical Reverberations', *JAOS* 114 (1994), 36–37 and n. 25; C. Cohen, 'The Literary Motif of Jacob's Ladder (Gen 28:12) according to the Interpretation of Ibn-Ezra and in Light of Parallels in Akkadian Literature', in: Y. Bentolila (ed.), *Hadassah Shy Jubilee Book. Research Papers on Hebrew Linguistics and Jewish Languages* (Eshel Beer-Sheva, 5), Beer-Sheva 1997, 21–26 (Hebrew); D. Lipton, *Revisions of the Night: Politics and Promises in the Patriarchal Dreams of Genesis* (JSOTSup, 288), Sheffield 1999, 80–92, 99–104.

[38] V.A. Hurowitz, 'Babylon in Bethel—New Light on Jacob's Dream', in: S.W. Holloway (ed.), *Orientalism, Assyriology and the Bible*, Sheffield 2006, 436–448.

[39] Hurowitz, 'Babylon in Bethel', 443.

Esagil at its centre, was the most prominent city in the empire. The transfer of the literary motifs from Babylon to Bethel indicates its importance
at that time, and should be seen as decisive evidence of the importance
of the place and its temple in the sixth century BCE.

Upon returning to the results of the excavations at Bethel, first we
should recall that unlike at many other Judahite sites, where clear destruction layers were exposed in the excavations, at Iron Age Bethel
no destruction layers were detected. This indicates that the process of
desertion and abandonment was gradual and took place over a long
period of time. Second, the location of the temple remains unknown,
so the sixth century settlement and cult place may be located in other
parts of the mound. Third, Bethel is located in the highlands, where
the bedrock is high and later construction and levelling works in the
Hellenistic to the Byzantine periods might have removed the remains of
older buildings and scattered the pottery away from its original location.

Nevertheless, several relatively sizeable fields were excavated at Bethel.
Since large amount of Iron Age II A–B pottery was unearthed at the
site, it is difficult to assume that late Iron IIC pottery disappeared almost
completely. The paucity of sixth century pottery at Bethel is in marked
contrast to the textual evidence presented above, so the lack of accord
between text and archaeology requires explanation.[40] To overcome the
difficulty I will bring analogies drawn from Mesopotamia, which might
suggest solution to the impasse.

According to the Sumerian King List, Eridu was the first city on which
kingship descended, and this is confirmed by the Sumerian flood story.[41]
Whereas the city was abandoned after the 'Ubaid period (late fifth millennium BCE), E-abzu, the great cult centre of the god Enki (Babylonian
Ea) continued to function for a long time.[42] Several south Mesopotamian
rulers of the second half of the third and the early second millennium
BCE mention the restoration of the temple, the final restorer being Hammurabi, king of Babylonia in the 18th century. Babylon then absorbed the

---

[40] Koenen (*Bethel*, 62) concluded that 'Bethel nach den archäologischen Quellen in
exilischer und persischer Zeit als Stadt oder nennenswerte Siedlung nicht nachgewiesen
ist'. Nevertheless, he suggested that Bethel was settled in the exilic period and did not
decide whether it was settled in the Persian period (p. 64).

[41] W.W. Hallo, 'Antediluvian Cities', *JCS* 23 (1970), 60–63; T. Jacobsen, 'The Eridu
Genesis', *JBL* 100 (1981), 513–527.

[42] For Eridu in the 'Ubaid period, see M.E.L. Mallowan, 'The Development of Cities:
From Al-'Ubaid to the End of Uruk 5', in: I.E.S. Edwards, C.J. Gadd, N.G.L. Hammond
(eds.), *Cambridge Ancient History* (3rd ed.), 1/1, Cambridge 1970, 330–350.

mythology and cosmological identity of Eridu and Marduk took the place of Ea, the god of Eridu.[43] The combined historical-archaeological picture that emerges is clear: 'Throughout the historical period the picture is thus one of a single venerable temple whose cult was entirely dependant on the patronage of pious kings. During all this time the local population of the site perhaps comprised only the personnel of this ancient cult-centre'.[44]

Nippur was the religious centre of Sumer in the third millennium and held the supreme religious position in Mesopotamia throughout most of the second millennium BCE. Enlil, the city's god, was considered the supreme deity in the Sumerian pantheon, and Ekur, his temple, the most important sanctuary in the country. The city carried the epithet Dur-anki, 'the bond of heaven and earth / underworld', and was considered the cosmic centre of the universe.[45] As far as we know, Nippur was never an important political capital, but was a thriving city in the third and early second millennium BCE. The city suffered great decline in the 17th century and was almost completely deserted in the 16th–15th centuries.[46] It was restored in the 14th century and its temple rebuilt.[47] In the late 13th century the city declined once again and by the end of the first millennium it had diminished to a village flanking Enlil's temple.

In spite of the city's great decline in the 17th–15th centuries, the god Enlil was considered the head of the Mesopotamian pantheon and Ekur, his temple, the navel of the earth. Enlil's and Ekur's places were appropriated by Babylon and Marduk only in the time of Nebuchadnezzar I (1125–1104), following his victory over Elam and the restoration of

---

[43] A.R. George, ' "Bond of the Lands": Babylon, the Cosmic Capital', in: G. Wilhelm (ed.) *Die orientalische Stadt: Kontinuität, Wandel, Bruch* (1. Internationales Colloquium der Deutschen Orient-Gesellschaft), Saarbrücker 1997, 129–133.

[44] George, "Bond of the Lands"., 132.

[45] W.G. Lambert, 'Nippur in Ancient Ideology', in: M. de Jong Ellis (ed.), *Nippur in the Centennial. Papers Read at the XXXVe Rencontre Assyriologique Internationale,* Philadelphia 1992, 119–120; J.G. Westenholz, 'The Theological Foundation of the City, the Capital City and Babylon', in: idem (ed.), *Capital Cities: Urban Planning and Spiritual Dimensions* (Proceedings of the symposium Held on May 27–29, 1996, Jerusalem, Israel), Jerusalem 1996, 45–46; W. Sallaberger, 'Nippur als religiöse Zentrum Mesopotamiens im historischen Wandel', in: Wilhelm (ed.), *Die orientalische Stadt*, 147–168.

[46] S.W. Cole, *Nippur in Late Assyrian Times* c. 755–612 BC (SAAS 4), Helsinki 1996, 7–12; George, 'Bond of the Lands', 132–133.

[47] E.C. Stone, 'Economic Crisis and Social Upheaval in Old Babylonian Nippur', in: L.D. Levine, T. Cuyler Young (eds.), *Mountains and Lowlands: Essays in the Archaeology of Greater Mesopotamia* (Bibliotheca Mesopotamica, 7), Malibu 1977, 267–289; Cole, *ibid.,* 7–12; George, 'Bond of the Lands', 132–133.

Marduk's image to Babylon.[48] However, the literary-theological conflict between the Babylonian priests and authors and their opposite members in Nippur continued for about a century, and literary works were composed in the struggle for religious seniority between the two gods, their temples and cities.[49] It is evident that the pre-eminent position of Nippur and its god was the acknowledged ideology in Mesopotamia until the late second millennium. Like E-abzu at Eridu, in time of decline and desertion the Ekur temple and its personnel formed the nucleus of the settlement at the site, and pious Mesopotamian kings continued to support the temple throughout the second millennium BCE.

Likewise, the temple of Bethel was the most important sanctuary in the Kingdom of Israel and must have kept its elevated status under the Assyrian empire (note the legendary story in 2 Kgs 17:25–28). Following Josiah's conquest of Bethel and its despoliation, the city probably suffered serious decline and even partial desertion. But the venerated temple was restored and formed the nucleus of the place, being supported by the government of the province, similar to the E-abzu temple at Eridu and the Ekur temple at Nippur. Since the location of the temple is unknown, it is impossible to evaluate the scope of settlement that was built around it. The sanctuary's elevated religious status was propagandized by the priests, who composed literary works that emphasized its great antiquity, its consecration by the Patriarch Jacob, and its religious importance as a bond between heaven and earth—parallel to the status of Esagil in Babylon.

The case of Bethel shows once again that we must be cautious in drawing conclusions on the basis of negative evidence. In view of the documentary evidence we had better assume that Bethel was an important cult centre in the sixth century BCE, and that its decline in the late sixth to early fifth century should not be separated from the rise of Jerusalem at that time.

---

[48] W.G. Lambert, 'The Reign of Nebuchadnezzar I: A Turning Point in the History of Ancient Mesopotamian Religion', in: W.S. McCullough (ed.), *The Seed of Wisdom. Essays in Honour of T.J. Meek*, Toronto 1964, 3–13; W.G. Lambert, 'Studies in Marduk', *BSOAS* 47 (1984), 2–5; W. Sommerfeld, *Der Aufstieg Marduks. Die Stellung Marduks in der babylonischen Religion des zweiten Jahrtausends v. Chr.* (AOAT, 213), Kevelaer / Neukirchen-Vluyn 1982, 182–189; A.R. George, 'Marduk and the Cult of the Gods of Nippur at Babylon', *Or* 66 (1997) 65–70.

[49] V.A. Hurowitz, *Divine Service and Its Rewards. Ideology and Poetics in the Hinke Kudurru* (Beer-Sheva 10), Beer-Sheva 1997, 16–19; V.A. Hurowitz, 'Reading a Votive Inscription: Simbar-shipak and the Ellilification of Marduk', *RA* 91 (1997), 39–47.

## 8. SUMMARY NOTES

In conclusion, it seems that in multi-strata mounds, especially in periods when the urban culture is at a low ebb and only a few poor structures are built, and these often on the foundations of earlier structures, the archaeological research can draw erroneous conclusions from the findings in the dig. This is especially true in the old city of Jerusalem, which was built on terraces and settled for thousands of years, each new city resting its foundations on the bedrock, destroying what had stood on it. In sites of a single stratum, or just a few strata, even poor, scattered structures may be well preserved. However, in multi-layered highland mounds, even the public and private buildings in periods of decline may disappear completely due to the extensive construction and developments carried out on the site in later periods. The old truth, 'absence of evidence is not evidence of absence', is particularly applicable for multi-layered highland sites and should always be taken into consideration.

I don't mean to belittle the importance of archaeology, which can shed light not only on aspects of the material culture, but also on other significant areas, such as economy and society, imports and exports, religion and the cult, among others. But in regard to multi-strata highland sites in such times as the 'United Monarchy' and the Babylonian and Persian periods, the results of the archaeological excavations should be treated with great caution.

The discussion of the documents and the archaeological finding vividly demonstrates the dangers of ignoring the limitations of either of these disciplines. Exclusive reliance on one of them alone can produce a distorted picture. Only the skilful use of both can lead to a balanced evaluation of the ancient reality.

# HISTORY AND PROPHECY IN THE BOOK OF JUDGES

KLAAS SPRONK

*Protestant Theological University, Kampen*

In introductory courses to the Old Testament modern teachers usually find it helpful to confront the student with the old Jewish tradition which reckons the book of Judges together with Joshua, Samuel and Kings to the part of the canon called the Former Prophets. This can be regarded as a useful contribution to the discussion about the right view upon this and other books which are in the Christian tradition called the historical books and interpreted as giving an accurate historical picture of the situations they describe. The name 'Former Prophets' would indicate that what we find written in these books is, as formulated by L.C. Allen in a standard introduction, 'not history as modern historians might write it. Rather it is history from a prophetic point of view'.[1] Allen gives three reasons why the books of Joshua, Judges, Samuel and Kings are called prophetic: '(1) There is a focus on prophetic messengers, especially Samuel, Nathan, Elijah, and Elisha and their role in history. (2) There is an anti-establishment perspective, like that of the preexilic prophets in the Latter Prophets. Failure and shortcomings in the leadership of Israelite society are continually exposed. (3) Events are analyzed in the light of the prophetic truth that YHWH is sovereign in history, both foretelling and fulfilling his prophetic word.' In this contribution I want to evaluate the arguments for this commonly accepted characterization of the book of Judges. To this I shall add a discussion of the different ways in which scholars nevertheless try to reconstruct the historical facts behind the stories told about the judges, because, as Allen hastens to add: 'To make such a statement, however, is not to denigrate the historical value of the biblical books'.

---

[1] W.S. LaSor et al., *Old Testament Survey: The Message, Form and Background of the Old Testament* (second edition), Grand Rapids 1996, 133.

## 1. The Origin of the Term 'Former Prophets'

The categorization of these books as prophetic is already known from the introduction to Jesus Sirach, which speaks of 'the Law, the Prophets, and the other books'. We also find it in Josephus' book *Contra Apion* 1:40: 'but as to the time from the death of Moses till the reign of Artaxerxes, king of Persia, who reigned after Xerxes, the prophets, who were after Moses, wrote down what was done in their times in thirteen books'. In 2 Maccabees 2:13 it is told 'how Nehemiah founded a library and made a collection of those about the kings and the prophets and those of David and the letters of the kings on the subject of offerings'. It is interesting that what is usually indicated as the Prophets is described here as the books 'about the kings and the prophets'. This hints at the subdivision into Former and Latter Prophets. It should be noted, however, that this subdivision was made much later. It is not known in Talmudic times. When the rabbis referred to 'former prophets' they meant the prophets who lived in the period before the destruction of the first temple. With the 'latter prophets' they meant the postexilic prophets Haggai, Zecheriah, and Malachi.[2] The name Former Prophets as a designation of the books of Joshua to Kings appears to be coined by the Soncino family in their edition of these books with the commentary of Rabbi David Kimchi.[3] According to Sarna and Sperling the subdivision between Former and Latter Prophets was made 'for convenience only', in order 'to differentiate between the narrative, historical works (...) and the (largely poetic) literary creations of the prophetic authors'.[4] So perhaps we should be more careful and make not too much of the qualification as prophetic.

The most important reason for this name is that according to old Jewish canonical tradition their authors were prophets, as is stated in Talmud Baba Bathra 14b–15a: 'Who wrote the Scripture?—Moses wrote his own book which bears his name and the portion of Balaam and Job. Joshua wrote the book which bears his name and (the last) eight verses of the Pentateuch. Samuel wrote the book which bears his name and the Book of Judges and Ruth. David wrote the Book of Psalms, including in it the work of the elders, namely, Adam, Melchizedek, Abraham, Moses,

---

[2] Cf. N.M. Sarna, D.M. Sperling, in: *Encyclopaedia Judaica* (second edition), vol. 3, Jerusalem 2007, 576.

[3] Cf. M. Avioz, 'On the Origin of the Term Nevi'im Rishonim' (Hebrew), *JISJ* 8 (2009), 1–7.

[4] Sarna, Sperling, *Encyclopaedia Judaica*, vol. 3, 576.

Heman, Yeduthun, Asaph, and the three sons of Korah. Jeremiah wrote the book which bears his name, the Book of Kings, and Lamentations. Hezekiah and his colleagues wrote Isaiah, Proverbs, the Song of Songs and Ecclesiastes …'.

In this connection it should be noted that also Joshua, the author of 'the book which bears his name', is regarded as a prophet in old Jewish tradition. Jesus Sirach 46:1 says that he succeeded Moses in his profession as a prophet.

## 2. The Prophets in the Book of Judges

One of the arguments mentioned by Allen for the prophetic character of the Former Prophets is that these books 'focus on prophetic messengers'. This may hold true for Samuel and Kings, but hardly for Joshua and Judges. In the book of Judges we only find two explicit references to prophets and both can be regarded as marginal. The first is in Judges 4:4–5 describing Deborah as 'a prophetess (אשה נביאה), wife of Lapidoth, was judging Israel. She used to sit under the palm of Deborah between Ramah and Bethel in the hill country of Ephraim; and the Israelites came up to her for judgment.' This is a remarkable combination of information about her person, family status, living place and function. Her title 'prophetess' stands by itself. It has no connection with what follows. The emphasis is on her work as a judge: that is what the Israelites expect her to do. The title prophetess seems to have been given to her later, as has been noted by a number of commentators. A reason for this could have been the place where she resided ('under the palm of Deborah'). This can be associated with graves and therefore with the forbidden way to contact the supernatural by necromancy.[5] Auld has shown that the title נביא was often added to the stories of the kings in a later stage.[6] This appears to have been done in Judges 4 as well. It makes the relation between Deborah and Barak look like the relation between Samuel and Saul, Nathan and David, Elijah and Ahab.

The second occurrence of the word נביא is in Judges 6:7–10, a part of the introduction to the story of Gideon. In the previous six verses it is told that YHWH gave the Israelites into the hand of Midian. It concludes

---

[5] Cf. K. Spronk, 'Deborah: a Prophetess: the Meaning and Background of Judges 4:4–5', in: J.C. de Moor (ed.), *The Elusive Prophet* (OTS 45), Leiden 2001, 232–242.

[6] A.G. Auld, 'Prophets and Prophecy in Jeremiah and Kings', *ZAW* 96 (1984), 66–82.

in verse 6 with the remark that 'Israel was totally humiliated before Midian'. Then the Israelites cried out to YHWH. According to the repeated framework in the book of Judges one would expect that this reference to Israel crying out to YHWH is immediately followed by describing YHWH taking action and raising up a deliverer, as in 3:9 (Othniel) and 3:15 (Ehud). But before we read in this situation of Gideon being raised up, a prophet enters the stage: 'When the Israelites cried to YHWH because of Midian, YHWH sent a prophet (איש נביא) to the Israelites.' This prophet reminds the Israelites of YHWH helping them out of Egypt and giving them their land. He had asked them 'not to fear the gods of the Amorites in whose land you are living', but they had not obeyed this command. Then, in verse 11, a messenger of YHWH comes, finds Gideon and starts persuading him to become the next deliverer of Israel.

These verses 6:7–10 are usually interpreted as a later added inter-mezzo.[7] It separates the cry for help from YHWH's reaction. Also the first words in verse 7, repeating the reference to Israel's crying for help in verse 6, can be interpreted as an indication that different pieces of text are glued together. In the Septuagint this repetition of the last words of verse 6 in verse 7 is missing. In the Judges scroll from Qumran cave 4 precisely these four verses appear to be missing completely.[8] This brings some scholars to the conclusion that we have here a rare case where redaction criticism is supported by textcritical evidence. The Qumran text would have preserved an early text form. One should be careful, however, with making too much from this fragment. Very little is known of the scroll as a whole.

When one takes a closer look at the text and its context it can be noted that leaving the verses 7–10 out does not result in a more logical text. Leaving out verses 7–10 would mean that the reference to Israel crying out was originally followed by the action of the messenger of YHWH. This is not what one would expect on the basis of a comparison with the stories about Othniel and Ehud, where Israel's crying out is directly followed by a description of the raising of a deliverer. Moreover, in his reaction to the messenger Gideon reacts to the words of the prophet, when he says: 'Where are all the wonders that our fathers told us about when they said, "Did not YHWH bring us up out of Egypt". But now YHWH has abandoned

---

[7] Cf. A. Scherer, *Überlieferungen von Religion und Krieg: Exegetische und religions-geschichtliche Untersuchungen zu Richter 3–8 und verwandten Texten* (WMANT 105), Neukirchen-Vluyn 2005, 197: 'spätsekundär-deuterokanonisch'.

[8] Cf. E. Ulrich et al., *Qumran Cave 4, IX* (DJD XIV), Oxford 1995, 161–164.

us and put us into the hand of Midian' (6:13). When we look at other stories about the judges we can note that there is a tendency in the book of Judges to deviate from the scheme presented at the beginning. In the story of Deborah and Barak the reference to Israel crying out to YHWH is not followed by the raising up of a deliverer. Deborah, the judge who is going to help Israel, is already functioning. In the story of Jephthah we see the same pattern as in the story of Gideon. When Israel cries out to YHWH because of the oppression by the Ammonites YHWH does not immediately send Jephthah but first speaks (directly, without a reference to a prophet or a messenger) to the Israelites in the same way as the prophet in chapter 6, referring to his help in the past (10:11–12). And before Jephthah can start his work as a deliverer some problems have to be resolved between him and his family and the people. So there are good reasons to see 6:7–10 as part of the overall 'systematic and tendentious shaping of the editing of the cycle'[9] and not as a late insertion.

Judges 6:7–10 has its closest parallel in the words spoken by Samuel addressing the people after he had anointed Saul as their king: 'He said to the Israelites: "This is what YHWH, the God of Israel says: 'I have brought Israel up out of Egypt and I delivered you from the power of Egypt and the kingdoms that oppressed you.'"' (1 Sam. 10:18). According to Scherer the text of Judges 6 is secondary, dependent upon 1 Samuel 10.[10] He also points to the relation between Judges 6:7–10 and the story of the messenger of YHWH at Bochim (2:1–5), in which the people of Israel are also reminded of the exodus out of Egypt.

### 3. The Prophetic Character of the Book of Judges

All these texts, which are not part of the stories about the deliverers and judges themselves but seem to be meant to introduce or supplement them, have been discussed extensively by scholars investigating the origin and possible redaction(s) of the book of Judges. There is a growing consensus concerning the book of Judges that its present form is best explained as a late interpolation between the books of Joshua and Samuel.[11] Old stories were put in a framework making them fit in

---

[9] Y. Amit, *The Book of Judges: The Art of Editing* (BIS 38), Leiden 1999, 251.

[10] Cf. Scherer, *Überlieferungen von Religion und Krieg*, 194–195.

[11] Cf. T. Römer, *The So-Called Deuteronomistic History. A Sociological, Historical and Literary Introduction*, London 2005, 137; K. Spronk, 'From Joshua to Samuel: Some

between the stories of the origin of Israel and the history of the monarchy. It is not necessary to assume all kinds of redactional layers or to give it a place in some kind of deuteronomistic theory. It is possible to assume one single, coherent redactional operation. The way in which the beginning of the book is related to Joshua looks like the way the last chapters are related to the books of Samuel, for instance, by the reference to similar place names. Very interesting in this regard is the special role of the messenger of YHWH in the book of Judges. In 2:1–5 the messenger of YHWH comes to the people of Israel to remind them of the covenant with their God which they have broken. This takes up Joshua 24, where it was Joshua who spoke about the covenant and the obligations for the people. The role of Joshua is taken over in Judges 2 by the messenger of YHWH. Something similar can be observed in the parallel passages about the birth of Samson in Judges 13 and the birth of Samuel in 1 Samuel 1. The main difference between these stories is that the promise in 1 Samuel 1 is given by the priest Eli, whereas in Judges 13 it was given by a messenger of YHWH. Similarly, in Judges 2 compared to Joshua 24 there is a kind of upgrade with regard to the mediator between YHWH and man.

One may note a pattern here in which also the aforementioned added references to the prophet(ess) fit. It makes Deborah look like Samuel and it also relates the story of Gideon to the story of the first king anointed by Samuel. It puts emphasis on the right relation with YHWH. This way of telling the old stories of Israel's heroes appears to be typical of the book of Judges. One could call it the prophetic character of the book. In fact, already the first verse of the book strikes this prophetic tone. After the death of Joshua the Israelites ask of YHWH: 'Who shall go up against the Canaanites first?' The expression used here (שאל ביהוה) is found only in the stories of the judges, Saul, and David. In the books of Samuel it can be called a 'Leitmotiv'.[12] It is decisive in the career of Saul. His downfall and also the rise of David are connected with the right and successful way to get advice from YHWH. It is hardly a coincidence that this expression is used here in Judges 1:1, where it is related to Judah, the tribe of David. It is also hardly a coincidence that it returns in the final part of the book

---

Remarks on the Origin of the Book of Judges', in: J. van Ruiten, J.C. de Vos (eds), *The Land of Israel in Bible, History, and Theology. Studies in Honour of Ed Noort* (VTS 124), Leiden 2009, 137–149.

[12] H.-F. Fuhs, *TWAT*, 7, Stuttgart 1993, 921; for the use of this verb in the Book of Jeremiah see B. Becking, "Means of Revelation in the Book of Jeremiah", in: H.M. Barstad, R.G. Kratz (eds), *Prophecy in the Book of Jeremiah* (BZAW 388), Berlin, New York 2009, 33–47.

telling dreadful stories about a situation when there is no king to keep the peace between the tribes. In 20:18 YHWH is asked again: 'Who shall go up first?', this time against the Benjaminites. Again it is Judah who is called up by YHWH. It is precisely what happens with David according to 2 Samuel 2:1. David asks YHWH: 'Shall I go up to one of the cities of Judah?'. YHWH assures him that it is safe for him to go up to Hebron.

The (prophetic) message of the book of Judges appears to be given at the outset, clear and simple: before acting you should ask YHWH and wait for his answer. The right example is given at the beginning and repeated at the end. It concerns Judah and this points forward to the greatest son of Judah, David. Others can follow this example, like the Danites (cf. 18:5–6). Things will go well with the help of a prophetess like Deborah, but in many cases things go wrong. Most of the time this has to do with bad communication or even a lack of communication with YHWH. An example of bad communication with YHWH is the story of Jephthah who does not ask the divine advice but starts negotiating with YHWH. The example of no communication is the story of Samson. He only remembers his god when he is on the brink of death.

### 4. Looking for a Historical Background

It would be wrong to set prophecy against history. In the Old Testament prophets are nearly always directly involved in political matters. Prophetic texts are best understood when they can be related to a specific historical situation. One of good things of the historical critical exegesis is that it teaches us that it can be helpful to differentiate between the historical situation of the story and the historical situation of the story teller. Some interpreters assume or state that this is not necessary with regard to the book of Judges and come with evidence that we are dealing with eyewitness accounts. Usually this is motivated by the conviction that as a sacred text the Old Testament must be a valid historical source. This was also suggested, for instance, by Allen in the quotation given in the introduction to this article. A good example of this approach was given recently by Bryant G. Wood. He is so convinced that he accuses scholars who not agree of being unscientific: 'As one schooled in the scientific method, it disturbs me that, in addition to the say-so of esteemed authority figures, many times opinions are driven by preconceived notions, received knowledge (...), arguments from silence (...) or majority opinion. In an objective, scientific inquiry, conclusions must be based on evidence, and evidence alone. Take the matter of the historical accuracy of the Hebrew Bible. Most scholars are of the opinion that biblical history prior to the monarchy is myth and fable.'[13] Unfortunately, the way he tries to prove his case appears to be more aggressive than convincing. For instance, he bases the historical reliability of Judges 3 on a rather superficial interpretation of the results of an old excavation: 'Judges 3 tells of Eglon, king of Moab, establishing a residency at Jericho and exacting tribute from the Israelite tribes for 18 years in the late 14th century. When John Garstang excavated Jericho in the 1930s he found a large palatial-like structure which he identified as Eglon's palace. An abundance of imported pottery and an inscribed clay tablet attest to a well-to-do occupant involved in administrative activities. Yet, there was no town to rule over. It was occupied only a short time in the late 14th century and then abandoned.'[14] He adds that the plan of the building excavated by Garstang matches a reconstruction by Baruch Halpern of Eglon's palace 'remarkably well'. This 'evidence' is not so hard as suggested by Wood and it certainly does not speak for itself. First, we have to assume that 'the city of palms' mentioned in Judges 3:13 as taken by the Moabite king Eglon was the same as the city of Jericho. Then we have to assume that Eglon made this into his residence and that Ehud went there to meet him. From the story in Judges 3 we do not get the impression that Eglon's residence was very special. So it comes as no surprise that one of the buildings of ancient Jericho looks like it, having also an upper room, a porch and a back door. This could have been the place where all this happened, but it is not likely and it certainly does not prove that Judges 3 gives a reliable account of something that happened there. What is 'speaking' here is Wood's conviction about the character of the Bible.

Sometimes archaeological evidence does speak for itself, namely with the discovery of written texts. Of course, texts need to be translated and interpreted and they often leave room for discussion. Nowadays we also have to reckon with forgeries by creative criminals trying to take advantage of the eagerness for material from the biblical period. This eagerness can also lead to too much creativity with biblical scholars. An astonishing example of this is the interpretation by William H. Shea of an ostracon found in Ashkelon.[15] This ostracon was presented first in

---

[13] B.G. Wood, "Let the Evidence Speak", *BAR* 33.2 (2007), 26.
[14] Wood, "Let the Evidence Speak", 26–27.
[15] W.H. Shea, 'Samson and Delilah in a Philistine Text from Ashkelon', *DavarLogos* 2.1 (2003), 73–86.

1996 by Frank Moore Cross.[16] He interpreted it as an administrative text, which he translated as: '... from the (cereal) crop which you (...) they shall pay to (...) (cereal) crop of Sapan ...'. Shea comes with a completely different reading. He assumes a remarkable mix of letters and pictograms and translates: 'To Hanno of Gaza: The head of the Hebrew Samson, (who belonged) to Delilah, I placed in the hand of Agga, the son of Achish of Ashkelon king.' According to Shea we are dealing with a letter from the king of Ashkelon, Agga, to Hanno, king of Gaza, about the movement of the head of Samson. There can be no doubt about the identity of the decapitated person: this is the Samson of Judges 13–16. In the letter we are informed of something not told in Judges 16. Samson was beheaded, just like Goliath by David.

It is difficult to take this seriously. One suspects that this is a hoax, a joke, or a test of the scholarly world. It cannot be excluded, however, that Shea is serious here. He may have been inspired by the inscription of Khirbet el-Qôm with regard to the use of pictograms, because this inscription is related to the picture of a hand. Shea took part in the discussion about the translation and meaning of the inscription, to which he contributed with a number of daring, so far mostly not accepted suggestions.[17] Whatever may have been his intentions, Erasmus Gaß took him seriously and did him the honour of completely tearing down this house of cards, returning to a translation closely resembling the one by Cross: 'From the (cereal) crop which you have let down one shall lift up for (...) son of Sapan.'[18]

This leaves the question: is it possible that we shall be confronted one day with a (more convincing) piece of evidence like this, with positive proof of the existence of Samson and Delilah as historical persons or of any of the other persons named in the book of Judges? According to most handbooks it should not be excluded. Although it is usually admitted that the text is relatively late, the possibility is left open that the stories refer to actual historical facts and situations. This is based on archaeological and sociological evidence. A recent example of this is given by Sperling: 'For all its theological tendentiousness, the picture presented by Judges of conditions in pre-monarchic Israel finds a good deal of archaeological support. In addition, despite the imposition of their own concerns by

---

[16] F.M. Cross, 'A Philistine Ostracon from Ashkelon', *BAR* 22.1 (1996), 64–65.
[17] W.H. Shea, 'The Khirbet el-Qom Tomb Inscription again', *VT* 40 (1990), 110–116.
[18] E. Gaß, 'Samson and Delilah in a Newly Found Inscription?', *JNSL* 32 (2006), 103–114.

later writers, Judges has preserved literary fragments of great antiquity and affords insights into the social and religious conditions of the period between the conquest and the monarchy'.[19] He finds this 'archaeological support' in an article by Bloch-Smith and Alpert Nakhai, in which they state: 'Given the rather late and tendentious nature of the biblical text, it is somewhat unexpected to discover that archaeological evidence presents a similar, though not identical, picture of the events of the period. (...) Excavated sacred sites of the Iron I are generally consistent with those descriptions preserved in the Book of Judges'.[20] Something similar can be observed with Ackerman when she states that 'the multiple women characters in Judges are depicted as fulfilling the exact sorts of economic, social, political, and religious roles within their communities that Meyers' examination of the archaeological, sociological, and ethnographic data available for the Iron I period predicts'.[21]

It should be noted that the data Sperling and Ackerman are referring to are no more than circumstantial evidence. No direct connection can made with any of the persons or events described in the book of Judges. The positive view with regard to the historical reliability of the book of Judges taken beforehand by scholars like Sperling and Ackerman can be regarded as the legacy of Albrecht Alt and Martin Noth and their theory about the settlement in Canaan. Alt and Noth have made it plausible that the book of Judges, especially the first chapter, gives a more reliable picture of the history of ancient Israel than the book of Joshua. Noth also created a fitting historical background for the stories of the individual judges with his theory of the Amphictyony, as a kind of irregular tribal league. Since the time of Alt and Noth much has changed in the scholarly opinions about the period before the kings and the books describing that period. The theory of the Amphictyony has been abandoned. Noth's theory of the Deuteronomistic History and the place which the book of Judges takes in it, is—to say the least—questioned. As a consequence one should be more reluctant with regard to the value of the book of Judges as a source for the reconstruction of the history of ancient Israel.

In his recent commentary on the book of Judges Trent Butler presents this topic as if it is likely that the book of Judges gives a good historical

---

[19] S.D. Sperling, *Encyclopaedia Judaica* (second edition, 2007), 11, 566.

[20] E. Bloch-Smith, B. Alpert Nakhai, 'A Landscape Comes to Life: The Iron I Period', *NEA* 62 (1999), 62–127, 118–119.

[21] S. Ackerman, 'Digging Up Deborah: Recent Hebrew Bible Scholarship on Gender and the Contribution of Archaeology', *NEA* 66 (2003), 172–197, 176, referring to C. Meyers, *Discovering Eve: Ancient Israelite Women in Context*, Oxford 1988.

picture of the period it describes between the lives of Joshua and David: 'The concept of outsiders coming in and David ruling from Jerusalem requires some type of interim period. Why not accept the biblical contours of this interim period as that of local heroes performing in ironic ways to become both revered in tribal memory and pictured as the ultimate cause of Israel's moral and political downfall? Does not the very human picture of the heroes provide some kind of authentication?'[22] One can, however, also ask: why not accept this book as made up to fill in the intermediate period between Joshua and Saul? Why not accepts that this was done on the basis of the books that had to be connected? The literary analysis of the book of Judges seems to point in this way. It may have been written or produced in the first place to connect Joshua and Samuel, not to document the pre-monarchic period, with heroes who are not pictured as 'very human' but as prefiguration of the following kings.[23]

### 5. EVALUATION OF SOME RECENT STUDIES ON JUDGES AND HISTORY

A number of recently published studies show different ways of relating the stories from the book of Judges to the history of ancient Israel. They also show how difficult it is to come to convincing results.

In discussing Judges 19–21, the stories about the rape of the concubine and the following battles between the tribe of Benjamin and the other tribes, Douglas Lawrie states that one cannot simply distinguish here between fact and fiction.[24] In his view this story is so bizarre that it is not plausible that it was invented by an author as an introduction to the stories of the kings. He also has his questions about the motives of scholars like Julius Wellhausen. He may have been too focused on demolishing any confidence in the narrative as an accurate historical account because of his struggle against the orthodox view on the Bible as a reliable source of historic information. According Lawrie it is possible to assume some historical truth behind these stories. Benjamin could have become, because of its geographical position, a nasty stumbling

---

[22] T. Butler, *Judges* (WBC 8), Nashville 2009, lxxi.

[23] Cf. M.Z. Brettler, 'The Book of Judges: Literature as Politics', *JBL* 108 (1989), 395–418. He speaks of judges as 'protokings' (p. 407).

[24] D.G. Lawrie, 'Figuring in and Figuring it out: The Historical Imagination at Work in and on Judges 19–21', *Scriptura* 96 (2007), 425–440.

block on the road between North and South. History also shows that it is possible that a relatively small incident, like the murder of one woman, can bring about a major war. He points in this connection to the incident of the murder of one man that lead to the First World War. Very important in the view of Lawrie is the rhetorical factor. It is clear that these chapters are part of an attempt to show that the Israelites are better off with David of Jerusalem than with Saul of Gibeah. But to convince the hearer the rhetorician should be able to point to things that really happened and are remembered as such by his audience.

Against this view it can be argued that it is not impossible to explain Judges 19 as fiction with a specific function. In the story everything is centered around the places Jebus/Jerusalem and Gibeah, cities that are related to David and Saul respectively. Gibeah is the place where hospitality is violated. The story telling this is not invented, but adapted from Genesis 19, the story of the people of Sodom showing no respect for the guests of Lot. The stories of the battles between the tribes show no details which make one think of a specific historic event. The same holds true for the story about the robbing of the girls of Shilo, because we are dealing here with a theme that is well known in many cultures.

More promising with regard to the question about the historical background is the attempt by Mario Liverani in his book about the history of Israel. He is able to relate these final chapters in the book of Judges to the situation in the Persian province of Yehud after the return from the Babylonian exile: 'The scenario of a diversified territory, dangerous to cross, of relationships that represented a balance between maximum security and maximum interaction, of regular meetings and dispersions, is set in a "founding" pre-monarchic past. It is, however, clear that both author and reader have also—and chiefly—the post-exile situation in mind, with the returnees spread throughout the whole territory, partly governed by them and partly in the hands of foreign, and clearly hostile, people, as well as partly controlled by groups that they were related to but who were not very trustworthy. It is no coincidence that the historical scene, restricted to the area between Bethlehem and the Benjaminites centres, coincides precisely with the territory that the Babylonian returnees occupied on their arrival.'[25]

However, we face the same problem as when trying to relate the stories in the book of Judges to the period before the monarchy: it is possible to

---

[25] M. Liverani, *Israel's History and the History of Israel*, London 2005, 307.

read them against this background, but it is no more than likely. Both attempts say more about the convictions of the interpreter than about the interpreted text.

When it comes to hard facts we are on more solid ground with the approach by Erasmus Gaß.[26] His search for the historical background of the stories of Samson and the Philistines is at first sight even less promising than that of Lawrie and Liverani with regard to Judges 19–21. The name of the hero and his lover, Samson and Delilah, seem to be invented: 'he of the sun' against 'she of the night'. The battles against the Philistines seem to meant as a kind of prelude to the stories of David: what has begun successfully but eventually remained unfinished is taken up by David who brings it to an end. The numbers used in the story point to an artificially constructed climax: first 30 men are killed by Samson (14:19), then he captures and tortures 300 foxes (15:40), and finally he ends his life taking 3000 enemies with him (16:27).

The interesting thing is that Gaß brings in external evidence which is not beforehand influenced by the wish to prove any kind of dating. He has studied the archaeological evidence concerning the places mentioned in the story: when were they occupied and known to the possible hearers of the story? Next to this he surveyed the remains of the Philistine culture. A problem, however, with this approach is that the Philistines and the places mentioned in the story do not have to be a physical reality to the hearers. They can also be part of a common memory, laid down in well known stories. The best chance to get a possible clue to a historic situation is with facts and names that do not seem to have a specific function within the story and its wider framework. In the case of the story of Samson the Philistines do not meet this criterion, but the placenames Zora and Estaol do. So the archaeological information that the site of Ṣarʿa, usually identified with Zora, was primarily inhabited in the period between 700 and 586 BCE may be relevant. It can be regarded as an indication of the time in which this story may have been told or invented.[27]

---

[26] E. Gaß, 'Simson und die Philister: Historische und archäologische Rückfragen', *RB* 114 (2007), 372–402. Gaß also contributed much in this regard to the commentary by W. Groß, *Richter* (HThKAT), Freiburg 2009.

[27] Cf. Groß, *Richter*, 742–743.

## 6. Conclusion

After this short study into the prophetic character of the book of the
Judges and the small survey of the mostly unsuccessful search for points
of reference to any known historical situation, it can be concluded that it
does not seem wise to expect physical evidence for any of the stories of
the book of Judges as historical fact somewhere between the 13th to the
11th century BCE, in which these stories are said to have taken place. It
is more more likely to find evidence of the historic situation of the story
tellers. The thorough literary analysis, on which this search for history
should be based, shows that the writer who is responsible for the book of
Judges in its present form can be called a prophet.

# RESISTING THE PAST:
## ANCIENT ISRAEL IN WESTERN MEMORY

KEITH W. WHITELAM
*University of Sheffield—Great Britain*

## 1. INTRODUCTION

The historicity of the Exodus, we are told, is a dead issue.[1] The cutting edge of debate on the history of ancient Israel has moved on, of course, to the monarchy and later periods; scholarly attention has become pre-occupied with the historicity of David and Solomon, or the question of when state-structures can be said to have appeared in ancient Palestine and the priority of Judah or Israel in the rise to statehood. So this is where one might point a student or someone from outside of the discipline who wanted to know what were some of the current historical issues exercising the minds of biblical scholars, and where they can see first hand the rhetorical skill, wit, and scholarly restraint exercised by all involved in these debates. It is a debate that has contemporary currency, as we know, feeding into modern competing notions of identity and sovereignty. Remembering and forgetting, as Yael Zerubavel reminds us, are intricately linked in the construction of collective memory.[2] The way in which particular images of the past move from centre to periphery and back again exposes the dynamic character of collective memory and its continuous dialogue with history.

While some biblical scholars have been content to pronounce the death of the historicity of the patriarchal, exodus or settlement/conquest traditions and focus their energies on debating the niceties of four-

---

[1] W.G. Dever, 'Is There Any Archaeological Evidence for the Exodus?' in: E.S. Fredrichs, L.H. Lesko (eds), *Exodus, the Egyptian Evidence*, Winona Lake 1997, 81, states categorically that '... I regard the historicity of the Exodus as a dead issue.' Elsewhere, he claims that 'with the new models of indigenous Canaanite origins for early Israel there is neither place nor need for an Exodus from Egypt' (Dever, 'Is There Any Archaeological Evidence for the Exodus?', 67).

[2] Y. Zerubavel, *Recovered Roots: Collective Memory and the Making of Israeli National Tradition*, Chicago 1995.

chambered gates, red-slipped ware, or what constitutes an empire or
mini-empire, we are constantly reminded elsewhere that these images
cannot be so easily dismissed. They are deeply-seated in the popular and
political imagination. Far from passing into the mists of scholarly debate,
they continue to exert a profound hold on modern notions of identity and
are central to a view of the past that is almost resistant to challenge.

A timely reminder of this power was illustrated in 'Unholy Land?', a
Channel 4 TV series in the UK, where one of the programmes followed a
young Jewish family from New York on their emigration to Israel. After
a visit to Hebron, the mother and son were filmed complaining that land
purchased by Abraham was now in the possession of Arabs: the biblical
story in Gen. 23 represented for them a 'title deed' to the land. Similarly,
Eviatar Zerubavel in *Time Maps: Collective Memory and the Social Shape
of the Past* recounts the view of an ultranationalist settler in Hebron as
saying:

> Here, *right here*, God promised Abraham the Land of Israel ... Just imag-
> ine to yourself that *I go to sleep at the very place where Abraham used to get
> up every morning!*[3]

Such an invocation of the past is an essential element in the way in which
collective memory creates continuity with the present, what Norman
Davies refers to elsewhere as 'the myth of seamless continuity', or Geary
terms 'the moment of primary acquisition', thereby providing a sense of
identity, belonging and legitimacy.[4]

Similarly, President Clinton revealed that the night before the meeting
of Arafat and Rabin on the White House lawn on 14 September 1993,
he had stayed up until the early hours of the morning reading the book
of Joshua.[5] It is a vision of the past so powerful and so ingrained in
western consciousness that President Clinton believed that his reading
of the Exodus narrative put him in touch with the history of the region.
Similarly, President George Bush, in his address to the Knesset on 15
May 2008 on the occasion of the 60th anniversary of the founding
of the modern state of Israel, described it as 'the redemption of an

---

[3] E. Zerubavel, *Time Maps: Collective Memory and the Social Shape of the Past*,
Chicago 2003, 43.

[4] N. Davies, *The Guardian, Saturday Review*, 13 November, 1999, 3; J.P. Geary, *The
Myth of Nations: The Medieval Origins of Europe*, Princeton 2002, 12.

[5] See M. Prior, *Zionism and the State of Israel: A Moral Inquiry*, London 1999, 167–
168. Nothing could symbolise better the claim of Israel to the land by divine gift and right
of conquest: a 'historic right' which Clinton appeared to endorse by his choice of reading
material.

ancient promise given to Abraham and Moses and David.' The lavish production 'The Exodus Decoded', directed by James Cameron and aired on the History Channel in 2006, shows how such traditions, like the unforgettable image of Cecil B. de Mille's Moses standing before the parting waters, are so deeply embedded within the political and popular memory that they appear almost resistant to critique or revision. Such examples illustrate Carl Becker's view that 'whether the general run of people read history books or not, they inevitably picture the past in some fashion or other, and this picture, however little it corresponds to [a] real past, helps to determine their ideas about politics and society'.[6]

What we have been witnessing over the last few years with the revival of the 'biblical history' movement—evident in volumes such as Provan, Long, and Longman's *A Biblical History of Israel*, Kitchen's *On the Reliability of the Old Testament*, Hoffmeier and Millard's *The Future of Biblical Archaeology*, or Kofoed's *Text and History: Historiography and the Study of the Biblical Text*, among others—is the intricate and dynamic relationship between collective memory and history.[7] These modern 'biblical histories' share the basic premises of collective memory, are shaped by them, and in turn help to further reinforce such memories. Those who march in their massed ranks under the banner of 'Biblical History' and to the refrain of 'absence of evidence isn't evidence of absence' represent the dominant paradigm in our discipline. They are determined to resist an image of the past constructed by critical historiography over the last 25–30 years or any counter memory on which it might draw. Their vision of the past has no room for scepticism, what some might see as an essential quality of the historian, espousing instead a principle of falsification whereby we are exhorted to accept the testimony of the biblical narrative unless it can be falsified.[8] They call for a return to orthodoxy and the power of tradition, including a return to the

---

[6] C.L. Becker, 'What are Historical Facts?', in: P.L. Snyder (ed.), *Detachment and the Writing of History: Essays and Letters of Carl L. Becker*, Ithaca 1958, 61. Also cited in Zerubavel, *Recovered Roots*, 3.

[7] I. Provan *et al.* (eds) *A Biblical History of Israel*, Louisville 2003; K. Kitchen, *On the Reliability of the Old Testament*, Grand Rapids 2003; J.K. Hoffmeier. A.R. Millard (eds), *The Future of Biblical Archaeology: Reassessing Methodologies and Assumptions*, Grand Rapids 2004; J.B. Kofoed, *Text and History: Historiography and the Study of the Biblical Text*, Winona Lake, 2005.

[8] For a more detailed treatment of this issue see K.W. Whitelam, 'The Death of Biblical History' in: J.W. Rogerson, D. Burns (eds), *In Search of Philip Davies: Whose Festschrift is it Anyway?*, London n.d [delayed publication from 2007; available in pre-publication format at http://tandtclark.typepad.com/ttc/2007/12/an-online-lhbot.html].

powerful images of the past embedded deep in western memory. Here
is a point where the popular, political, and academic imaginations meet
and become mutually reinforcing as the focus returns to the patriarchs,
exodus and settlement / conquest. Issues which only a few years ago were
dismissed by some as dead issues for biblical studies now return from
the margins of academic discourse to the centre of attention, providing
the rallying points to resist a past envisioned by critical historiography.
Thus it becomes important to understand the power of these images of
Palestine's past if we are to understand why histories of ancient Israel are
written in the way that they are and the oppositional rhetoric that sur-
rounds them. It is important to try to understand why this remembrance
of the past is so robust, so deeply ingrained in western memory, that it is
virtually immune to critical engagement. Yet examining the roots of this
memory may also provide some indication of where the sites of resistance
might be located that offer alternative memories and thus alternative histories of ancient Palestine.

## 2. John Speed and the Representation of Palestine

In 1611, John Speed produced his magnificent *The Theatre of the Empire
of Great Britain* which included detailed maps of the counties of England,
along with those of Scotland, Wales, and Ireland. It was later expanded in
1627 with A *Prospect of the Most Famous Parts of the World*, containing
maps of other parts of the world, including a map of Palestine at the very
end of the volume (fig. 2).[9]

This map is strikingly different to his earlier representation of Palestine, 'Canaan as it was possessed in both Abraham and Israel's days with
the stations and bordering nations', published in 1595. His work of 1611
onwards is fascinating for a number of reasons. Given its location in an
atlas 'presenting an exact geography of the kingdom of England, Scotland, Ireland and the Isles adjoining', it is puzzling that he chose to include
the Exodus and tribal divisions along with an inset of Jerusalem surrounded by the Temple vessels rather than a map of the monarchy of
David and Solomon. Similarly in a work claiming to offer 'an exact geog-

---

[9] J. Speed, *The Theatre of the Empire of Great Britaine: Presenting an Exact Geography
of the Kingdomes of England, Scotland, Ireland, and the Iles Adioyning: with the Shires,
Hundreds, Cities and Shire-townes, Within Ye Kingdome of England, Divided and Described
by Iohn Speed*, London 1611.

raphy', he does not attempt to depict the geographical features and towns of Palestine of his own day. Why, in a volume supposedly dedicated to the king, would Speed choose to represent Palestine through the exodus and division of the land among the tribes rather than as the royal domain of David and Solomon? What would be more natural in an atlas, supposedly dedicated to and sponsored by the house of Stuart and incorporating its terminology for the land ('the empire of Great Britain'), than a map of the monarchy, a representation of the land as the possession of the crown?

Speed's work drew on a long tradition in western cartography and was inspired by the innovative atlas of Ortelius, *Theatrum Orbis Terrarum*, first published in 1570. Ortelius declared in his 'Address to the Reader' that 'Geography is ... and not without good cause called the eye of History'. He then set out what kinds of events are best suited to geographical illustration:

> Especially ... the expeditions and voyages of great Kings, Captaines and Emperours ... the divers and sundry shiftings of Nations from one place to another ... the travels and peregrinations of famous men, made into sundry countreys.[10]

Ortelius's magnificent map of the 'Peregrination of Abraham the Patriarke' illustrates his view of the proper subject of geographical illustration. It is adorned by narrative and pictorial devices on or around the map, including 22 vignettes depicting various episodes from the life of Abraham. Another of Ortelius's maps depicted the location of the tribes.[11] Interestingly, his inclusion of Tilleman Stella's earlier map of sites in Israel and Judah appears to downplay the notion of the land as the possession of the crown by retaining the tribal divisions. Noticeably, unlike his own map of Abraham's journeys, it is devoid of biblical references or vignettes illustrating the stories of David, Solomon, or later kings adorning the edge of the map.

The longevity of these themes of the patriarchs, exodus, and tribal divisions is seen in a series of maps from the great cartographers of the sixteenth and seventeenth centuries. Mercator's map of Palestine in six sheets from 1537, for example, depicts the Exodus. Nicholas Vischer the Elder's map of Palestine of 1659, which became a common feature of

---

[10] Cited in J. Gillies, *Shakespeare and the Geography of Difference*, Cambridge 1994, 71. The quotation is taken from the English edition of 1606, R.A. Skelton (ed.), *The Theatre of the Whole World*, Amsterdam 1968.

[11] See K. Nebenzahl, *Maps of the Bible Lands: Images of Terra Sancta through Two Millennia*, London 1986, 87.

Dutch Bibles, portrays the Israelites encamped during the Exodus, with
the 12 tribes deployed around the edge of the inset along with population
numbers, the tabernacle in the centre, Moses standing to the left holding
a staff with Aaron opposite in priestly robes.[12] The popularity of these
themes is confirmed by Catherine Delano Smith's studies of maps in
sixteenth century Bibles where we find five traditional subjects depicted:
the Patriarchs,] the Exodus, the twelve tribes of Israel, Christ depicted in
the Gospels, and the spread of Christianity as described in Acts.[13]

As with Speed's atlas, what is striking about these early European maps
or maps in sixteenth century Bibles, which reached very wide audiences,
was the almost complete lack of interest in the monarchy. It appears to
hold no significant interest for cartographers until the eighteenth century. Georg Seutter's map from 1725, showing the kingdoms of Judah
and Israel superimposed on a map of the tribal divisions, is not unlike
Tilleman Stella's earlier map used by Ortelius. Seutter was well known
for his maps of German states, eventually becoming the official geographer of the Kaiser of the Holy Roman Empire.[14] The most explicit representation of the early monarchy is to be found in Gilles Robert de Vau-
gondy's magnificent 'Map of the Land of the Hebrews or Israelites' from
1745. It includes an inset in the upper left corner entitled 'the Monarchy
of the Hebrews' displaying the administrative structure under Solomon.
The larger map continues to show the divisions of the twelve tribes.
The smaller inset map has twelve districts, roughly corresponding to the
tribal divisions, with the names of the officials in charge. At the bottom is a small vignette showing Solomon's judgement, unlike Ortelius's
earlier map of Israel and Judah which lacked any additional decoration.[15]

It is not insignificant that such maps only began to appear in significant numbers in the eighteenth century: the time of the rise of the
European nation-state. It would appear from the evidence of cartography and common Bibles that the monarchy was marginalized in western memory before this time and only began to form a significant ele-

---

[12] See Nebenzahl, *Maps of the Bible Lands* 1986, 132.
[13] The first Bible map was of the route of the exodus in Zurich in 1525 and Antwerp
1526 in Lutheran Bibles. C. Delano Smith, 'Maps as Art and Science: Maps in Sixteenth
Century Bibles' *Imago Mundi* 42 (1990), 65–83, deals with the history of the Exodus map
in various Bibles. See also C. Delano Smith, *Maps in Bibles, 1500–1600: An Illustrated
Catalogue*, Geneva 1991; Nebenzahl, *Maps of the Bible Lands*, 1986, 105.
[14] See Nebenzahl, *Maps of the Bible Lands* 1986, 144–145.
[15] See Nebenzahl, *Maps of the Bible Lands* 1986, 148–149.

ment of collective memory during the period of the triumph of the European nation-state. This has been reinforced since 1948, of course, in the context of Israeli-Palestinian conflict and particularly in disputes over the sovereignty of Jerusalem. It is only as the present changed that the past was remembered differently or elements of that past that had been marginalized became more important in questions of identity. But what does this marginalization of the monarchy and popularity of the exodus and settlement / conquest in the sixteenth and seventeenth centuries tell us about the roots of western collective memory and the representation of Palestine?

The map forms part of what we might term 'the media of memory'; as such, it is important evidence for the configuration of collective memory in earlier centuries.[16] It is also offers an opportunity to trace the roots of contemporary collective memory in which the image of the exodus and settlement / conquest have proven to be so robust and resistant. Maps, as Harley demonstrated so effectively, tell us about the world in which they were created, the aspirations, and identity of those who created and consumed them.[17] They also offer us a glimpse of the roots of images that continue to have such a profound effect upon our own world.

### 3. Marginalizing Monarchy

Speed's work appears at an interesting juncture in English and British history; he was born in 1552, six years before the accession of Elizabeth I (1558–1603), the last of the Tudors, and his work spans the last years of her reign, those of James I of England and VI Scotland (1603–1625), who forged the union of the kingdoms of England and Scotland, and the early part of the reign of the ill-fated Charles I (1625–1649). Speed's atlas continued to be published for well over a century, being reissued in

---

[16] The phrase is taken from W. Kansteiner, 'Finding Meaning in Memory: A Methodological Critique of Collective Memory Studies' *History and Theory*, 41 (2002), 179–197.

[17] See, for example, J.B. Harley, 'Maps, Knowledge and Power' in: D. Cosgrove and S. Daniels (eds), *The Iconography of Landscape*, Cambridge 1988, 277–312; J.B. Harley, 'Secrecy and Silences: the Hidden Agenda of Cartography in Early Modern Europe' *Imago Mundi* 40 (1988), 111–130; J.B. Harley, 'Historical Geography and the Cartographic Illusion' *Journal of Historical Geography* 15 (1989), 80–91; J.B. Harley, 'Deconstructing the Map', in: T.J. Barnes and J.S. Duncan (eds), *Writing Worlds: Discourse, Text and Metaphor in the Representation of Landscape*, London 1992, 231–247.

the reign of Charles II (1660–1685), significantly well after the English civil war (1642–1651) and the struggle to reduce the power of absolute monarchy.

What strikes the viewer of Speed's map of Palestine, in the context of its inclusion in *The Theatre of the Empire of Great Britaine*, is that it is drawn as though it is a typical English county. Like Lincolnshire (fig. 3), for instance, it includes an inset of its major town and is decorated with the same symbols for towns and villages, historic events, ships and large fish.

I chose Lincolnshire from Speed's maps not just to show the symbols for towns and villages or the coast line with the ship and fish, not just because this joint meeting is being held in Lincoln, its county town, which is depicted in the bottom left hand corner, though that is a very convenient coincidence. But because, on an autobiographical note, if you look closely at the south of the county around the edge of the Wash, to the area labelled as Holland, fittingly again for this meeting, the empty spaces there outside the village of Gedney are where I grew up and where my ancestors have been written out of history.

Speed describes Great Britain as 'the very Eden of Europe'; it is for him a land flowing with milk and honey, teeming with game and abundant produce. He then adds that ' ... whereby safely may be affirmed, that there is not any one kingdom in the world so exactly described, as is this our Island of Great-Britain, that only accepted which Joshua conquered, and into Tribes divided.' The division of the land, with each of the tribes represented by a coat of arms, is particularly significant. Here we see the land 'in all its particular divisions'.[18] Palestine is, in effect, rendered like England with its county boundaries. The production of Speed's atlas along with others before, such as that of Saxton, allowed the viewer to take visual and conceptual possession of the physical kingdom in which they lived.[19] Palestine, drawn in the manner of the English counties with all its divisions, became such a familiar landscape through the constant repetition of this image that it was already appropriated in western memory long before the period of European expansion.

In contrast to Saxton's earlier atlas, the royal coat of arms on each of the county maps in Speed's *Theatre* (36 of the 42) is reduced in size and joined by arms of the local gentry. The atlas also contained a chorographic

---

[18] R. Helgerson, *Forms of Nationhood: The Elizabethan Writing of England*, Chicago 1986, 93.

[19] See R. Helgerson, *Forms of Nationhood*, 1986:51.

description of the land and people of Britain, focusing on the local, which largely ignored the existence of royal power.[20] Chorography, the study of local history, was one of the most important branches of geography at the time. As Helgerson notes, 'more and more, chorographies became books where country gentlemen can find their manors, monuments, and pedigrees copiously set forth. In just a few decades, chorography thus progressed from being an adjunct to the chronicles of kings to become a topographically ordered set of real estate and family chronicles.'[21] Speed's maps, with the concentration on the manors and coats of arms of the gentry and other local features, direct attention away from the king and his claim to the country. England had become, in the words of Helgerson, a 'land-centred nation'.[22] Chorography was particularly attractive to the newly empowered classes of landed gentry and merchant families: 'The close self-identification with place that chorography provided, as well as its practical utility, gave these increasingly important members of early modern English society a sense of their roles and location in the political and social sphere.' It allowed them to be located in place and time, explore their identity, thereby helping to define the growing sense of who they were. As Cormack notes: 'This study of local history was particularly important in the development of an attitude that favored things English, adding to an ideology of separateness and superiority.'[23] The way in which this ideology of separateness and superiority is embedded in such maps, including the map of Palestine, is also important in tracing the roots of a conception of ethnicity that has informed many of our histories of Israel.

The audience for such books, the mnemonic community as Zerubavel would term it, was the landed gentry of England struggling to diminish and replace the power of the king. What we see in Speed's atlas, including his map of Palestine, is the struggle for power at a critical juncture in the shifting relationships between the monarchy and the landed gentry. What we are viewing here is the tension involved in the transition of power

---

[20]  See R. Helgerson, *Forms of Nationhood*, 1986, 58.

[21]  See R. Helgerson, *Forms of Nationhood*, 1986, 135.

[22]  See R. Helgerson, *Forms of Nationhood*, 1986, 62. It is interesting that Thomas Fuller's *A Pisgah-Sight of Palestine and the Confines Thereof: With the History of the Old and New Testament Acted Thereon*, London, published in 1650, contains individual maps and chorographic descriptions of each of the tribes. He states in his introduction that 'the eye will learn more in an hour from a Mappe, than the eare can learn in a day from discourse.' Each section of the book is dedicated to a member of the landed gentry. It is, in a sense, a chorography of Palestine, again along the models of such works on England.

[23]  L.B. Cormack, *Charting an Empire: Geography at the English Universities, 1580–1620* Chicago 1997, 163.

from the monarchy to the landed gentry. What is at the centre of these maps is the land in all its divisions: diversity within unity. There is no suggestion that this is the possession of the monarch, hence the lack of interest in David and Solomon. Each of the tribes is represented by a coat of arms just like the English landowners in their own counties.

The ideological effect of these maps is to strengthen 'the sense of both local and national identity at the expense of an identity based on dynastic loyalty.'[24] Compared with Saxton's maps, those issued in the decade after James's accession to the throne of England show 'a diminution of the place accorded the insignia of royal power and a corresponding increase in the attention paid to the land itself.'[25] The struggle for power and control of the land evidenced in Speed's atlas was to end on the battlefields of the English Civil War. For the mnemonic community that sponsored and consumed these products, the monarchy of David and Solomon was a forgotten memory. It could play no role in their remembered past as they struggled to overturn the power of absolute monarchy and claim control of the land for themselves.

### 4. The Imperial Impulse

While Speed's maps contributed to the developing power of a particular ruling class in England, the other mnemonic community for whom such maps were significant were the growing merchant class. It was merchants who often funded the cost of the rapid expansion of cartography as much as government.[26] A close examination of his map of Palestine in the *Theatre* reveals that the ship off the coast is flying the English ensign. In Speed's original map of 1595, this was a land still to be possessed, by 1611 it had been visually incorporated as an English county with an English ship patrolling off the coast. As Brotton notes these maps 'had only ever really been based on the ability to speculate and to conjecture

---

[24] See R. Helgerson, *Forms of Nationhood*, 1986, 56.
[25] See R. Helgerson, *Forms of Nationhood*, 1986, 56.
[26] P. Barber, 'England II: Monarchs, Ministers, and Maps, 1550–1625', in: D. Buisseret (ed.), *Monarchs, Ministers and Maps: The Emergence of Cartography as a Tool of Government in Early Modern Europe*, Chicago 1992, 59, notes that: 'Thus, when discussing the patronage of cartography in late sixteenth-century England, one is talking not of royal/ministerial *or* merchant/gentry patronage but of a continuum extending from, in a few cases, complete and direct royal patronage to a few cases of patronage by merchants or country gentlemen alone.'

on the imaginative possession of distant territories'.[27] Yet the reprinting of maps of Palestine—Ortelius's atlas alone reached 40 editions and was translated into several languages—and their dissemination in the most popular Bibles of the day meant that this was now a familiar landscape. The implied claim to global authority was to be realised in the following centuries. What had been appropriated visually, was to be occupied physically in the coming centuries.

This new imperial ideology, claiming the supremacy of the English nation and its right to seize control of new trade routes was articulated in many books on geography written in the last twenty years of Elizabeth's reign and the first twenty of James's.[28] Noticeably it was not the monarchy or empire of David that came to represent this expansion overseas. These were not the king's lands, anymore than England was the possession of the crown. These were the merchant's maps and so these were the merchants lands. This was a divinely-sanctioned creation of an English empire, hence the importance of the exodus and the tribal division of Palestine. The map of Palestine which completes *The Theatre of the Empire of Great Britain* condenses historical time and thereby helps to create that myth of seamless continuity in which Speed's England stands as the culmination of a divinely guided universal history.

---

[27] J. Brotton, *Trading Territories: Mapping the Early Modern World*, London 1997, 186.

[28] See L.B. Cormack, *Charting an Empire*, 1997, 1. Again the context and reception of Speed's atlas is important for understanding the ideological components which inform the shaping of collective memory. Cormack outlines the importance of works such as this in stimulating and sustaining the imperial impulse that would eventually lead to the physical as well as the visual appropriation of Palestine, and other territories:

The study of geography was essential to the creation of an ideology of imperialism in early modern England. Large numbers of young men destined to be part of the governing elite began to converge on the English universities just as the English were searching for an identity independent of the Roman Church and focused on the autonomy and superiority of England. These young scholars found in the study of geography as set of attitudes and assumptions that encouraged them to view the English as separate from and superior to the rest of the world. Geography supplied these men with belief in their own inherent superiority and their ability to control the world they now understood. The men who studied geography proceeded from the universities to positions of importance in government, law, mercantile activities, and court positions, and the worldview they had gained at university aided them in their climb through patronage connections. This development of an imperial ideology for a group of men so closely concerned with England's internal and external relations would help create the future history of the English and British Empires.

## 5. Conclusion

These images of Palestine became a familiar, if imagined, landscape throughout Europe with the constant reprinting of the maps of Speed, Ortelius, Mercator, the Vischers, and many others, and their dissemination in the most popular Bibles of the day. Ortelius exhorted his reader in the following terms:

> … the reading of Histories doeth both seeme to be much more pleasant, and indeed so it is, when the Mappe being layed before our eyes, we may behold things done, or places where they were done, as if they were at this time present and in doing.[29]

Those who purchased his and other volumes or opened their Bibles were able to experience Palestine as the place where the biblical events, particularly the exodus and conquest, were continually played out. A few centuries later, European tourists on Cooks tours to the Holy Land were able to experience the contemporary land and its inhabitants as a series of biblical scenes that acted out their reading of the Bible. 'Every day', writes William Leighton in a letter to his family in 1874, 'we meet some incident which throws an unexpected light on the Biblical narrative.'[30] Yet for those unable to afford such journeys works such as Rev. William M. Thomson's *The Land and the Book; Or, Biblical Illustrations Drawn from the Manners and Customs, the Scenes and Scenery of the Holy Land* took the reader on a journey through Palestine experiencing its colours, smells, and costumes; enabling them, in their own homes, to experience Palestine as performed space.[31] The maps of Speed and Ortellius, with their dominant images of exodus and conquest, functioned in the same way. As the English geographer, William Cunningham wrote in his *The Cosmographicall Glasse*, in 1555, the benefit of such maps was that they could be experienced 'in a warme & pleasant house, without any perill of the raging Seas: danger of enemies: loss of time: spending of substaunce: weriness of body, or anguishe of mind'. Or as one pur-

---

[29] Abraham Ortelius, *The Theatre of the Whole World*, R.A. Skelton (ed.), Amsterdam 1968, cited in Gillies, *Shakespeare and the Geography of Difference*, 71.

[30] W.H. Leighton, *A Cook's Tour to the Holy Land in 1874: The Letters of William Henry Leighton*, London 1948.

[31] Rev. William M. Thomson's *The Land and the Book; Or, Biblical Illustrations Drawn from the Manners and Customs, the Scenes and Scenery of the Holy Land*, London 1888. For a detailed treatment of Palestine as 'performed space' in works from the nineteenth century, see K.W. Whitelam, 'The Land and the Book: Biblical Studies and Imaginative Geographies of Palestine' *Postscripts*, n.d.

chaser of Ortelius' *Theatrum* wrote to him, you have 'made the earth portable'.[32] Palestine could be experienced and appropriated in European homes long before its physical possession. As we trace the line that runs from Speed to our contemporary biblical histories we begin to discern a dense network of materials—maps, chorographies, travel diaries, travel handbooks, and academic textbooks—that have constructed, disseminated, repeated, and reinforced an imaginative geography of Palestine that prepared the ground for its textual and visual appropriation and eventually culminated in its physical possession. We also begin to see that their imaginings of space or their reading strategies are not relics of the past, dead issues, but continue into the present and hold a dominant position within our discipline, as well as being deeply embedded in the popular and political imaginations.

---

[32] Brotton, *Trading Territories*, 175.

FIGURES AND MAPS

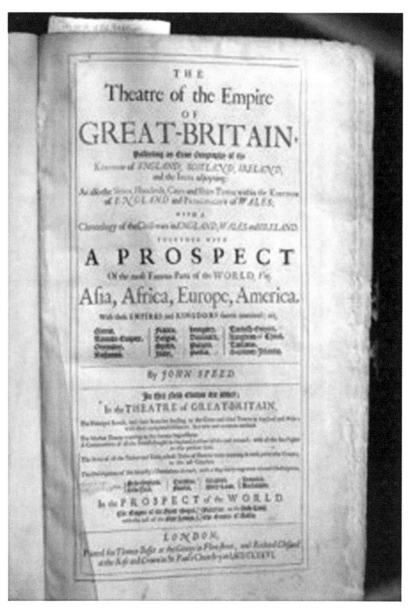

*Fig.* 1. Title page from John Speed's *The*
*Theatre of the Empire of Great Britaine*
Courtesy of the University of Sheffield Library

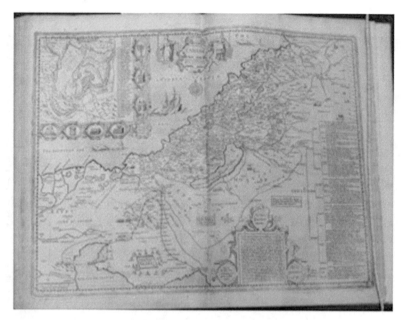

*Fig.* 2. John Speed's Map of Canaan
Courtesy of the University of Sheffield Library

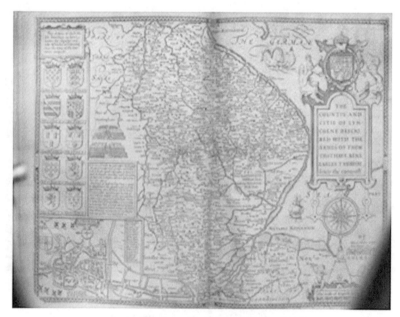

*Fig.* 3. John Speed's map of Lincolnshire
Courtesy of the University of Sheffield Library

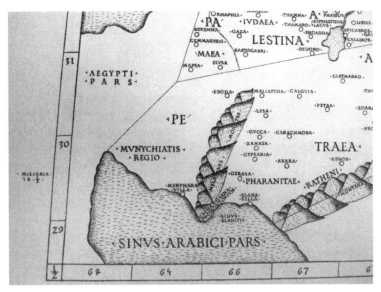

*Map* 1. Section from Ptolemy, Quarta Asiae Pars
(Rome, 1490) (Board of TrinityCollege, Dublin)

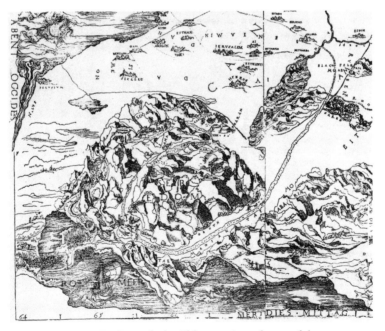

*Map* 2. L. Cranach the Elder, section of map of the
Holy Land, c. 1522–1425 (Kunz 1995) (Armin
Kunz and *Print Quarterly* 12.2 (1995), 124)

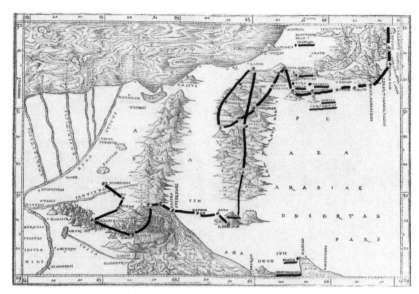

*Map* 3. J. Ziegler, Tabula Septima, from *Quae intus continentur*
(Argentatori, 1532) (Board of Trinity College, Dublin)

*Map* 4. Miles Coverdale, section of map from *Biblia.*
*The Bible: That is, the Scriptures of the Old and New*
*Testaments, faithfully translated into English* (Zurich, 1535)

*Map* 5. G. Mercator, section from 'Amplissima Terrae Sanctae Descriptio ad Utriusque Testamenti Intelligentiam' (Louvain, 1537) (Perugia, Biblioteca Comunale Augusta, I.C.94 [3])

*Map* 6. G. F.della Gatta's reduced version (Rome, 1557) of W.Wissenburg, 'Descriptio Palestinae Nova', 1538 (British Library)

# INDEX OF AUTHORS

# INDEX OF TEXTUAL REFERENCES

## Septuaginta

## Pseudepigrapha and Deuterocanonical Literature

## West Semitic Inscriptions

## Classical and Early Christian Sources